Elegant Parenting

(How To Do It Right The First Time)

Strategies For
The Twenty-First Century

A Seminar With
Beth and John Gall

Illustrated by Christine Lux

Elegant Parenting*

* For Grandparents, too!

Printed at Ann Arbor, Michigan by General Systemantics Press.
All rights reserved.

Library of Congress Cataloging In Publication Data

Gall, John, 1925-
    Elegant Parenting
    Bibliography: p.
    1.
I. Title

For hardcover edition: ISBN 0-9618251-2-X

For paperback edition: ISBN 0-9618251-3-8

Library of Congress Catalog Card Number: 92-090582

Published by: The General Systemantics Press
            3200 West Liberty, Suite A
            Ann Arbor, Michigan 48103-9794

Acknowledgements

We want to express our very special appreciation to Barbara Anderson and David Thomas—charter members of the Parenting Classes—to Dan and Mary Carlson, to Rick and Francoise Jaffe, to Christine Lux and Steve Wells, to Dick and Lois Shaw, to Peg Hoey and Val Daniel, and to Professor Edward M. Schwartz for critical readings of portions of the manuscript at various stages of completion. They have offered pertinent and constructive criticisms that have rendered the final product much more coherent and readable than it would otherwise have been.

Our two sons, Duane and David, responded with tolerance, good humor, and love to our fumbling attempts at parenting, and we owe them a special debt of gratitude for allowing themselves to be identified in some of the anecdotes in the text. Also, they and their wives Barbara and Kim respectively, have provided valuable feedback by sharing their reactions to the manuscript in the stages of its evolution.

Special thanks are also due to the many other members of the Parenting Classes who by sharing their own struggles, insights, and successes over a period of more than ten years have provided much of the material that has made this book possible.

Foreword

All children are born little. Their instructors for becoming fully functional people are the adults already there who shepherd them from the time when they are born, when no child can take care of him or herself, to the time when they can.

These instructors (parents) can present only what they have learned. If their learning for how to be fully human is incomplete or distorted, that is all they have to pass on.

These instructors do the best they can. Since very little attention has been paid to developing fully functioning human beings, most of us build ourselves on non-credentialled staff. The curriculum has been focussed largely on conformity and obedience, which is a fertile soil for developing decisions and conclusions about oneself that are often detrimental.

—Virginia Satir[1]

About the Authors

JOHN GALL, M.S., M.D., F.A.A.P., is Clinical Associate Professor of Pediatrics at the University of Michigan. He is in private practice of Pediatrics in Ann Arbor, Michigan.

BETH GALL, R.N., M.A., C.P.N.P. (deceased), was a Pediatric Nurse Practitioner. Until her retirement she was in full-time practice with her husband. John and Beth have two married children and currently have two grandchildren.

CHRISTINE LUX, B.A. (University of Michigan), has worked in the fields of education and the media in addition to being an artist and illustrator. Together with her husband, Steve Wells, she has two daughters, aged 3 and 8 years.

CONCH

Hold a baby to your ear
As you would a shell:
Sounds of centuries you hear
New centuries foretell.

Who can break a baby's code?
And which is the older—
The listener or his small load?
The held or the holder?

—E. B. White[2]

In Memoriam

Beth Gall
1929–1993

Beloved wife, colleague, and companion
through thirty-seven years of
loving and growing.

Table of Contents

Preface: Parenting as a Performing Art

"My Forty Years as a Pediatrician"

During my student days there was a rather pompous doctor at the medical school who used to preface his observations by saying, "In my forty years of experience . . ." We students were put off by that phrase, because it seemed to imply that no matter how logical we might be in our reasoning, no matter how up-to-date our knowledge might be, we were no match for the authority of forty years of clinical experience. But we didnt know how to counter this formidable ploy . . .

So it was with a good deal of relief and actual enjoyment that some of us overheard that doctor in an encounter with another teacher in the medical school, who said in a voice loud enough for us to hear, "Roscoe, you haven't had forty years of experience. You've had one year of experience repeated forty times."

One year of experience repeated forty times . . . so you're not going to find any references in this book to "my forty years as a pediatrician." No pronouncements from on high. The skills and techniques presented here must stand on their own. They must stand the test of your putting them into practice and finding out for yourself whether they can work, and when and under what circumstances.

Now, when I first started out in practice (and it really was almost forty years ago!) I experienced a rather severe shock. Pediatric practice wasn't at all like what I thought it was going to be. My technical, scientific training was all very fine, but what my patients and their parents needed and wanted was something different, something more. I soon realized that my own professional training was almost totally lacking in whatever that something was.

I don't mean to imply that my teachers were uncaring. Many of them were very caring, and some were the most dedicated human beings I have ever known. But—except in the few cases where they figured some part of it out for themselves—they simply didn't know specifically what to do to communicate that caring. They didn't know how to make their presence an effective instrument of healing. And what they didn't know, the medical school could not teach.

In fact, I had been scientifically trained with only minimal attention to the art of healing, the art of human communication.

But I didn't know this at first. How can the student know that the curriculum is incomplete?

I only knew that I wasn't satisfied. I just didn't feel right day after day as I practiced my profession. I decided maybe I just wasn't cut out to be a practitioner, so I resigned from the big clinic where I was located and took a postdoctoral fellowship in Human Genetics; and for nearly ten years I pursued a career as a specialist in medical genetics, specializing in mental retardation and problems of growth and development. I became an Associate Professor and wrote learned papers and I still wasn't satisfied.

So I resigned my position and went into solo private practice, on my own.

As luck would have it, that move coincided with an opportunity to learn the art of therapy without taking a residency in psychiatry. Because I did not want to be a psychiatrist, I wanted to be a healing person, a therapeutic person, in my own profession of Pediatrics. My wife and professional colleague, Beth, who is a Pediatric Nurse Practitioner, joined me in the training program.

For six years we practiced pediatrics by day and took our training in the evenings and on weekends at the Huron Valley Institute in Ann Arbor, under the tutelage of our charismatic teacher, Kristyn Huige, M.A., M.S.W., to whom we gratefully acknowledge our indebtedness. This experience introduced us to individual therapy, group therapy, and family therapy, and to the major schools and styles from Gestalt to systems theory. As a result, our practice began to change.

We began to gain our first glimmers of understanding about what was going on. We began to learn how to listen to what our patients were saying. We began to learn how to analyze their problems in terms that could lead to actual resolution of those problems. We began to build a repertoire of interventions that actually work.

Parenting as a Performing Art

We gradually began to realize that if our patients were to be successful in raising their own children, they really ought to learn those skills, too. The revolution in psychotherapy is more than thirty years old now. Why not use those marvelous skills and methods for childrearing? Why not teach them to parents? Why have they not been applied to childrearing?

Why shouldn't parents have the benefit of those skills? The skills of the therapist are the same skills needed by anyone who wants to be effective in human relations. They are the same skills needed by parents for effective interaction with their children.

We also remained painfully aware of our own deficiencies, our own inability to respond adequately to the parent who, at the end of the visit, pleadingly asked for more specifics on how to cope with their child's tantrums, their child's eating or sleeping problems, with sibling rivalry, fearfulness, a thousand and one things.

We thought that there must be some specific knowledge somewhere, some source of tried and true pragmatic methods. We searched the literature of a century of pedagogy without much success. We cut across cultures, we read Margaret Mead on childrearing in Samoa and learned that there, too, in that seeming paradise, childrearing was simply left to chance and tradition.[1] No provision was made for collecting, enhancing, perfecting specific techniques.

But what about the bestselling popular books on childrearing? Aren't the bookstores loaded with such books?

True; and they perform a valuable service in translating into popular language the current scientific understanding of the principles of child development. But if you have read those books, you know that most of them don't tell you specifically what you really need to know. They tell you to be consistent and loving, for example—but they don't tell you what that translates into in terms of the argument you are having right now with your eight-year-old. Or they give advice such as, ''Keep the communication channels open. Talk it over''—which is fine if your child is old enough to talk and willing to talk and sophisticated enough to perform verbal manipulation of abstract ideas. That's a pretty tall order! And what does it mean, anyway, to ''keep communication channels open?'' Just exactly how do you do such a thing?

Some books do provide some specifics, of course. One book that we like a lot is ''How to Talk So Kids Will Listen and Listen So Kids Will Talk'' by Adele Faber and Elaine Mazlish.[2] Another useful text is ''Without Spanking or Spoiling. A Practical Approach to Toddler and Preschool Guidance'' by Elizabeth Crary.[3] A third is ''Self-Esteem: A Family Affair'' by Jean Illsley Clarke.[4] And Dr. Thomas Gordon's ''Parent Effectiveness Training'' provides a number of specific verbal formulations for use in specified situations.[5]

But few if any books teach the actual art of influencing the behavior and attitudes of your children by both verbal and non-verbal means in such a way that they will spontaneously and of their own impulse do the things that are constructive for them and for the peace and tranquillity of the family. What most books don't teach is exactly what to do and say when your child won't eat the sandwich you have just made for them because it wasn't cut into two exactly equal halves. What they don't teach can be summarized in the phrase: Parenting As A Performing Art.

We finally decided to conduct our own parents' classes and learn while teaching.

So were born our Sunday afternoon Parents' Advanced Strategy Seminars. We called them Advanced Strategy Seminars because the focus was on acquiring a set of specific strategies rather than on good advice and fine general principles.

To provide the kind of learning environment we had in mind, we structured the classes as a small intimate interaction group. We met on Sunday afternoons from 1:30 to about 4, so people would have enough time to explain in detail the kinds of problems they were having with their children and to consider the various possibilities for solutions. Nursing mothers were encouraged to bring their babies with them, but older children were not invited. These seminars were for the parents.

After ten years of Sunday Seminars, here is the book drawn from those ten years of experience.

We have kept the seminar format for this book because the small group process "flows" more naturally than a didactic presentation, but since this is an amalgamation of many seminars, the material has been compressed, extended, modified and blended to give a logical coherence to the whole thing. The names of the participants have of course been changed, and, where necessary to preserve privacy, certain details have been altered.

We are especially grateful to the many couples and individual parents who have attended our seminars over the years, who contributed many of the examples cited in this book, and who served as guinea pigs for some of our early efforts. In a very real sense, this book has been made possible by them.

Specific Parenting Strategies

The specific strategies presented here are well known to practicing therapists. In all probability they have been used on occasion since the early days of humanity. However, their recognition as specific strategies has come much later, in most cases in our own era. We have gleaned them from scattered references, in the field of therapy and from other sources. We have given credit wherever we could find a printed source.[6] We have tried them out and have retained them because they work—not infallibly, not every time, but often enough to be worth learning.

Learning to improve parenting skills is obviously an ongoing process. As parents, we individually have the capacity to improve our parenting skills over the course of our own lives. Similarly, society has the possibility of improving parenting skills over the long term of the centuries. While some advances have been made over the long term, progress in this area is much slower than it could be. One major reason is the discounting of the importance of deliberate study of parenting skills. It just isn't considered very important. You're not likely to find it in the curriculum in any school. There is a general belief that there isn't much to it, anyway. Obviously, we disagree. We feel that parenting is important. We are convinced that it can be learned, just as any skill can be learned.

Others—including some child care specialists—may feel that it is a mistake to put such potent tools into the hands of parents who lack lengthy professional training. Our reply is that no one can avoid influencing others. The only question is whether we are going to do it knowingly or unknowingly. We believe that knowledge is better than ignorance.

This book is our attempt to make a constructive contribution to a world where improvement in the quality of human interactions may be a deciding factor for our very survival as a species. As Watzlawick and colleagues have so clearly stated:

> ''. . . *the world of human behavior clearly stands out today as that area in which our understanding and skills most need revision.*''[7]

This is not a book on child care techniques. In these pages you will not learn how to diaper a baby or take a toddler's temperature. Neither is it a do-it-yourself child psychiatry text. It is a book on parenting, for ordinary parents meeting ordinary problems in raising their children. It is intended to teach easy and elegant ways of interacting with children in order to achieve parenting goals. It is full of recipes and specific instructions and it presents general principles only when they can actually be put to practical use.

But the book is more than a set of recipes. If the spirit and method of approach used here are properly absorbed, you can learn from them new ways of finding elegant and easy solutions for yourself. Then you will be on your way to enjoying the mastery of Parenting As A Performing Art.

How To Use This Book

Readers who learn best from lists will find the Strategies, General Principles, and Case Histories listed separately in the Appendices, beginning on Page 333. A word of warning is in order: while many of the strategies can be picked up and used ''off the shelf,'' it's probably wise nevertheless to read the text for a better understanding of how, why, and when to use a given strategy.

The text is divided roughly into three parts: Chapters 1 through 8 develop basic concepts of parenting as a communication skill, with emphasis on communication as a feedback (cybernetic) process. Chapters 9 through 18 consider strategies in relation to child developmental levels, inborn temperament, the ''parent factor'' (the limitations and hangups of parents themselves), and questions of discipline and autonomy. Chapters 19 through 21 are freewheeling tours of the use of advanced strategies for larger goals of self-esteem, competency, and sense of success in life.

We have deliberately avoided organizing the text around ''problems'' such as ''toilet training,'' ''obedience,'' etc. Readers who get beyond the first eight or nine chapters will probably understand that such ''problems'' represent self-defeating definitions that simply get in the way of successful parenting strategies

Chapter 1

In Real Life It's The Fox

Key Ideas

JG: Let's begin by introducing a few key ideas that are basic to the kind of approach that I like to use. You've probably gathered by now that I'm not very much on theory. I'm willing to take a technique here and a technique there from whatever source and use whatever seems to work. So this is not going to be a Freudian psychoanalytic or an Erikson child development seminar or—you name it, it's not going to be it. It's going to be more like a recipe book. We're aiming to get a repertoire of techniques that you can actually use—things that you can actually do in the real setting where you are, rather than fine general statements such as—

BG: ''Be consistent.''

JG: Right, ''Be consistent, be firm, be nurturing, be understanding.'' What do those words mean? How do you carry them out, operationally? Why not have the flexibility to be a little unfirm, a little inconsistent if circumstances require it? How about a new principle that says: Be consistent when it's useful and inconsistent when that's useful? So you can see how pragmatic this is going to be.

Repertoire

The basic idea that we're talking about here is repertoire—which means having a bag of tricks that you can use.

Arthur: Strategies?

Strategies

JG: And strategies. These two things go together. The strategies are what you want to have a repertoire of. I emphasize the repertoire part because if you learn about strategies and don't know how to use them—if you don't have them available—it doesn't do you much good just to know them. Repertoire means being able to switch very quickly from one pattern of reaction to another pattern of reaction.

Observer Mode

If you think about this, it gets you in the habit of stepping aside from your own behavior and taking a look at it, by making a mental comment about it: "Oh, I'm doing this now. I'm going with the compliance or I'm going with the resistance or I'm doing a reframe"—that kind of thing.

That's very unfamilar for most people, to think about it like that. If you're like me, you were raised with the idea that behavior is just something that you naturally do. If a situation happens in a certain way and you get angry or sad or scared or even happy, well, that's just natural, there's nothing else that could possibly happen. It's inevitable, it's just fate, or, worse yet, "This is the way the world is."

But when you start thinking about your response as a specific pattern and one of a series of choices that you might make, then you can get into a position where you can criticize your own performance and say, "Oh, I see, the angry response didn't get me where I want. Maybe I'll try this other response."

In Real life It's the Fox

It's like that story, the Fox and the Hedgehog—you know, Aesop's Fable—or was it La Fontaine? I can never remember. The Fox is the one that has the bag of tricks, the Hedgehog is the one that does the one thing only. Now I happen to feel that Aesop turned the moral of that story just backwards, because he had the hedgehog being the one that won out every time. But in real life it's the fox with the multiple options that succeeds in the higher percentage of cases, so what we're going to aim at is having a repertoire of multiple options—options for responding in any given case.

Reynard the fox got in trouble because he had too many tricks in his bag. There were too many things that he knew how to do. But that's not our problem with raising kids. Our problem is that we don't know enough things to do. In particular, I think for many people *the idea that there is a set of strategies* is the really new idea. I think for many people the belief is that you just act natural, or you just do what you're supposed to do, or something like that. Really that locks you in to doing one thing and if it doesn't work then you do it a little harder, and then maybe you remember,

"Oh, yeah, my mom always told me, 'Try, try again'." So you try again and it still doesn't work and after a while you're frustrated because you're using one strategy and it's not working.

Only One Strategy

Now all over the world there is one very popular strategy, which is called, "Asking for what you want." You ask the person directly and if they do it, great, it's wonderful, you have succeeded. But if they don't do it, if they say, "No, I don't want to," then, well, you might try again or you might think, maybe it works if you yell at them, or if you stamp your foot, or if you add a cookie to it. Basically, you're stuck with it, it's one strategy.[1] What we're aiming at here is having a multitude of strategies—or at least a nice set of 10 or 20 or more so that you can go from one thing to the next, try something else.

Now there's a problem with this, and that is that it involves deliberately doing something that you wouldn't spontaneously do. It involves thinking of another way to do a thing and then deliberately doing it differently from the way that you might spontaneously feel like doing it. For some people that's a very uncomfortable thing to do. They get an uncomfortable feeling that they're play-acting, or that they're not being real, or that they are manipulating their child. I just want to tell you these things because you might experience that at some point.

Believe me, that feeling goes away. After you have succeeded three times, the new strategy becomes your spontaneous response. Then you don't feel as if you're manipulating anybody at all, and you don't feel uncomfortable, you just spontaneously do it. So stick with it. It's like playing the piano. Eventually you learn how to do the scale by putting your thumb under and you don't think about it any more. The first time you try, it seems unreasonable.

Technique

So what I'm talking about, the basic approach here, is having some repertoire. It's just like playing the piano. If you can only play one tune, you're kind of limited. Do any of you know a natural musician, a person that can just sit down and play the piano, by ear?

They sound wonderful. But after a while it gets boring, because their repertoire is limited and they don't have the technical skills to do the really difficult stuff. You have to study!

Learn! Learn! Learn!

Remember Pinocchio when he went off to the island of donkeys? And what was the message he was given before he went? Learn! learn! learn! I can't remember—was it Jiminy Cricket that said that? Who was it that told him that? But that's it—Learn! learn! learn! You have to learn how to do this.

A Bigger Bag Of Tricks

So the basic idea is repertoire. If you've ever had anything to do with children, you know that if you want to be successful in dealing with them

"You've got to have a bigger bag of tricks."

you've got to have a bigger bag of tricks than they have. You need to know a substantial number of specific strategies if you want to have any satisfying percentage of successes in dealing with children. You really need a repertoire of specific strategies that have a proven track record of successes.

Practice! Practice! Practice!

Having a repertoire that you can use means that you have to practice. It means that you actually have to deliberately practice some of these things until you can do them swiftly, because in a typical situation with a child, your response time has got to be within a certain number of seconds or ideally within half a second, to get the best results.

Time Bombs

Well, that's not strictly true. You can get long-term effects. For example, if you want your child to go to college, you can start that process in infancy. Then you're going to have to wait a long time to see the result, if any. But you can actually set off these slow-fuse type of reactions so that your child might decide that yes, they do want to go to college. You start that very early on. Remind me of this later on and I'll tell you some true stories about kids that were primed many years earlier. One went on to college and graduate school, and one never did go to college and still turned out well, because that was his decision, that was the life pattern that he chose.

Supplementing Instinctive Parenting With A Disciplined Set of Strategies

So what we're doing is supplementing instinctive parenting with a disciplined set of strategies where you learn what to do even though it doesn't coincide exactly with your maternal or paternal instincts. You may have a feeling that you just ought to do a certain thing—particularly with Moms, if the baby cries they say, ''Oh, I have to go and comfort that baby.'' That is what has made the human race survive for thousands of years but it's also made for very noisy babies.

If you want to have a baby that survives, of course you have to know how to protect them and meet their basic needs. But you can do more than just survive. You can survive comfortably, even elegantly—if you know specifically what to do.

Choices

This doesn't mean you don't pay attention to your own intuition or trust your own instincts. It just means that now you have some choices. If you want to have a baby that does a lot of smiling and relatively little crying, then you have to know the skills of reinforcing the behavior that you want and skipping the reinforcement of the behavior that you don't want. You don't deny them your love and affection. You just add on this new skill in human relations.

So our aim here is not to take away anybody's strategies, but rather to add twenty-five or thirty-five or even fifty new strategies to them. If you have strategies that work, if you have strategies you're comfortable with, you keep 'em. But you may want to reshuffle the order of priority that you use them in. And that's OK. That's your decision. Our function here is to give you that repertoire.

Feedback

The second key idea is feedback. Engineers know what feedback really is, I mean real feedback, honest-to-gosh feedback, where the output of the machinery feeds back to control the operation of the machine, more or less. Well, the way I'm using the term is not quite the same thing, but it's close.

What I'm talking about with feedback is—looking with your two eyes to see what is happening when you do what you do. This is the part that is so hard for us as human beings to get accustomed to, because we are told, "You should do such and such," and it's often presented to us in terms of moral principles, "You should *always* do such and such."

So in interacting with the child, you are looking at your child and something inside tells you, "Now in dealing with your child you should be firm and you should be consistent." So you're being firm and you're being consistent or whatever you think that is, and if you're not looking at what the kid is doing you may fail to see that his chin is sticking out farther and farther and he's gritting his teeth together and his neck is getting very stiff, and it's quite clear that kid is never going to do what you are recommending to him at the moment. In fact, he's being just as firm and as consistent as you are!

The feedback is being sent to you but unless you take it in you won't be seeing what's going on as a result of what you're doing. You get the idea? Feedback. Sensory Feedback. So what we're going to do is practice this in the next few sessions until you get to be about a hundred times better at feedback than the average person is right now.

"The feedback is being sent to you but unless you take it in, you won't see what's going on as a result of what you're doing."

The Other Person's Behavior
Is Your Feedback

That's really the central fundamental idea that I use in talking about human interactions. The thing to remember is, no matter what kind of interaction is going on, the other person's actual behavior is your feedback. That's what tells you whether you're succeeding or not.

If you've read other books, standard books on childrearing, you know that they are very heavy on the program side. They tell you what you as a parent ought to do. So people come at the interaction with their children with this idea that they should do X. But in your particular case X may not be working at all. And if you don't have the feedback to pick up the fact that program X is not working, you will continue to use program X, or if you're like many of us you'll then do program X twice as hard. It's supposed to work because the book says it works, and so the reason it isn't working must be because you aren't doing it hard enough.

Do Something Else

Most of us have been taught, ''Try, try again, if at first you don't succeed,'' and all of that. I'm teaching you the reverse. If something that you're doing isn't working, for crying out loud don't keep doing it. Do the thing that's going to work, or at least do something else, because then you'll have a better chance of getting the results you want. So feedback is a very basic concept. It helps you to make your next move.

Infant Signals

One of the ways to start is with babies. Babies, it turns out, for thousands of years have been signaling with their bodies and their faces, sending messages to parents which parents react to, but with rare exceptions hardly any parent ever knows consciously that they're getting a signal and responding to it.

Now some of these signals are pretty obvious, right? And some of them get a pretty quick response! Have I talked to any of you about baby signals before? It's incredible that the first papers on this topic were published in the 1970's. The first time that anybody ever tumbled to the fact that babies are sending messages to their parents, and that you can read those messages by the movements of their body, was only twenty years ago.

So we'll be talking a little bit about what babies actually do and how you can pick up their signals. Then you know where they're at and what they're doing, what state they're in and the probabilities that they would respond favorably or unfavorably to a given action on your part.

Chapter 2

He Just Gave A Little Chirp

Baby Signals

JG: Well, the thing about baby signals is that they exist. That was a giant step forward for mankind when it finally dawned on us that babies give signals, when we started thinking about their spontaneous behavior in this way. Of course they're not giving them deliberately and consciously. And if you don't know that there is such a thing you won't look for it. It doesn't mean that you won't respond to them, because it's impossible not to respond to another person.[1] Trying not to respond is just another form of response.[2] So the baby has an effect on you, whether you know about signals or not.

You get these little short sequences of behavior that they run through over and over again. A paper came out in 1978, written by—

BG: David Givens.

JG: David Givens, published in *Sign Language Studies*.[3] I always thought that it should have been published on the front page of the *New York Times*, because he described twenty signals of infants, repetitive signals that consistently convey the same information. The way it happened was a classic example of serendipity. It wasn't a grant project. It hadn't been thought up in advance. He was invited to review some video tapes of mothers and babies, and as he was going over the tapes, all of a sudden it dawned on him that the babies were repetitively producing certain movements.

BG: They were initiating interactions.

JG: They were initiating interactions or they were trying to announce something about their own state. So he wrote down twenty signals that he could see, wrote the paper, and sent it to *Sign Language Studies*.

> **Donald:** *What are some of the signals that he observed? Can you remember any of them?*

JG: Yes! I use them every day. And when couples come to me prenatally to talk about their future baby, I make a point of telling them specifically which signals they are going to see in the delivery room, and how they can respond appropriately if they know what those signals are and what they mean. They can respond appropriately. I point out that the baby will understand if an adult responds appropriately to a signal.

BG: They understand that there is intelligent life out there, in this universe!

Tray-Pound

JG: That's right. I looked back into the literature and discovered that Arnold Gesell had spent twenty years at Yale studying children under laboratory circumstances and had failed to stumble on the fact that they signal with their bodies, nonverbally. He even described in detail one of the signals and apparently didn't realize that it had communication value. It's the so-called tray-pound signal. You've probably seen your own kid do this, if they have a high chair, banging on the tray or banging their hands on the table top, or if they don't have anything to bang their hands on they just do this with their hands in the air.

BG: —or with their hands flat, like this.

JG: —or flat. That signal has two meanings, depending on the emotional tone connected with it. If it's a positive emotional tone it means enthusiasm, if it's a negative emotional tone it means frustration. Kids that are being fed too slowly or too fast, or being stuffed too full, will often bang on their tray. That's tray-pound. That's a signal. I've seen it done in army mess halls! That is a communication. Not necessarily deliberate and conscious. Depending on their age, there may be some conscious awareness of the fact that they are trying to influence Mom. But it is a faithful reflection of their internal state. At that moment they are in a somewhat agitated state.

BG: I grew up in the country, and there were mothers who could tell you stuff about their own children. I think women and mothers have been discounted through the ages because there have always been mothers who could interpret their baby's signals.

JG: Absolutely!

BG: I think many mothers did this sort of thing intuitively, but it never got in the literature.

JG: Many parents have known this stuff at an unconscious level, maybe even the conscious level, but Establishment Science just discovered it in 1978. Now it's officially known. It has been known to tens of thousands of parents down through the ages, but now it's officially true because someone has reported it and put it in a refereed journal.

Intake Mode

The very first signal, or one of the first signals, is Intake Mode. This occurs within minutes after delivery. You can see it better if the overhead lights are off. Babies usually keep their eyes closed if the light is too bright. If you get the ambient lighting down low enough, their eyelids will automatically open and then you can see that they have a search pattern that starts within a couple of minutes after delivery and continues until they actually locate a parent's face. The first face that comes into their field of view, they will lock onto and study it. It's usually Mom or Dad. And in that process a lot of very interesting things happen. It's obvious that they are taking in huge amounts of visual information, because within five or ten minutes of this process going on, they will have adjusted their own facial muscles to more or less match your face, so that they begin to look like you.

The signal connected with that is called Intake Mode. The baby does a kind of slow dance with movements of arms, legs, fingers, and toes. That signal tells you they're open for business—they're ready to take in information. That's when you can actually exchange information with the baby. If you bring your face up close and make a sound, the baby will hear it and sometimes even repeat it.

The Signal, ''Hello!'' (Interaction Signal)

From a signal standpoint, when a baby looks into your face, it has the same meaning as it does when any other person looks into your face. It means, ''Hello!'' It means, ''I see you and I am letting you see me and see that I see you.'' It's an exchange of validation, it's an Interaction Signal. The response, of course, is any kind of response. Any kind of response that you give will be an adequate response because it will tell the baby that they have been seen, that their gaze has in fact encountered another person, and that person recognizes that there is somebody there, namely the baby. That's probably the very first validation or, at any rate, a very early, very powerful validation of the existence of the baby.

BG: I guess it's something like the old system when they first started having radio or telegraph: ''Acknowledge!'' ''Roger!'' ''Over!''

JG: Exactly! "I see you, do you see me?" If the other person acts as if they don't see anything, that is a negation. That is saying, "You don't exist," or "You're not important enough to be responded to."

So the mere act of looking back at your baby completes that first communication, that first exchange. You can actually see the baby responding to your gaze with body signals that indicate comfort. They relax and typically they look away and then they look back again. Then they do it again. When they look at you, you look back or smile, then they look down and you wait for them for a second or two and then they look back. After you have done this little dance a few times they realize that not only do they exist, but also that the other people think that they are so wonderful that they are willing to dance with them, they are willing to pace them. You send powerful nonverbal messages through these signals.

Parents can't help doing this. In the delivery room, when you see your baby in those first few minutes, there's no way that you cannot react. It may not be by a deliberate conscious response, but you are going to do something, you are going to turn your body, alter your posture, raise an eyebrow —something is going to happen and that is all the baby needs to get that first validation.

So when a baby looks in your face, that's a signal. And if they really want to interact they'll look right in your eyes, and then at that point it's almost humanly impossible to avoid responding. It's very difficult not to do something when a baby looks you right in the face. Parents always respond in some way. Even if it's just a frown, they will respond to a baby who is trying to make contact in this way.

Breakaway Signal

And when they look away, that's another signal. That signal is probably equally as important as or even more important than the interaction signal, because that's the one that says, "Give me a break." That's the one that says, "Lay off!" That's the Breakaway Signal, which means that they've had enough interaction and they need to stop interacting. That's just natural for human beings. You run awhile, then you've got to stop and catch your breath. You think awhile, then you've got to stop and relax your mind, and so on.

Bon Appetit!

The signals that have been identified so far represent maybe one out of ten thousand, one out of one hundred thousand. We think we know what it means when a baby roots from side to side; but David Givens noticed that there's a signal that a baby gives even before they start rooting. That's this signal:[4] hands together in the midline, knuckles touching, moving up and down like this. A baby that's doing this has not yet reached the stage of grinding hunger pangs, they're starting to think about food, but they're not hurting.

So, if a mom knows this, and offers to nurse at this stage, the entire process of feeding now operates at the level of pleasure, rather than hunger pangs. That's a very important difference. Many moms pick up early signals without knowing what the signal is, they just feel that the baby needs to be nursed, and they will nurse before the hunger pangs appear. Those are the lucky babies, who have the sense of power because they understand all they have to do is give this signal and they have the nursing thing under their control. They can influence mom. They can even influence Dad—a bottle fed baby can influence Dad. Of course it's not conscious and deliberate.

He Just Gave A Little Chirp

BG: We had a baby in our practice a few years ago who hardly ever cried at all and we tried to find out why this was. I went to visit the mother and baby at home one time for another reason. We were sitting there and I hadn't heard anything, the baby was asleep when we arrived, and suddenly Mom said, ''Oh, there's Jeremy, time to get him up and feed him,'' and I hadn't heard anything, but what he did was, he just had a little signal that went like this [BG makes chirping sound], and that was all. He had woke up and was wet, and he needed to be changed and fed. We were commenting on this and she said that he's always done that because they had had the lecture that John gave prenatally. She used to nurse him whenever he'd start chirping like this. Then he associated it with these sounds, and he seldom cried for anything. He would signal her, ''Hey mom, hey!'' and she'd figure out what it was that he needed, and he was just a very happy baby.

Is He Ready To Communicate?

Linda: With Kevin, the first thing he does when I look away is to make a face.

JG: He doesn't like it!

Linda: and then he looks away.

JG: And then *he* looks away!

Mark: Well, if you're not going to communicate with me!

JG: Incredible volumes of information passed back and forth!

So when a baby looks away, fine!! You don't say, He doesn't love me. You just say, He's looking away! And you wait until he looks back again. With babies that's real important. With older kids, too, if there is not a readiness to communicate, you may have difficulties.

Mark: You certainly will!

Awareness Of Feedback

JG: This brings us to the other component of communication, and that is, picking up your feedback.

The child—every baby—has this repertoire. They can give you ten ways or a hundred ways of saying, "Leave me alone!" But if you don't pick it up, if you don't detect the feedback, then you will continue to try to interact at a time when the child is saying, "I'm not ready to interact." So what I'm talking about is awareness.

The thing to be aware of is the feedback that you're getting. If you send out a signal—whether it's a verbal or nonverbal signal—and you don't notice what the child does in response, you're operating blind. You're like the ship at sea at night in the fog. If you don't know the feedback, you don't know which direction to go. So awareness of feedback is the missing link that has been left out of the textbooks of pedagogy throughout the eighteenth and nineteenth and twentieth centuries.

So we're going to talk about picking up the feedback, what kind of feedback we get, but most particularly being aware of it, because most of the signals that kids give are quite plain and all you have to do is to notice them and you'll know where you're at.

Pay Attention!

In terms of interacting with babies and other people, the crucial question is, "Are they in Intake Mode?" "Are they paying attention to you directly, or have they gone off somewhere?" If you try to feed in information when a person is processing internal stuff, it's really pretty ineffective. You've probably all had the experience of talking to somebody who wasn't listening to you. You can see they're gone, you talk louder, it doesn't help!

"Awareness of feedback is the missing link that has been left out of textbooks."

Turned Off

With kids, too, we get in the habit of yelling at kids and telling them what we want, and half the time they're turned off. If you notice that they're turned off, you can say, "Oh, yeah! Nothing being taken in, so why broadcast?" It'll save you a lot of unnecessary vocalizing.

> *Bobbi:* *Aaron would be really quiet while he was doing something and he was so into it that when I would say something to him, he didn't hear me. I'd say it louder, and he wouldn't hear me. I could stand right next to him and say it, and he still would not hear me. When he gets into his own thing, it's just as if nothing is happening around him at all but what he's doing.*

Charlene: Lily is like that to the extreme. We frequently have to hold her head, look in her face, and say, "Do you hear me? Say yes or no!" Literally! You have to go that far to get her to pay attention.

Tuned In, Tuned Out

JG: Now, of course, we, on the other hand, have been trained for twelve years, sixteen years—however many years of school we've had—to do what's called, "Pay attention!" The teacher says, "Pay attention!" the first day and sixteen years later the teacher is still saying, "Pay attention!" and we're still striving to pay attention. Which really means: "Disregard all the cues that you would ordinarily respond to and pay attention to the cue that the teacher is giving."

That's a very artificial thing for a human being to do. It's truly difficult to learn, and it's learned at a great sacrifice because it means that we make a decision to please the teacher. We agree to turn off ninety-nine percent of our experience, things that we would ordinarily have paid attention to. Especially with regard to human beings, we're only supposed to notice what is actually being said, in so many words. We're not supposed to pay attention to their posture or their eyes, we're not supposed to consciously notice that they're bored, that they're anxious or nervous or have something else going on inside. We're just supposed to listen to what they say. We're not even supposed to notice what's going on inside ourselves.

This is a very artificial state of affairs and kids don't do it. When they do, it's only with great difficulty. You really have to get their attention somehow and persuade them. Part of the art of childraising, I think, involves getting in touch with all of that 99% within ourselves that we have learned how to disregard, because that's what the kids are tuned in to. We can say to them, "X", but they see by our bodies that "Y" is what's happening, and so they'll respond to that. I think learning to be really effective with kids, to be good parents, is for us to become aware of the "Y" that's going on with us and also to be able to see the "Z" that is going on with the kid, and tune in to that and make use of it.

Pay Attention To The Carts!!

Karla: Where I see that happen is when I take my two older kids to the grocery store. I used to walk in and say, "Now you guys have to pay attention to the carts around you." They're five and seven, and the last thing they're worrying about is whether some lady is going to knock them down with her cart. They're looking at everything on the shelves. I realized, by watching them, that they just can't pay attention to so many things at once. I always thought, "They're old enough to pay attention now," but in that situation, they just can't. If I don't want to get frustrated, they have to stay home unless I'm only going to pick up a few things.

JG: It's very difficult to direct your conscious attention. It wants to go where it wills. If you've ever tried to pay attention when you don't want to, you know how hard it is. The kids are paying attention, but not to what you want them to.

Karla: Well, they can do it for a minute, but they can't keep it up through every aisle unless you remind them, "Now pay attention!"

JG: Now, there are certain things you can do. It's a fact of life that if a person is hungry, one's conscious attention is going to be directed toward food. You will walk into a room and the first thing you will check out is whether there's anything edible in it. You may try to forget that because maybe it's your purpose to sit in the room and study for two hours; but if your stomach is gnawing at you, you'll notice the crackers on the shelf and pretty soon you'll notice them again. There's this irresistible return of your conscious attention to that which is the uppermost need for your total self.

It's real hard to fight that. It takes a lot of practice. But if, instead of fighting it, you use it, you can get incredible results. It's sometimes even useful in childrearing. For example, if you feed your kids a big meal before you take them to the supermarket, you cut down to some extent on the amount of physiological motivation to be interested in the items as food.

You still have the problem that it's a beautiful visual display. It's just so interesting. There are so many new things happening in the supermarket that their attention is going to be just seized by all those interesting things. It's very hard to fight against that. So, how could we use it?

Karla: Well, one thing has helped. The markets have the little baskets that you can carry. If I give each kid a basket, they wait for me to tell them what to get. They're more in tune to what I'm doing and sticking closer. But you can only do that when you're in a good mood and have a lot of time. Then it's more of a privilege for them to go with me and be able to do that. It really helps all of us because they're waiting for me to tell them what to do and not just running all over looking at everything.

Indirectly Directing Another Person's Attention

JG: Most of us haven't had much experience in directing other people's spontaneous attention.[5] We've had a lot of experience in sitting in classrooms and hearing the command, ''Pay attention!'' So we tend to use that by telling our kids, ''Pay attention!'' But deliberately practicing the specific technical skill of indirectly directing another person's attention—we usually don't do that.

They Can Just Shut Down

Sally: Talking about babies wanting to turn away—a friend of mine had a friend with a four-month-old daughter. One day we were all together and she complained that she didn't understand why her baby would fall asleep on her. She said, ''I'll be in the middle of playing with her, and she'll fall asleep!'' To be around that woman was painful for me. I mean—I was just tense! I could see the kid turning away and arching back and then it would just fall asleep.

BG: It was interesting for you to see how sometimes a person doesn't always pick up the meaning of those cues when they're one of the actors in the scene.

JG: Being so involved you don't see it—good point.

BG: And babies do have another step back.

JG: They have a step beyond screaming and crying: they can pass out. That's right, they can turn off, go into a coma, they can become catatonic, that's what that is.

Sally: It was a really strange thing. The kid didn't scream or cry—but then, she was only about 4 months old. I got this feeling that maybe her Mom hadn't listened while she was younger and she just learned that that didn't work.

Graded Series Of Negative Responses

JG: ''No use crying, I'll just turn everything off.'' Right. Those stages are:[6] first, breaking eye contact, that's the first thing babies do to tell you that they've had enough. It was fun but they've had enough, so they break eye contact, they drop their eyes. If you miss that signal, they drop their eyes further and turn them slightly to the right. If you miss that signal, they drop their eyes way down, slide them to the right, and turn their head to the right. If you miss that one, they'll turn their head farther, if you miss that one they'll go into Maximum Gaze Aversion, their head 90 degrees to yours, looking off to the side. That's the same signal that dogs and cats give when they don't want to obey you, and they want to pretend that you're not there, as if to say, "If I can't see you, I don't need to respond."

After that, a baby will begin to turn their head beyond 90 degrees, the arm toward which they're turned begins to stretch out, the other arm begins to bend up toward their body, the head begins to go back, the back begins to arch, and eventually they are literally trying to arch backwards to get away from you. Ten stages of withdrawal. They are trying to say, "Please, leave me alone, I need a little free time here to integrate the previous experiences," that's what they're trying to tell you, in baby language.

You can eventually drive them into that posture, and from there, their inborn repertoire goes directly to crying and screaming or even, as Sally said, into a catatonic state where they're shutting off their sensory input, and that's obviously not a healthy situation for the baby to be in. It might be all right for the oppossum, which does that as a matter of evolutionary development. When danger threatens, the oppossum goes into a coma. For human beings it's not a very useful thing, especially for learning.

Feeding Him Backwards,
Not Even Seeing His Mouth

You see this often with relatives who want to play with the baby. They've only got two hours—they really want to get the most out of their time and they begin to move in on the baby while the baby is trying to move away.

There's also a videotape where a baby about 9-12 months of age is being fed in a high chair. The mother is trying to feed the baby, the baby doesn't want the food, is not only clamping his lips together but is turning his head, farther and farther. Finally his head and body are turned around 180 degrees in the high chair, and mom is bringing her arm around and feeding him backwards, not even seeing his mouth. Now that's to be in the grip of an idea, right? That's to be possessed by an idea, instead of paying attention to the feedback.

The Hardest Step Of All
(Shift Your Basic Orientation)

JG: So signals are not necessarily subtle. You don't require superhuman vision to see that your baby has got himself twisted 180 degrees away from you. All you have to do is look and say, "What am I seeing? What is this?" The reason I dwell on this over and over again is that this is the hardest step of all. It's the shift in orientation from what we want to what is actually happening. We tend to reference some kind of program in our head[7] that says, "You should be nourishing this child, you should be feeding this child, this child should be eating his green spinach." It's real hard to shift from that orientation of referring to our internal needs and the program in our head, to looking at the child and seeing, for goodness' sake, where's the child at.

My Agenda Or Your Agenda?

That's the secret of the power, when you begin to habitually look and pay attention to where the other person is at, where the baby is at, where the child is at. You need that information. Even if it's just so elementary as this, that your child is just doing what you tell him because you are telling him to do it, you need to know that. What they're doing at that moment is protecting themselves against the interaction with you, by doing what you demand, but at the cost of shutting out what they really feel like and maybe what their real needs are. When you learn to tune in to their agenda, to feel the current of their life and what's up next for them, rather than referencing your own anxieties—that's the key.

Infant Scientists

During the break Louise brought up a point that I thought was very pertinent. She was talking about how babies and toddlers often know what they want to do but they lack the resources or the skill or the practice to carry it out. If they have savvy parents, they can even set up an arrangement whereby the parents can indicate by pointing or otherwise what it is that the child wants, and carry out the necessary procedures and then the child feels very gratified because they've been able to get something done that's actually physically beyond their capacity. They've been able to order it done. It's quite clear that their intelligence, even at a very early stage, is highly advanced and what they lack is skills. They lack practice in doing things.

There's one thing that I'd like to leave you with, and that is the awareness that the baby, even the newborn baby, is a complete human being with a functioning intelligence.[8]

I want to tell you a story about Doctor T. G. R. Bower of Edinburgh. He is a baby student—a baby scholar—and a very honest one, because he admits in his book that he didn't believe that babies under five months of age reach for things.[9]

Parents kept coming to him and saying, "We know our baby does this," and he would say, "That's nice, yes, go away!"—until finally one day a five-day-old baby was right in front of him and the baby did this and he saw it, and he said, "My God, this baby is really reaching, it is true."

Contingency Detection

Dr. Bower reports some fascinating studies done by some of his colleagues in the field. What they did was to take newborn babies and rig up an apparatus whereby they would put a little yarn thread around one wrist and attach the thread to a mobile, so that when the baby moved its wrist the mobile would move and make a sound. Of course, babies being what they are, they spontaneously move, and pretty soon they move the mobile. Dr. Bower's colleagues found that the average baby in the newborn stage takes 20 minutes to learn that it is the left hand that will make the mobile move. Then they will move their left hand to make the mobile move. They will do it over and over and over, and as they do it, they will smile.

Then the researchers would put the yarn on the right hand, and 20 minutes later, the babies would be moving their right hand and smiling. Then they set up a sophisticated series of electronic switches, so that if the babies turned their head on the pillow twice to the left and once to the right, it would make the mobile move. Inside of 20 minutes, the average baby, in the newborn stage, had figured out how to jerk their head to the left twice and once to the right, to make the mobile move. These babies were smiling, long before the textbooks say the social smile comes in.

Now this is a very interesting experiment. Anything that a baby spontaneously does, anything that is in their spontaneous repertoire, movement-wise, it only takes them 20 minutes to figure out what it is that they have to do, to produce a result that is gratifying, that they can see. And when they do that, when they master that, they smile. You can think of this as the proof that human beings have an instinctive reward system built into themselves, for figuring out that X produces Y. In other words we are intrinsically rational, logical, and scientific and we enjoy it. OK? I don't want to read too much into this but nevertheless you get the idea. It's called Contingency Detection. The ability to discover, "If I do X, the outside world will do Y."

Nice experiment. So, whenever you're dealing with your baby remember this. This is a human being with real, rational, scientific powers of observation, of making connections between cause and effect—not the kind of scientific cause and effect that a professional scientist would understand, but the simple cause and effect that if behavior X is located in time just prior to event Y, then behavior X must have produced event Y. And there's a smile with doing it that way. This drive to learn about the world is what we're trying to tap into. Babies like things to be predictable, understandable. What they don't like is to be crossed up, is to have something work, and then not work.

Baby Sonar

Now one of the babies that Doctor Bower had in his laboratory, one time, was a baby that was born totally blind. It had been a preemie, and at the time of the studies it was approximately forty-six weeks gestational age—that is, equal to about six weeks old. This baby vocalized in a very strange way, making sharp, clicking noises with his lips and tongue. On a hunch, Professor Bower—in total silence—dangled a large ball in front of the baby. The baby produced a series of clicks and then turned his head toward the ball. Now matter how the ball was moved, the baby would click and then orient toward the ball.[10]

This baby was using sonar, echolocation, to find that object in his environment. When the baby was four months old, Dr. Bower fitted him with a sophisticated electronic chirp generator. Within a few minutes, that baby was responding appropriately to the signals and by six months of age had learned to detect an approaching bottle, find the nipple, reach out and grab the bottle appropriately and feed itself, using the chirps.

So this is built in. The human being will use everything that they have, all the sensory modalities, all the motor abilities. They will use everything to learn about their world, and to find out what they need to know, in order to detect these contingencies, these regularities of pattern. Our job is to not turn that process off. Our job is to encourage that process, to help them find out what they can do and encourage them to do it.

When I read that, I had to think about what I have seen over and over and over at the medical school, with the medical students, in the training for the physical exam, for the examination of a baby. Here are these little babies that utilize the feedback that is coming to them, whether it's auditory, visual, whatever it is, they will pick it up, they will use it, and they will find out what's going on in the outside world around them. Then they will change their behavior to accommodate.

How The Professor Does It

I've seen a professor examining a newborn baby to show a student how to do it. Here's the baby, lying on the table, waving his arms and legs, looking around, opening and closing his eyes, opening and closing his mouth, yawning, sneezing, doing everything. Then here comes the professor! He wants to look in the baby's mouth. He takes a tongue blade and jams it in the baby's mouth, and the baby promptly clamps his jaws together, so the professor has to force the baby's jaws open to look in the mouth.

Then the professor wants to look in the baby's eyes with his light, so he takes this real bright light and he shines it right into the baby's eyes and baby clamps his eyes shut. Then the professor has to take his fingers and pry those little eyelids open. Which is what they all do, every day, I guarantee you, I've seen it forty times a day—just to look in those eyes.

Now, you know and I know that you can get a baby's eyes to open spontaneously by turning off the lights. Then you don't have to pry their eyes open.

Every mother in this room knows how to get a baby to open their mouth. You probably know three or four ways.

BG: One mother in our practice knows that her baby likes to suck on his own big toe, so she puts his big toe up there and he opens his mouth.

JG: There are so many ways to do anything. You're only limited by what you can think of. The one that I like to use is to bring the light up over their head, because when they try to look over their head, their mouth falls open!

The professor wanted to look at the baby's fist, to look at the baby's palms. You know they look for these creases. So he pulled on the baby's fingers. What happened? The baby makes a fist. Then you have to pry the fingers open to see what's going on there.

You can touch the back of a baby's hand, and their hand opens like this.[11]

In every case the doctor was producing the defensive reaction that made his task difficult. He was not utilizing the feedback that he was getting from the baby, to be a signal to modify his own behavior. This just went on and on and on, through the complete physical exam. The doctor was doing what he had been taught. He had been taught how to examine a baby from head to toe. He was using an internal model, a program, a sheet, a protocol, and he was going down that list item by item. Meanwhile the baby was yawning, but the doctor was examining the feet. The baby's mouth was open, you see, but he was examining the feet! Now it's obvious that somewhere between the first week of life and age forty or fifty, something rather serious happens. We stop using our feedback.

BG: We're carefully taught!

JG: We're carefully taught to pay attention to the program inside our head, instead of what's happening in the real world.

Sally: I've taken quite a few art courses. One of the first things they had to teach you to do was to not draw like what you knew to draw. To actually look at what you were drawing. We actually had to unlearn what we had learned before.

BG: That's the hardest thing to do.

JG: Isn't it the truth?

Is This Really Necessary?

It's a re-orientation to where you pay attention to what's really happening, rather than to the program inside your head. We all have that program. By now—age thirty, say—it's probably ten thousand pages of protocol. When you're dealing with your baby, learn to be aware of what your protocol says, and then ask yourself of each and every item, Is this really necessary right now, or is this producing the opposite of what I want?

I hope that some day medical schools will teach the right way to examine a baby.

The same thing applies when you're interacting with your baby. It's not a physical exam, but it's the same basic category, you're interacting. So instead of using this protocol in your head that says, ''You must make them do this, you mustn't let them do that,'' you look at the baby, see what's really happening, and then take your cue from that, and adjust your behavior to what's really happening.

Stonewalling The Baby

JG: That famous experiment where the parents, the mothers, were instructed not to respond to anything that the baby did—basically to stonewall the baby—have you ever seen that movie?[12]

Mark: No.

JG: I sometimes wonder how they have the heart to continue the experiment. A baby—one of their primary signals is the interaction signal where they look into your face. That's one of the first things they do after they're born. They look into the face of the nearest caretaker. The value of this signal, the signal quality, is, ''Hello there! respond and validate me!'' There's no mother on earth who can fail to respond to that unless she's been instructed by the researcher not to do it.

But if you do train yourself to stonewall, you will see it has a very adverse effect on the baby. They will try three or four times to interact with you, and then they will give up, and when they give up their whole body slumps, their head goes down, their eyes go down, and they look like they've just given up. Again, this is almost impossible for human beings to endure, parents just do not allow this to happen.

Well, it's incredible, it's terrible. Here are these Moms with this absolute stone face, shoulders not turning, eyebrows not raising, nothing is happening. The baby looks up into their face, gives them the big eliciting look, you know—

Cora: God!

JG: and they hold it for a second or two, nothing happens, they drop their head, and a few seconds later they come up again and try again. The third time their eyes slide down and to the right, their head goes to the right, their bodies slump, and it's really obvious that they have given up. It's really clear that there's a powerful negative emotion connected with that experience of not being validated. It's as if they don't exist.

So when a baby looks at you, it means, I'm ready for action. I'm ready to interact with you. Do something. It doesn't matter what you do, they're not particular. You can raise an eyebrow—

Louise: Our baby, she's always looking to see what kind of a mood everyone has, to see if her brother is in a good mood—

Morilla: Ah!

Louise: —or if he looks concerned—

JG: and how old is she now?

Louise: She's eight months old now; but even before, when she was only five months, she was always looking to see what mood we were in. If we are happy, smiling at her, she smiles right back. If not, she looks concerned and worried, especially with her brother, whom she adores. You can just see it, she's always worried, because she gets very moody unless he's lovingly heard from, then she's always looking to see, ''What is he going to do now?'' It's amazing!

JG: With your next baby, you can observe that this will happen within five minutes of being born. They actually look into your face, in the delivery room, and when they get that smile back, then they relax.

Morilla: Well, that would argue then that it's very important for your child to be placed with you immediately after the baby is born instead of with somebody that's busy doing testing or—

Cora: Yeah, they always run away with them to do the Apgar tests—

Infant Bonding

JG: I don't know how important five minutes is, or even six hours; but when it gets beyond two days, or three days, there could be trouble. However, that's where Dads come in, you see, because babies can bond with Dad just as well as with Mom. If they have bonded with both Dad and Mom in the first two, three minutes, they will then tolerate an interruption of maybe a day or two for both, but if Dad is around; if Mom is the one that has to be away and if Dad is around, he can keep that contact, so that the baby knows that the caretakers have not abandoned him.

> *Louise: I remember when Kyle was born, his father was holding him a lot, and he was really quiet, like he knew his father's voice, and he was just making cooing noises, he wasn't crying at all, he was just looking at things and getting to know the world. It was really neat.*

The Power Of The Bonding

JG: You can verify this objectively. I've seen it so many times. The baby has to be whisked off in an Isolette, with monitors, and so on. If Dad is there and puts his hand in the Isolette, the baby will grab hold of his finger, and you can then see the monitors come back towards normal. They will pull their own heart rate down, and their own respiratory rate, and they can maintain that for thirty seconds, sixty seconds. They can't cure lung disease that way, but they can demonstrate really objectively the power of the bonding.

> *Cora: Would that be true only if it was one of the parents? For instance, if there was a nurse who had been spending a lot of time over the first two weeks with the baby, if she puts her hand into the Isolette, wouldn't the baby react to the smell, or whatever—?*

JG: I get the impression that if a baby is separated from both caretakers at birth, within a couple of days they are trying to bond with every nurse that walks past their bassinet. They have to bond with someone.

He Would Only Take Breast Milk

> *Kay: Something happened with our baby. He did not want to eat and he was put on IV, and the nurses tried to get him to eat the formula, and he would throw it back up and throw it back up, and then they encouraged me to pump my breast milk and then give him that, and there was one day—I guess it was about three days before he was dismissed—we gave it to him in the bottle. It was about the*

first time that he had breast milk since I tried to breast feed him when he was born—and he just drank it down immediately—everything—and then from then on he would only take breast milk. I wish I had known more at the time about what was going on.

JG: The process starts instantly and automatically. Babies know their mother on the olfactory channel, and they never make a mistake and they never forget. Bonding is powerful.

I Knew That He Was Going To Be Able to Roll His Tongue

Ralph: There was another thing we noticed about our boy and the visual channel. Immediately after he was born—this was before they put him in the Isolette—I knew that he was going to be able to roll his tongue, like that, because both Kay and I can, so I did that and he did it back to me!

He Won't Perform On Cue

Ralph: But he has never in his life done it again! That's the only time—

Kay: He won't do it now. He did it for me one time after we brought him home, and he won't do it again.

Ralph: the only time in his life.

JG: That's right. He just wanted to give you a little taste of what he could do—so to speak!

Cora: Incredible.

Ralph: But we can't get him to do it now!

BG: He won't perform on cue.

He Lifts His Left Eyebrow

Ralph: Even if you do it to him, you never see him do it, for any reason. But immediately after he was born, he did it. Also he lifts his eyebrow.

Kay: I don't know if that sort of thing is characteristic—but this is something that they asked us about, just to make sure that he was really Ralph's child or something! Ralph has always lifted his—what?—left eyebrow?—

Ralph: Yes, left eyebrow.

Kay: and the baby did that within the first day, and it was always the left one.

Once You're Tuned In To It, It's Plain As Day

JG: So we're talking about responses that, once you re tuned in to them, they're plain as day. I mean, you look for these things, they're there; but if you don't know that that's the kind of thing that you have to look for, you'll miss it, and with that, you may miss a cue in the interaction with your baby.

Infant Competency

These are fully competent human beings at the moment of birth. They're nothing like that ''little vegetable'' myth that they used to put in the textbooks. They used to say that babies are blind at birth. There used to be some question as to whether they could see up to the age of three weeks. Can you guess how they arrived at that conclusion? They used a complicated instrument and they found that the refractive acuity of the baby's eye is 20/600, and since that's the legal definition of blindness, therefore they're blind. But if you get up close to your baby and watch as the minutes go by in that first forty-five minutes, you will see your baby altering their facial features to match yours. They literally do this.

> *Priscilla: Does that also throw out the notion that if the baby smiles it's just gas?*

JG: It's not gas!

Inborn Disposition

> *Louise: Don't you think also that it depends on the nature of the child? Our son didn't smile for a long time—and he's very bright. I'm sure he got everything right away. But our daughter, she was smiling from the beginning. She was just such a good natured child—I don't think she's more intelligent than he is, she's just—*

JG: —more demonstrative—

> *Cora: —sunnier disposition—*

> *Louise: I don't know, just different disposition.*

JG: That will make it easier or harder to see their signals, easier or harder to tell what they're doing. You know how some scientists are—they work for a year on a hard problem and then when they solve it, they just grunt. They don't leap up and run out the front door and yell, "Eureka!"

That's inborn temperament.[13] As you train yourself to pick up these signals, you need to be aware that a given child may give them in very muted form so they're hard to see. You really need to be able to see as well as the baby, who can pick up a movement of your eyebrow as small as a tenth of a millimeter. They learn that Daddy does this, or Mommy does this. They learn that Mommy makes a dimple on the left cheek as she begins to smile and then it spreads to the right. Whatever it is, they see those tiny, tiny changes, and in forty-five minutes they have put them into their own body, so that now they look like you and they react like you.

Cora: Meaning that their smile is your smile?

JG: A part of their smile comes from you.

When He's Angry He Speaks Through His Teeth

Louise: You know, that's true. My son, when he's angry, speaks through his teeth, like this, and I just hate it. Then I realized I was doing it, and that he was imitating me the whole time—and I thought, "Oh, my God!"

Kay: It makes you feel really small, doesn't it?

Cora: That's probably why it grated on you so.

Awareness

JG: When you see yourself reflected back in the person of another person, without realizing that that's what's happening, it has strange and weird effects. If you know that's what is happening, then you are in charge of it, you can do it or not do it or you can do more of it or less of it. That puts you in charge of that interaction.

But you have to know that it's happening. That's the essential element of communication, you have to be aware that it is taking place. Otherwise it will operate at the unconscious level and it will not be under your control. You will be doing stuff that you don't know you're doing. The child will be having an effect on you that neither you nor they are aware of. So it's utterly essential to develop your sensory awareness beyond the level that we use it in everyday life. You have to develop it all the way back to the level that the newborn does, where they respond to everything. Well, you don't have to be that good. Ten percent of that is still a lot!

Tracking

I want to leave you with one final thing, and that is; the reason for studying the sensory channels and body language and things like that is to be able to know what's going on with the other person, your child, and because you can't pace a person if you don't know where they're at. If you want to use techniques that will work, you have to be able to track them and pace them. You've got to know where they're at.

These are the ABC's of doing interventions that actually work. You need to be aware of what they are doing. After that, we'll have a session on how to be aware of what you are doing, because you may be doing things that sabotage and undermine your own requests. You need to be aware of where you're at and what you're doing, you need to be aware of where the other person is at and what they're doing.

Pacing

Then you go to deliberately pacing into that system. You enter their universe because you can only change them from inside. You cannot change them from outside—unless you've got a very compliant and understanding child. You can sometimes do that, but basically, the problems come about when they won't change from outside.

Confrontation Versus Pacing

If you want to lead a person into the kind of behavior that is best for them, this is the way to do it. That's not to say that confrontation should never be used. There are times when it's really useful; but the other approach, pacing, which is kind of the opposite of confrontation, is the one that's got the real power. The other one's good for emergencies. This is the one that's got the power.

The Dance Of Interaction

In the dance of life, interaction and resting, interaction and resting, or socializing and being alone, they alternate. It's a pattern of involvement and then stepping back, involvement, stepping back. When you do that deliberately to match the other person's pattern, that's called Pacing.[14]

With a newborn baby, when they're in intake mode and they're looking for your face, you interact with them, you smile, you coo, you play with them, whatever they like, whatever you like.

Then comes the moment when you find that they're not looking at you. That's the moment to back off, because they need a little time to themselves. They need to integrate the experiences that they have just had, they need to make a memory of that happy time. You give them that break, and it may last one second or two seconds or five seconds or they may fall asleep; but usually it's just a couple of seconds and then the next thing you know they are looking in your face again, so you interact again, and, after a few seconds of interaction, lo and behold, they're looking away, so you back off and give them a little time to themselves, and then interact a little again.

All of life is like this—interaction and then stepping back. That's the way human beings operate. You can't do 100% one thing straight through for 8 hours a day, and then turn it off for 16 hours. Industrial civilization thinks that we can function that way, but we don't, we have to have those breaks, coffee breaks, moments of inattention, what's called daydreaming. Daydreaming is probably the most important thing that a human being does—because that's the time when all this stuff, this flood of experience, is integrated and organized and made meaningful in our lives. It's put away in such a way that it can be useful to us. It's useful for babies too.

It's the pacing that tells them that the other person really cares. Awareness is that state of alertness where you know that there is such a thing as feedback and you are looking for it. Tracking is noting your feedback in real time, moment by moment, to determine what is actually happening with the other person. Pacing is when you use it to decide when to interact or to stop interacting, to dance with the other person. What that does, whether it's a little baby or another adult, when you pace another person, that other person feels comfortable, they feel security, because they're not being interrupted and confronted and forced to do something that is not spontaneous for them.

In the case of a newborn baby, you can register it objectively, as a slowing of the heart rate, and slower and deeper breaths and who knows how many thousands of biochemical, metabolic factors are involved. With a person who's old enough to give you verbal feedback, they'll tell you, "Gee, I feel so good around you, I really like to be with you, I always feel comfortable." That's what they say.

Leading

After you have gotten inside their system and walked with them in their system, then you can introduce a change. That's called Leading, just like in dancing. That's the fundamental plan. And to do tracking, pacing, and leading you have to be tuned in on all your sensory channels. That's what we'll be doing next.

Chapter 3

A Sore Spot From Your Own Past

The Two Faces Of Awareness

JG: Well, we're still just at lesson one, and we're talking about awareness of the feedback we're getting from our child. The other side of it is the awareness of your own personal feelings. I think it's really useful to know how you yourself are feeling, because you have to be comfortable as well as the child. It's hard to raise a kid if everything you do creates uncomfortable reactions inside of you. The situation has to be compatible with your needs, too. So when we talk about awareness, we mean awareness of the child's feelings and the child's needs, and awareness of your own feelings, your own needs. In other words, feedback doesn't only come from the child—it comes from inside yourself too.

You need to be aware of that in order to pick a strategy that will meet your needs as well as the child's needs. At this point, I don't think it's useful to try to say, "One ought to feel this way," just as it's really not useful to say about the child, "He ought to react this way." The more relevant question is, "What's actually happening, and what can I, as the parent, do to bring about a state of comfort for myself and for my child?"

It's really useful to be tuned in to your own feelings—to know how you feel; and when you have strong feelings, you've got to have an arrangement that's going to take care of your feelings.

(Bobbi's baby lets loose with gleeful yell!)

After all, there are two, three, or more people involved here. It's Mom and Dad and the baby; and if there are three kids, it's Mom and Dad and the three kids. Sometimes it's Grandma, too, so you have to think about your feedback from every source.

Sally: Well, yeah, if you're feeling bad about something he's going to pick up on that.

BG: If you're feeling bad leaving him, he's going to pick that up sooner or later. I'm not saying, "OK, you've got to be really good about hiding your feelings!''—but somehow there has to be an arrangement so that you can leave him and feel good about it so he doesn't say, ''Hey wait a second—when I'm going off with somebody, it's supposed to be bad 'cause look how bad Mom's feeling.''

A Sore Spot From Your Own Past

Quentin: That's our problem, we—we've never let Jimmy cry. We can't.

Raven: There's always something to pacify him, like his pacifier.

JG: You hurt inside when you hear him cry.

Quentin: Ordinarily we just pick him up. We can't let him cry, it's like neither one of us can.

JG: It's hard, isn't it?

Raven: It's really hard.

JG: You find that it gets to you somehow.

Charlene: I felt that way. I thought I couldn't stand it, and then when we finally did let Lily scream—we were so exhausted that we finally reached a point where we couldn't stand not ignoring her. We did the same as you, we went to sleep when she was screaming mad. We were just so exhausted.

Quentin: We're at the point now where we just let him wear himself down. Last night he didn't go to bed until almost 11:00 at night.

JG: I'm glad you brought this up because this is a very important issue. That is: how you feel about doing a certain routine. There are some routines that for some reason tie into something in your own personal approach, your own personal background. They're touching a sore spot somewhere in your own past that you maybe don't even know about, and you find it very difficult to do that. Somehow doing that particular approach to your kids seems like—well, it just hurts. I think it's worth while to respect that and to stay away from that if it doesn't feel right for you—to just look for other methods because there are lots of other methods. You don't have to stay locked in to one particular approach.

Quentin: Yeah, because we didn't want to let him cry.

BG: Well, especially when he was so sick that you were afraid you were going to lose him. I think you get a different feeling about a child, too, when you've had that close a call. It's real hard to think about letting him just cry.

JG: There's a lot of parent savvy that can be passed on by didactic classes and seminars like what we're doing now. There are also problems that do not respond particularly well to material that you read or that you hear somebody else like myself talking about. Sometimes it is necessary to do a one-on-one consultation about a particular problem, and to attack that individually. This class doesn't do that, so we will not have a total solution of all your problems just because I'm sitting here talking. Keep that in mind. If you find that there are problems that simply don't respond to your use of the principles or strategies that you're learning here and you still want to deal with them, it's possible to do that in a one-to-one way. We can actually get together individually, and work on a particular problem, or I can refer you to someone.

Sometimes it turns out that the problem is that for one reason or another parents are simply unable to go into a certain region of behavior because it's too emotionally charged for them. It may turn out that there are areas of your own experience in childhood that get activated. Sometimes a person doesn't even realize this until they have actually experienced it in connection with their own child. The solution of that problem is not some type of strategy such as we're presenting here. The solution is to deal with the problem in connection with the parents, and that frees the parents to apply new methods. I just want to put that in perspective. I'm not sitting here telling you that you can do anything and everything just by learning strategies; but once I've said that I want to make it real clear that there is an awful lot that you can do—a great deal more than you would suspect.

Spontaneous Fractures Of Infancy

When I was a medical student and intern and later a resident in Pediatrics, way back in the fifties, there was a very strange disease called ''spontaneous fractures of infancy.'' A lot of time was spent in serious speculation about what sort of metabolic disorder could result in spontaneous fractures of the long bones, spontaneous fractures of the skull, spontaneous bleeding over the surface of the brain. I can remember seeing a one-year old child hospitalized on the pediatric ward with simultaneous spontaneous fractures of both legs, and I wondered what sort of disease could produce effects like that. A baby would be admitted for an illness such as pneumonia, and X-rays of the chest would reveal what really looked very much like healing of the long bones, the arm bones, the rib bones, the kind of healing that would occur after a fracture. Such babies would be sent home after they got well, only to be readmitted a week later or a month later with collections of fluid over the brain, just as if they were recovering from some sort of injury to the head.

When I went into my residency at the Mayo Clinic, and later when I was practicing at a well-known medical center, we would see such patients and wonder just what sort of mysterious disease it was that could produce such strange effects.

It wasn't until a young radiologist by the name of Caffey looked straight into the eyes of the monster and called it by its true name that we began to understand that we were seeing battered children.[1] Even then, it took a full generation more for doctors and nurses everywhere to realize that child abuse is not some rare and esoteric event.

Now Sigmund Freud knew about child abuse. He had seen the evidence at the Paris Morgue, but when he realized how many of his clients gave histories of parental seduction and abuse and as the evidence accumulated, he apparently shrank back from acknowledging that so high a percentage of children could have been actually physically abused by their parents. He seemed to retreat into a theory that the child's fantasies of abuse are more important than real-life events.[2]

This is probably the reason why it was not the psychoanalysts of the world who made us aware of child abuse, but a radiologist, who stumbled into it while trying to make sense of the strange occurrence of what looked like healing fractures in the bones of children whose parents had brought them to hospitals for quite other reasons. I guess the analysts were busy trying to confirm Freud's theory that it was not real child abuse, but the child's fantasy of being abused, that was the real cause of mental disorder.

They Don't Remember
What Was Done To Them

Now people don't procreate children with the deliberate intention of abusing them, but they have been raised in a certain way, they have a certain set of attitudes, they have a certain repertoire for dealing with situations, and that repertoire is what they themselves learned as children.

When they have tried everything they know, and they still have a screaming child or a fussy baby, or when the baby won't eat or the toddler keeps running away, they revert to what was done to them in similar circumstances. It's a matter of unconscious learnings from the distant past. When they find themselves striking their child, or shaking their baby, that behavior is a surprise to them—or they may consider it simply "natural"

"It's a matter of unconscious learnings from our distant past."

to do that. They don't know where that behavior of theirs came from. They don't remember what was done to them.

We Never Had To Spank Him Again

Do you remember, Beth, the family that were old-fashioned disciplinarians who believed in spanking? They also tried to be enlightened and use time-outs first. The father had sent their three-year-old son to his room for some misbehavior and Eric had taken a one-pound jar of sticky, smelly A&D ointment and smeared it all over the four walls of his room, as high as he could reach. And mother discovered you can't wash A&D ointment off with a washcloth, it won't come off with detergent, you can't even scrape it off because it soaks all the way through the wallpaper and even into the drywall. They had to have Eric's room completely redone from the walls out. They were afraid of what they might do to Eric if he continued his misbehavior, so they agreed to come to the parents' class.

Dad came, too, dressed in a blue pinstripe business suit complete with vest and tie, and he made it clear that as a business executive and a reserve officer in the military, no one was going to take away his rights as a citizen to discipline and to spank his own child in the privacy of his own home.

We agreed completely. We were not there to limit him in his options. We merely wanted to offer him a broader range of options, some of which might offer him a better chance of success in guiding his son along the right path.

They stayed and listened and thanked us and went home and they didn't come back to the next class, and Beth and I reminded ourselves that you can't win 'em all. If they don't stay to learn you can't blame yourself for that.

But then they did come back, a month later. Dad reported that they had missed the previous class because his own father had died and he had gone to the funeral, and at the funeral he realized he couldn't even cry for the death of his father, because he kept remembering the spankings and the mean, cruel things his father had done to punish him when he was only a little kid.

A wave of determination swept over him that he didn't want Eric ever to feel that way about him. And as he told us this, in the class, he broke down and cried. And they stayed for the whole series of classes.

Recently—which was now five years later and Eric was eight years old—Beth met them socially and asked if the classes had been helpful and Mom replied: ''Oh, we never had a chance to try out the things you taught us. After that episode with the A&D ointment, he changed so completely that we never had to spank him again.''

Mark: Whoa! Wait a minute! Back up just a minute! You can't end that story just like that! What do you mean, he never misbehaved again?

JG: That's what the parents thought. That's how they saw it. The way they saw it, he just spontaneously got better, began to behave himself. That's typical with nonverbal interventions. The people involved may not have a clue as to what happened. You and I might say that Dad, after that profound emotional experience at his own father's funeral, gave off ten thousand nonverbal signals that he was a changed person, that he was not going to be so heavy around his kids. Would he have changed if he hadn't come to our parents' class? Who can say?

Child Abuse And
Therapeutic Communication

Now what does child abuse have in common with therapeutic communication, and why am I bringing up such an unpleasant subject? Well, child abuse is what happens when parents lack the resources for elegant and effective communication with their own offspring. Also, child abuse forms a kind of model for adult communication. Mostly, we adults don't dare openly abuse another adult when our communication techniques fail, but we do become hostile and negative toward that person. This happens because in the modern high-tech world of the twentieth century, we are still locked in to using one, and only one, strategy of communication with our fellow human beings. We tell them what we want and if we don't get it we threaten them with our disapproval. If that doesn't work, we escalate and threaten to punish them. Eventually we threaten them with bodily harm, which leads on a larger scale to warfare. And now, in the Nuclear Age, in a perfect spasm of escalation, we threaten our enemies by telling them if they don't do what we want, we will blow up the whole world, them and ourselves too. The problem is, basically, that we have only one strategy for interacting with others, and when that doesn't work, we try even harder to make it work. We fail to realize that what we need to do is to stop trying to force success out of a failing technique. We need to try something else, something that will work.

The fact is, there are many elegant and delightful ways to communicate with other human beings in such a way as to cause them to spontaneously desire to act in ways that are also congenial to ourselves. We don't need to limit ourselves to direct demands.

But people who don't know about alternative strategies don't feel that they have a choice. They feel compelled to act as they do. That feeling of being compelled, of having no choice, is only dispelled by actually having some other choices, some alternative strategies, some other options.

Now some of you already know what it is to be an abused child, but others of you have not understood that you *were* abused children, and this is where the unspoken assumptions come in. Most of us were raised by methods that relied heavily on negation and forbidding, to the point where some of us will take that as the standard and actually feel upset when someone suggests that child rearing can be done from a positive approach. If you can learn to recognize the abusive component in your own childhood experiences, then you will be better able to move on to a more positive approach for yourself and your child.[3]

Chapter 4

How Do You Get Into
Another Person's World?

Channels

JG: How do you develop the power to know and feel what's happening inside the other person? How do you get into another person's world?

Well, being aware of how you feel inside of yourself is a certain kind of awareness. Being aware of what the other person is doing is a more objective kind of awareness. You get the awareness of what's going on inside of yourself by paying attention to your own reactions; that is, how you feel, what your own gut reaction is, your intuition about the situation, as well as your thoughts. You get the awareness of what's happening with the other person by using your eyes and ears and checking it out. You look and see, that's how you get your feedback. You listen, and you get your feedback from that. You get your feedback from the visual sensory channel, from the auditory sensory channel, you can get feedback via kinesthetic too. If somebody pushes you, or carries you, or lifts you, or rocks you, you get kinesthetic feedback. You can also get feedback from smells and tastes. These are the major sensory channels on which you get your feedback: Visual, Auditory, Kinesthetic, Olfactory, and Gustatory.[1]

The Whole Picture

So if you want to know how your child is experiencing the world you have to know what sensory channels he or she is operating on and you have to have at least enough sensory awareness on those channels to build a similar experience for yourself. You also need to know your own strengths and weaknesses, so you can compensate for your own lack of data on the channels where your child has more variety than you have.

Babies, infants, and young children have almost unlimited potential because they're using all their sensory channels. What I'm trying to suggest is that we look at our kids with a new sense of the wonder which kids have themselves. We can come back to that ourselves as grownups: ''Wow! This kid sees the whole picture! Wow! This kid really heard what I said, or heard something I didn't even hear.'' It's fun to start reexploring the world from the sense of the kid's possible perceptions.

> *Kay: You're right. I've learned so much and I'm surprised that kids know as much as they do. I always thought that kids were just sort of—that we were supposed to teach them, rather than the other way round.*

BG: It works both ways!

JG: They're still in contact with stuff that we've lost contact with.

Auditory Channel

> *Kay: That's true. I didn't realize how much noise pollution we have in this world until Tony—every few minutes—he says, ''There goes a plane,'' or, ''There goes this,'' and I thought, ''How did he hear that—I really had to strain to hear it, and I don't know if he has better ears now, he probably does . . . but he's probably more open to learning or hearing that—''*

BG: But you've learned to shut it out in order to concentrate, because it would be overload for us.

JG: The people of the Kalahari desert, as they age, don't have the hearing loss that is regarded as normal in our society. Their hearing stays super-acute. But they rarely hear a sound that is over twenty or thirty decibels. It's really quiet.

> *Kay: It's probably also very important that they hear those sounds—I mean, for survival.*

JG: Exactly.

BG: When your lunch consists of a mouse—you gotta know where it is!

JG: Now auditory is a very strange double sensory channel, because there's the kind of auditory that delights in music and in the sounds of nature—that's Auditory Tonal—and there's the kind of auditory that processes language. That's called Auditory Digital. Those two functions are probably on different sides of the brain—a person who's had a stroke and can't speak, can sing a song or recite a nursery rhyme even though they can't say, ''Bring me a glass of water.''

Kay: Is that memory—something that's already been learned, or is it—

JG: There are two different areas of the brain—one for speech, and the other for the non-speech auditory, like music.

Kay: Is that like that one country and western singer who can hardly talk because he stutters so badly, and then when he sings, he sings perfectly?

JG: He's using the other side of his brain.

You're OK, Charlie Brown

BG: If you ever get a chance to see the video about Charlie Brown going to the spelling bee—do any of you remember that? I think it's called, "You're OK, Charlie Brown!" He goes all the way to the finals, even gets on the bus to go to New York.

Well, in this particular film, the adults never clearly speak a word, it's only, "Mmmm-mmmm-mmmm." It's never a word, just the sound, the tonality. If you ever get a chance to hear that film, it bears listening to, because the kids are the only ones doing any dialogue, but the grownups are influencing things quite a bit by their tonality.

I think kids that get talked to and yelled at a lot, tune out the words, the meaning, and get the tonality and then they react to that rather than the meaning of the words that the adults think they have given.

Voice Tones

JG: One of my favorite topics! How many television announcers have voices that are totally dead! You hear them talking about the most fascinating stuff in the world—the wildlife series, particularly. But the voice—it's the voice of the corpse from the tomb. You listen to that and you gradually get more and more depressed! They may be talking about how beautiful the creatures are.

BG: I just go—"Oh, turn it off! Turn off the sound, I'll just watch the picture."

Performances

Louise: With Kyle, he'll hear anything when we're talking at the table during dinner. He can be in the other room and he hears everything that doesn't concern *him, and he'll ask questions and it's amazing how well he understands. But then when I tell him to do something—*

JG: He doesn't hear!

Louise: Kyle, repeat, what did I say?

JG: There you go!

Louise: He'll just mumble the phrase—and then I say, ''Open your ears!'' and he'll cover them up like this. I have to repeat five times before he hears it and when I know that he can pay attention—

JG: Obviously, all of this blends into questions of performance. Kids usually refuse to perform. If they've done something—even if they've just done it right in front of you and have enjoyed it, and then you say, ''Do that again,'' the answer is almost automatically, ''No!''—because they don't want to be artificial; they don't want to put on a performance—as a rule. Some kids are little hams—they'll do it. They will repeat it a thousand times, and when you tell 'em, ''Stop!'' they will keep on doing it.

Repetitive Cognitive Exercises

BG: We have a four-year-old in our practice, a bright little kid in nursery school, whose father called up one day in great distress and said, ''Help! He won't do his Repetitive Cognitive Exercises!'' These were highly educated parents and essentially what they were trying to do was to get their kid to repeat all the so-called educational stuff he had learned that day as soon as he got home.

I said, ''Repetitive Cognitive Exercises? Yukk! I wouldn't do it either! Forget it!'' I don't know if they took my advice or not. They were very serious about education.

JG: ''Say this, say that.'' ''Tell Auntie what you did.'' Reminds me of son Dave's remark. One day after a hard day in first grade, he said, ''Dick and Jane, Dick and Jane! Dick and Jane make me vomit.''

Turn Down The Signal, Turn Up The Gain

Priscilla: When you mumble something under your breath to another adult that you don't want them to hear, they always hear that!

JG: Well, naturally, when you turn down the decibels, the other person, if they're auditory, turns up the gain so that they can hear it! That's why if you really want somebody to notice what you say, you whisper it.

Louise: *That's a good idea!*

JG: Make it difficult to hear!

BG: And do it only once!

Auditory Digital

When your child says something, you can hear the tone of it, but it's also worthwhile paying attention to what they're saying, because sometimes the actual linguistic message that they are giving you is important! So listen to it.

Ralph: *We found out at a certain point that almost everything Tony said was actually a word and we just weren't picking it up because it didn't sound like it. Every day we'd be driving along the road and he'd say, ''There's a something or other'', and we'd look around and say, ''No, he's crazy. No such thing!'' Then the next day, at exactly the same point on the street, he'd say the same thing, and eventually we'd figure out what he was talking about, and be all embarrassed because he had noticed it and we hadn't.*

Muzak In My Head

Cora: *I have a question about something that I do and this is an annoyance to my husband. It's like I have Muzak that goes on in my head all the time, so I've got this one part—*

Ralph: *I have that!*

Theodore: *Yeah, I have that!*

Cora: *—going like in a loop round and round, and it doesn't interfere with my ability to listen to what you're saying or what anyone else is saying or what I'm looking at, but it's always going on back there.*

JG: Your mind can handle two channels at once. You're in good company. Lots of people do that.

Morilla: *Why—not to get personal—but why does that annoy your husband?*

Cora: *Because he finds me singing when he's talking to me!*

Priscilla: *"You're not listening to me."*

Cora: *Right. It infuriates him. Also my husband can't sing to save his life. Our older child tells him not to sing. I can sing, but Dad can't sing. So, for all these reasons, singing gets some tension going sometimes.*

Garbage On Auditory

JG: So you can understand that a little kid who's that sensitive on the auditory channel, if he gets harsh words a lot, he's gonna be hearing a whole bunch of garbage, that is to say, unpleasant auditory experience. It's not just the one time or the five times or the ten times that the parent says it, but he'll hear it on his own internal tape a thousand times, maybe, in the course of a day.[2] Here's the potential to convince a person that they're rotten, that they're no good, just by telling them a few times.

Cora: *You mean when you find someone that's got that tape?*

The Sound Of Mother's Voice

JG: If they've got that tape—and a lot of kids have that tape, because auditory is very fundamental, it's very basic. The kids start with hearing their mother's voice. I think in many cases auditory tonal is even more important than what is actually said, because it is information coming in on a channel that the person is not consciously monitoring. In other words, this is a hypnotic influence. This is an influence that is taking place without your awareness.

Samantha: *With what you said, I'm beginning to think that Peter is probably an auditory person because he—I've always been concerned about this—he never makes eye contact with us when we're talking to him about anything or even when we're reprimanding him. We've gotten into the habit of grabbing his chin and trying to make eye contact and lately he's gotten into this thing of walking around the house like this, with his hands over his ears. (Samantha puts her hands over her ears.)*

JG: That's a pretty good feedback! That's really telling you something! Junk on auditory! Look out!

Samantha: *Maybe I should change my methods.*

JG: That's right, you can look for other methods.

"Junk on auditory!"

Overload

If you're constantly talking to a kid, you reach the point of overload and then you discover they've switched off, they're not hearing it.

> ***Theodore:*** *Our son will say, ''Be quiet!'' or ''Don't say that!''*

JG: Isn't it neat how straight they are about these things? They just tell you right out.

This direct read-back of where they're at is really helpful because you know—at least when they're young enough—that what you get is what they are really experiencing. That makes it easier to interact with a child.

Shutting Down

JG: A child who is constantly scolded, endlessly scolded from morning to night, can turn off the auditory channel and they can go through grade school, high school and college and not hear anything that was said. So one of the things you need to check is, "When I'm communicating with my child, is he tuning me out, is he turning off this channel?" If he is doing that, it means that he's getting a lot of unpleasant experience on that channel and he's decided, "Gee, it isn't worth while to listen in this world—all you hear is junk." People who have encountered terrible scenes in their childhood—or who have been hit from behind—will sometimes turn off the visual channel. They just won't bother to look at things anymore.

Mismatched Channels

Beth and I had a couple in therapy with us a few years ago who were so mismatched on their sensory channels, they fought like cats and dogs. In fact, they reminded us of our dog Smitty and his problem with cats. Smitty was a very small, very fuzzy, very nearsighted dog who had been separated from his mother at a very early age and who grew up without much contact with other dogs. I think that is the reason why he never learned to regard cats as enemies. He kept trying to make friends with them. And there was a cat in our neighborhood that wanted to be friends with Smitty, but they had this absolutely insurmountable problem. When Smitty feels friendly, he wags his tail. But tail-lashing amongst cats means, "Watch out, stand back or else!" The cat wanted to play with Smitty and would reach out with its front paw and take a swipe at Smitty; but to Smitty this was definitely not a friendly gesture and he would leap backwards. So when these two potential friends would try to get together, each would run toward the other and give the signal that caused the other one to fall backwards and run away. It was hilarious, it was comical and it was also kind of sad, because they really did like each other.

Well, this couple was like that.

Tone-Deaf Wife

The wife I think was tone-deaf, that is, she was not aware of the quality of her own voice. She had been raised in a very scrappy household, where you had to keep your voice raised all the time in order to be heard or to get any food. She had married a wonderful man—and she was a wonderful woman too—she had married a wonderful man for whom the definition of love was the soft soothing sound of his mother's voice. When he asked, ''Do you love me?'' what he wanted to hear—it didn't matter what the words were—he wanted to hear this low cooing sound. Have you ever heard a baby that's happy? They make that cooing sound. That's what he wanted to hear, but what the woman would answer to this question was, ''I'd be a damn liar if I said I didn't love you!'' in a high screech that set his teeth on edge. This poor guy would find himself reflexly grabbing the frying pan. You could trigger him into outbursts of rage by assaulting him with this horrible auditory tonal experience.

It was kind of sad, because they really did like each other. This case was one of our failures, because neither Beth nor I could get the wife to stop talking long enough to listen to the sound of her own voice, and her husband was not about to sit still for what sounded to him like another angry scolding from his mother.

Incongruity

JG: That's called incongruity,[3] when you simultaneously send two opposing messages, one in the words and one in the tone. Of course your body kinesthetically transmits a message too, so you can be sending three or even more messages at one time. If you're not tuned in, if you're not aware of the messages you're sending, you won't understand the reactions you're getting. The child will be responding to signals you send, but you won't realize that. You're likely to think the child is just contrary.

So if you want to be in charge of the actual messages that you are sending to your child, it behooves you to become a little bit aware of each and every one of these channels. You need to know what channels the child is using, you need to know what channels you're using, because this is communication back and forth. And in order to avoid incongruity you need to be aware of all the messages that you're sending.

But They Said They Would

Woman: I read an article about this and it was saying that women, more so than men, tend to think of the feelings and go from that and that that sort of relates to how they'll do with children. They were giving an example. It's the end of a really long day—father is getting on the children's case because they don't want to do what they said they would—but mom is saying, "Hey, they're tired, they're overworked, leave them alone!"

JG: She feels it.

Sally: And the father is just sitting here going, "But they said they would!" Right?

JG: Dad is operating out of auditory digital—he's only tuned in to the verbal channel. He probably didn't notice their body language or their tone that was saying, "We're tired. We're hungry."

Matching Channels (Pacing)

All right! You need to know what channels the other person uses best[4] and what channels they are awkward on. If you want to match yourself to the other person so that they feel comfort, you need to know what their model of the universe is. Of course there's a lot more to pacing than just matching channels, but we're just getting started. This is how you begin to learn how to pace. You have to know, "Are they visual?" and if they're visual, then you will talk to them about getting the picture. You will talk to them in visual terms.

BG: And with due respect.

Telephone Ear

JG: Right. Which means eye-to-eye contact. But an auditory person may not want to make eye-to-eye contact. When they want to really hear something, they put their head down so they don't have to be distracted by seeing stuff. They stick up their telephone ear[5]—the one that they hear best with—and they listen like this. Now that annoys a visual person, because the way a visual person knows that you're paying attention to him is if you're looking at him.

In a classroom, all the little visual kids stare at the teacher, and the teacher's just delighted and gives them an A but the auditory kid has got his head down like this and sort of tilted and the teacher doesn't know whether he's paying attention or not.

Change Your Basic Orientation!

JG: You don't have to look at their eyes—you can do this from the left eyebrow. Don't think that the eyes are the only source of feedback. The whole body, the posture, anything, the back of their hand; if you tune yourself into the feedback that is available, you will be able to pick up these responses from whatever sensory data is available. The thing that you need to learn to do is to change your basic orientation from your own agenda to noticing what's happening with the other person—because you can't influence them properly if you don't know where they're at. So that's the lesson for today—it's sensory awareness. This tremendous mass of information that comes in is your source of knowledge about where the other person is at—and if you're going to pace them, which is the next step, lesson two—if you're going to pace them you have to notice what there is to pace.

If you are going to deliberately modulate your voice so as to produce a state of comfort in a baby, you need to know that in fact they do respond that way to your voice—and you need to know whether they respond better to this pitch and tonality or to a different pitch and tonality. How fast should you speak, when you speak to a baby? How loud? What tones do you use? How much variation in pitch? These are things that people—they just do it automatically—but if you want to be really effective, particularly if you've got a problematic situation, you've got to be able to vary your behavior to pace the other person. That's how you do it.

[The baby just cried out].

JG: Being auditory I picked that up! And being olfactory—

Sally: You'll pick it up soon!

Response Time

BG: We went to visit our grandson Nathan last year and he was sixteen months old. His parents would ask him a question; and if he didn't know what to say, he would just sit there. He had a pacifier in his mouth, and he wouldn't answer anything but his eyes would move. You could see that he was thinking. Then they'd ask him another question and if he didn't know what to say or he didn't want to say, ''Yes,'' he wouldn't answer at all. When they finally hit on the right thing that he really wanted, he'd say, ''Yek!'' because he had the pacifier in his mouth. That meant, ''Yes!'' But it was a much longer time interval than you would have with an adult. Even some adults need more time to process than others do. If you learn to watch when you are interacting with your coworkers, they'll let you know.

The minimum time required for an adult to be able to respond adequately to a question is about eight seconds, or longer sometimes depending on the question and its emotional impact. Infants require a minimum of sixteen seconds to complete a response cycle when they are interacting with an adult. So when you are going to interact with an infant, you really need to slow down.

Wait Time

JG: How do you know when the other person has finished their internal processing and are ready to interact again? First you tune your eyes in to where you see that the other person has dropped their eyes. That's the equivalent of the withdrawal signal that the baby gives. They're processing what they just experienced. Then when they are ready to interact again, their eyes will come back to the present moment and you can see that. Whenever you interact with somebody—whenever they take in a signal, there is a time lapse during which they have to process the experience they have had of your signal or of you. They have to process it. They have to make sense of it, then they have to come out of that internal process and come up to contemporary again, to ''up-time,'' to get ''on-line'' again or however you want to say it. So if you really want your message to be taken in, if you want it to be integrated into the other person's experience, you've got to allow that time for them to do that. The good news is that all you have to do is watch them and you can see them doing it, and when they come back, they're ready.

> *Donald: In Education it's called Wait Time.*

JG: Wait Time, yes!

> *Donald: It's a typical mistake of first-year teachers, because you know exactly where you are going with your lecture, you know exactly the answer, and you ask this question and look around you and you're expecting somebody to go just like this and answer your question instantly, but that doesn't happen, because they need that time. It's very uncomfortable to wait, because if there's silence in the room people get very uncomfortable, especially if you are asking the question. You can't stand that silence, but you have to give them that time.*

JG: And it's fairly long.

> *Donald: Yes. Especially for the asker of the question!*

Internal Processing

JG: Right! It feels like a long, long time. Now that state is technically a trance. That's a moment when the person has gone inside and is processing data internally, is processing experience internally. So when you ask a person a question, you are putting them into a trance. If you really want to have effective communication and if you really want to do something more than simply rehearse your own agenda verbally in the presence of another person, it behooves you to know that. You need to know what they're doing while they're in that state and you need to know when they have come out. If you do it with kids, you can start when they're born, and start this process of waiting for them to come out and look at you again, and you interact. When they obviously go away, you wait for them to come back again.

Comfort State

One major characteristic of a trance state is its comfort. When you wait and allow the other person to experience that state of comfort, they feel gratitude to you. They feel good around you. They may not know why it is that they feel so good, but they will feel this feeling of gratitude. That's when you get this bond of solidarity. I'm sure that a lot of what's mystically called ''bonding'' in the first hour of life is actually this mutual experience of quiet comfort.

When you turn on your TV and see an interviewer and an interviewee frantically talking and jabbering as fast as they can with no pauses between, what you're looking at is just the worst kind of anti-communication that you can imagine. The interviewer needs time to generate a real question about something that genuinely puzzles them; and the person being interviewed needs to take that question seriously, needs to think about it and come up with a real answer. Commercial TV thinks that silence is dead time, it isn't earning any money. They are always in a hurry, and so the opportunities for real human interaction are lost.

Fred: You say a lot of time. Do you mean one second, two seconds in between?

JG: It really depends on the people who are participating. Certainly five seconds, ten seconds.

Fred: You very seldom see that happening.

JG: You very seldom see that. You can also tell because if you watch the eyes of the interviewee, they have this glazed look. They have a memorized spiel and they are just waiting for the interviewer to finish the question, because they know what they are going to say, they've memorized it, and they're not listening. That's not real experience. When a person is dumping a canned speech, that's not real experience. The whole thing is an exercise in artificiality and unreality.

> *Donald: The so-called "debates" in the last presidential election were a perfect example of that. You would hear a question and the answer sometimes seemed only a tiny bit related to the question, and then the speaker would go off on some long explanation, a totally different aspect.*

JG: There is a so-called art of debate, in which it is supposed to be a good thing to be able to take a question and glide into a different topic without the questioner realizing it. Then you don't have to answer the question. But that's not real communication. You do that to a kid and you will drive them away. They won't know why they dislike you but they will distance themselves, because of your unwillingness to tap into the real experience of the other person. We all start with this utter willingness to share experience with our newborn baby, we want to interact person to person.

> *Donald: I think a lot of the rebelliousness of the teenager is in great part—I teach teenagers and there are teachers in our school that have just unbelievable problems with kids because they don't know how to listen to them, they don't know how to respond to their needs somewhat. You could learn where they are coming from and respond a little to their needs as well as your own.*

> *Fred: With our daughter, when we ask her to do something, her immediate response is "No!" Is she digesting what we're saying when she says, "No" immediately or is it just a phase or what do you think is happening? She's almost two. Everything is "No!" "Are you feeling OK?" "No!" "Do you love us?" "No!"*

JG: At that age, "No!" often means, "Yes!"

> *Donald: Juan went through the same thing you're talking about. He went through a stage probably six to eight weeks when everything was "No!" But he would have smiles on his face. "Do you want some soup?" "No!" But if you put it in front of him he would just gobble it right up. Maybe it's because it's just such an easy word to say. We worked for such a long time to get him to say, "Yes" and now he's saying, "Yes" all the time. He now knows the difference between yes and no and it's just a real joy now. Our response was just to turn it into a game, a lot of the time.*

BG: You might notice that the response time is so fast, it's almost like being on automatic pilot. Just—the parent asks a question that goes up at the end and the answer is, "No!"—whatever. It's a canned response.

> *Sabrina: Timmy does that too sometimes—he's over three. But then in a few more seconds he'll say something else that isn't "No!" I mean it's positive or*

it's different. It's kind of like, ''Zoom!'' and then he's thought about it and he's got his real response.

Face Approach

Kim: *When someone Margaret's age—11 months old—touches her ears, rubs her ears, would that be a sign that she is auditory, or that she just likes her ears?*

Sally: *It could be an earache!*

JG: It's not always a channel signal! You might want to watch what happens to her muscles of expression when she hears something—see if she smiles or frowns or gets sad because of it.

Most kids are pre-programmed so that the smiling face or anything that remotely approximates it is pleasant for them. They're highly visual and that's the visual configuration that makes them feel better. You can get a lot of mileage out of just deliberately putting on a smiling face. Moms will often do Face Approach to the baby, move their face up close and then move back—and then move up again.

He Knows He's Heard

Sometimes a sputtering sound or some sort of little trilling sound combined with that, will just drive them into ecstasy. They just love it.[6]

Woman: *He's started now—he makes the trilling sound.*

JG: If he does it, then he has the extra power, the control.

Woman: *He knows he's heard.*

JG: He knows he's heard!

Amadeus

Remember the movie ''Amadeus''? How Mozart drove his poor contemporary—what was his name?—Salieri—right out of his mind without even intending to? Mozart didn't have to rack his brain to think up tunes and then figure out the correct harmonies, he just listened to what was happening inside his own head and wrote it down. He didn't even have to erase, he always heard his music in its final, perfect form. He was so sensitive to the finest nuances of pitch and tone and shaping and phrasing that on one occasion he fainted dead away when someone played a bad note on a trumpet. On another occasion he went to a concert in a distant city, liked it a lot, and came straight home and wrote it out, note for note, all the instruments of the orchestra, just exactly as the author had composed it and as the orchestra had played it.

Now of course a person like Mozart only comes along once in a thousand years, but there are many people who have musical talents that are enough to make me simply amazed. Beth, for example, can sit down at a church organ, play a few chords to get familiar with its tone, and then improvise the most beautiful music for hours on end. Ask her to transpose it into a different key and she just does it.

Sometimes she will say things like, ''This instrument is a quarter tone flat,'' and I will say, ''How on earth do you know that?'' She will say, ''Well, can't you hear it?'', and I will say, ''Hear what?'' She will say, ''Listen to that A. It isn't anywhere near 440,'' and I will say, ''What in the name of goodness are you talking about?'' ''The A! The A! Can't you hear it?'' And of course I have to say, ''I'm hearing the sound when you play the 'A' key on the keyboard, but I can't tell you how many vibrations it has or whether it's too high or too low. In fact, if you play two notes in a row, I can't tell you for sure if the second one is higher or lower than the first unless they are a long way apart. Of course, I can peek at the keyboard and see what note you are playing.''

What is happening here is an example of the problem of one person being able to make a larger number of sensory distinctions than the other. Beth just has a richer repertoire of distinctions on the auditory channel than I do. The world that she lives in is rich and varied in auditory experiences. She actually has auditory experiences that I simply cannot experience, and because of this capacity she is able to modulate her voice in such a way as to convey nuances of mood or interest and caring that speak directly to the emotional life of another person in a way that seems magical to me. Even animals, like dogs and horses, respond to her voice and instinctively turn to her, because her voice tells them that she really understands and really cares. I don't know what she is doing or how she does it, because I just can't hear those auditory tonal distinctions.

Visual Channel

But let's just shift over to the visual channel. We're in the kitchen and Beth says, ''Now what did I do with the butter?'' and my mind's eye flashes me a picture of the inside of the refrigerator and I say, ''It's on the second shelf of the refrigerator.'' She says, ''How did you know that?'' And I say, ''Well,

I saw you put it there,'' and she says, ''When did I do that?'' and I say, ''Last night, after supper.'' She says, ''Well, who would ever notice a thing like that? I've done a thousand things since then. How could anybody remember so many details?'' And I say, ''But it's easy. I saw you do it.''

How many people here believe they are visual?—These are the folks that get the picture. When you talk, you talk about bringing things into focus, getting the right perspective—

BG: You demand respect—

JG: —seeing things objectively.

> *Morilla: Demand respect, did you say?*

BG: Demand respect.

JG: Demand respect, which means you want the other person to look at you, re-spect, to look back. It's amazing but true. A person's vocabulary does tell you what sensory modality they're using at that moment.[7] If you sample their vocabulary over time, you'll find out when they go into kinesthetic, when they go into auditory, or whether maybe they're fixed on auditory or fixed on kinesthetic. I can't imagine a person who only used one sensory channel, but there are some visuals who come close. There are visuals who are so highly visual, they just don't comprehend a thing until they can see it, either in front of their eyes or—up here (looking upward).

BG: In their memory or in their creative part of their brain structure.

> *Kay: I knew a girl when I was in school who was a spelling bee champ and we used to make fun of her. In some ways she was really good and we were always amazed, but she'd be doing this, eyes up in the air, spelling the word out before she ever said it; but it was always amazing to watch her because she would have the word spelled out in the air. If we could see what she was seeing then we would get it too.*

JG: She was seeing something, right!

Accessing Cues

JG: Now you can actually watch this process taking place, if you're aware of the fact that a person's eyes move in the direction of the cortex that they are using. This is a powerful tool for looking right into your own child's mental processes.[8]

If you ask a visual person a simple mathematical question like, "What's four times four?" or something like that, quite often they will look upwards and if it's something that they've heard many times and they know about it, they access the memory side of their brain, the programmed side, that's the left cortex in a righthanded person.

You don't have to remember this because everybody varies, but typically with a righthanded person their memory is located up there to the left if they're visual. But if they have to make it up or derive it, if they don't know what four times four is, they will go and look up to the right and construct the picture. You can actually tell whether a person is constructing their response, creatively or fraudulently, or whether they are bringing out a memory. That's real useful information.

Theodore: Is it admissible in court?

JG: This is not even soft science, but pragmatically it's useful. Think of an auditory person, accessing auditory cortex. Where's the auditory cortex? Right here, just above the ears, so their eyes go horizontally left or right. For example, does anybody here know the Star-Spangled Banner? Can you hum the first line?

BG: (Hums the first line)

JG: Eyes a little to the right. You accessed your right auditory cortex, the musical side.

How Visuals Get The Picture

Now Visuals are always looking. They find it out before the teacher starts to talk. Isn't it true, you get one look at that lesson and you know what it's going to be about?

How do you study for an exam, those of you who do! Those of you who remember . . .!

Kay: Yeah. Trying to cram as much as possible, photographically, I think, is—I did it, a lot, and trying to recall it during an exam, I can see the words on the page but I can't quite put 'em together—

JG: You would not try to remember what you heard the teacher say—never in a million years—

Kay: Un-unh.

Cora: It depends on the teacher. Some teachers, yeah.

Kay: I had a Shakespeare teacher who was an actress and she would get up and act, so that way—that was visual for me, and that was something that—

Cora: —was reinforced.

JG: That's a combined multi-channel, visual and auditory and maybe kinesthetic too.

Kay: It always helped me, too, to put my notes in different colors, underlined, or whatever, in my notebooks because you could sort of see what colors—this I put down in this color. For some reason, that worked.

JG: Creative use of color!

Morilla: I need to physically rewrite everything and organize things in my own way but it—most of it was involvement, the writing of it—recreating it—

JG: So you get some memory through the kinesthetic act of writing the letters.

Theodore: That helps a lot. I could never use flash cards. I could sit there and I could repeat things over and over again, and it would bounce right off. I had to rewrite it.

Morilla: You had to do something with it.

Kay: Flash cards always worked for me!

Cora: My field is visual. My job relies on visual, and yet I'm one of these people who can walk past kiosks and announcements and so forth and not see any of them. When I focus I think I'm very good visually but if I'm not paying any attention, if I have no reason to pay attention to something I can just completely blot it out.

JG: You have the option of switching it on or off.

Cora: Apparently I switch it off a lot!

BG: It helps you to avoid overload.

JG: Yeah! For a lot of people that's not an option. They're locked in to a particular channel, and that's the channel.

Switching Channels

JG: Beth and I spent a lot of time being locked in on auditory with our son Dave. It took us years to realize that we weren't getting through very well on that channel. Every time we tried to talk to him it seemed the situation would escalate and we'd end up in a shouting match. Then one day Beth—just spontaneously, out of nowhere, apparently—wrote him a note and pasted it to the door of his room. He wasn't home at the time.

We Reached Him On Visual

To our amazement, next day there was a written reply pasted to his door. It was well written—printed, actually—polite, witty, and agreeable, and it was responsive to Beth's requests. It was amazing! We could reach him on the visual channel! That is, we could access that witty, polite, good-humored person that we knew he really was. We used that method all through his high school years and afterwards. Now he lives in Florida and sends us wonderful, loving letters and cards.

Kay: Did you say Visual Channel?

JG: Oh, you're right! That's not just Visual—it's Visual Digital. And there's another channel for you! People usually call it, ''Reading!'' A very underrated channel!

Soap Opera

You know what's really fun. I seldom get a chance to do this, but the soap operas in the afternoons—turn on a soap opera and turn the volume down to zero and then practice your skill at reading the interactions that are going on—just from their eye patterns and their body language. If you really want to get good at this, that's a good way to do it, because the people who play in these soap operas are—either they're very intuitive or somehow they have picked this up—and they have learned to do it very well and they telegraph the stuff—it's pretty pronounced.

Then comes this marvelous discovery that you can tell that they are not actually feeling the feelings that they are acting. When you get to that point, you are a graduate in this field. Then you can tell the difference between the body language that occurs congruently with the internal states and the body language that is subjected to conscious decision.

After you've done that for a while then you will start becoming aware of your own body language, your own accessing. That's when the fun begins, because once you've become aware of the way in which you telegraph messages, the possibility exists of control—of doing the thing in order to get a specific result, so that when you speak to your child, your body language is consistent with the message you want to send.

Chapter 5

That Lovely Feeling
Of Being Understood

How To Talk To Animals, Children,
And Other Loved Ones

JG: Now, Beth is one of those people who can talk to animals. I didn't know that when I married her. This is one of things that began to fascinate me after I met her and we'd gotten married. I began to notice some very strange behavior. Strange to me, that is!

It took me a long time to realize what was going on, because Beth didn't realize that what she was doing was anything out of the ordinary. She thought everybody was like her. Also, she didn't call it "talking to animals" because she never thought about it at all. As far as she was concerned, she wasn't doing anything. So how could you put a name on something that wasn't anything? But let me tell you what I began to notice.

The Three-Kitten Strut

The first thing I noticed was something just a little bit strange about her way of talking. We'd be taking our usual walk around the neighborhood on a Saturday morning and she'd look up at a tree and say, "Look at those two poor robins, sitting there shivering in their overcoats."

I'd say, "What do you mean, overcoats?" but she would just go on and say, "And the Daddy had better get busy and build her a nest, because she's just about to pop, she's so full of eggs." I'd be asking, "Which one is the female? Is it the one with the slightly duller colors?"

She'd say, "The pregnant one, of course," and then I would usually just give up. I couldn't figure it out! For a while I thought it might have something to do with sex, because she knew the pregnancy status of every cat, dog and gerbil in the neighborhood, and she knew it the very first time she saw them. She would look at a cat crossing the street—a hundred yards away—and she would say, ''Oh, that poor cat! She's so pregnant.'' And I would say, ''How do you tell?''

Usually she wouldn't listen to me, she'd just go on and say, ''She's got three kittens inside of her.'' I'd say, ''My God, I can't even tell that that's a female cat up there. What are you seeing?!!'' And she said, ''Look! She's got that three-kitten strut—she walks harder on one side than the other—her paws are hitting the ground harder on the left than on the right, so there's two kittens on the left and one on the right.

Woman: *Are you sure it's not five kittens?*

BG: Three or five. An odd number.

''*That three-kitten strut.*''

Tough Bugs

JG: But gradually I began to realize that this thing was bigger than just sex. We'd go walking out at Thurston pond in the springtime. All the little frogs would be chirping, chirping, chirping, and all of a sudden Beth would stop and say, "Ouch." I'd say, "What happened, did you hurt yourself?"

She'd say, "No, that frog!" I'd say, "Well, what about that frog?" She'd say, "Didn't you see how he swallowed a real tough bug just then?" I would say, "Well, I thought I saw his tongue flick out and he caught a fly or something, but—what do you mean, a tough bug?" She'd say, "Well, didn't you see his eyes bug out when he swallowed it?"

She didn't know—and I didn't know, but it's really true—a frog crunches its prey by pushing its tongue up against the roof of the mouth. The eye sockets are part of the roof of the mouth, so when they swallow a tough one their eyes bug out. Scientists only discovered that only a few years ago. Beth didn't know the scientific explanation, but she just naturally knew that their eyes bug out. She took it for granted that everybody knew that.

Kinesthetic Channel

And as the years went by Beth taught me to notice that a lost kitten has *bewildered ears*, that ducks coming in for a landing on the pond *backpedal* as they touch the water, that the robins in our front lawn are *listening* for worms. And when our little dog Smitty submitted to a scolding she explained that his body posture meant that he was in the *Adapted Dog ego state*.

When we're walking down by Thurston pond and I see a flight of ducks landing on the pond, that's a beautiful sight to me because I see the colors. I see this platoon, so to speak, landing all in order and it's a mosaic pattern of colors to me.

But Beth doesn't experience it that way at all. What Beth is feeling is the pumping of the wings and then when they get close to the water they stick their feet out, right? She says, "Look at that, they're back pedalling, they are coming in to land, they're back pedalling."

She was seeing—but seeing in a feeling way. She could feel what was going on inside of that frog, and that gives her a rapport with living creatures that I just don't have to anywhere near the same degree. The amazing thing is that living creatures recognize it instantly. We'll be taking our walk and a dog will appear at the end of the block. He takes a look at us and hesitates for a second and then comes running up—he runs right straight to Beth.

"Seeing in a feeling way."

He doesn't run to me. Now, I like dogs and I like to pet them, but I don't know what's going on with them—Beth does. Now this kind of being tuned in is one of the greatest assets that a person can have.

You Can Sit With Wolf

One year we took our kids to a music camp in the state of Maine. It was pretty far back in the woods and we needed a car. The auto rental agent drove out to the camp with a car for us to rent. He was going to drive us back to town so he could get off at the agency.

So he hopped out and opened the car doors and Beth said, "I'll sit in the back." He said, "OK, you can sit with Wolf," So Beth slid into the back seat.

Meanwhile, when he said "Wolf" I glanced into the back seat and my eyes encountered this massive snow-white animal head with slanted yellow eyes glowing out of the darkness of the back seat. I said, "Oh, my God, that's a real wolf!" But Beth was already getting into the car and I was on the wrong side to stop her.

What happened next was so subtle I almost missed it. I saw Beth turn her head and neck in a very strange way as if she were looking up at the animal from below and she was smiling and saying something like, "Well, hello there, may I sit beside you?" and the next thing I knew she was in the seat. The animal was actually sitting on his haunches next to her and he lifted one enormous paw—bigger than my entire hand—and placed it firmly on her thigh as if to express his dominance, and then dropped his huge head right on her shoulder and closed his eyes.

And we rode like that for thirty miles on the back roads of rural Maine until we got to town.

A Nice Relationship With Animals

BG: Yes, I don't know how it happens, but I do seem to have quite a nice relationship with most animals except cats.

Ralph: I have pretty much the opposite—I really like cats, but whenever I—

Kay: They come to him. I mean they—I've never heard of cats following people home—a stray cat or whatever—but they follow him.

BG: Oh-hh!

Ralph: But whenever I get in a stall with a horse it will try to crush me. It realizes that I hate it and—figures out that he hates me!

Cora: Well, then, do you think that most people to whom animals respond positively are by nature kinesthetic?

JG: I don't know! I'm not good on kinesthetic!

Cora: —their body language, they lean forwards towards dogs more—

BG: It can be a liability, you know—like poor old Midas. Everything he touched turned to gold. He kissed his daughter and she turned to a gold statue.

JG: That's the pitfall of being on the kinesthetic channel—you feel everything. Your mental model is made with kinesthetic experiences. What was it we did one time? We thought of your vocabulary. You have a marvelous vocabulary, but how is it you access a word?

BG: You mean to speak it out or—

JG: —to comprehend it.

BG: I know I do a lot of feeling. If there's a new word that I don't know or if I'm coming into something new, I do a lot of internal feeling processing—

JG: —Um-hmm. To get to the meaning of the word. I remember one time we were talking about this and what I remember is that for you a vocabulary—your dictionary—is something like a large warehouse where all the objects are on the shelves and you actually have to go and pick that object up and feel what it feels like in order to know the meaning of that word.

BG: Yes.

JG: So if I say a heavy word to you, you actually feel it.

> *Cora: It just seems heavy and dense?*

BG: Well, for example, longer words are harder to process than short ones, because they have more weight!

> *Cora: More visual weight?*

JG: A visual person might say they take up more space on the screen.

BG: No, I mean ''weight'' weight. A long word. It's as if the words are carved out of wood, you know, the letters are all carved out of wood. So if you have a large number of them, that weighs a lot more than with fewer.

JG: The kinesthetic person uses words like ''vibes'' or ''tuned in'' or ''handle'' or they ''feel good'' about a situation.

The Magical Number Seven, Plus Or Minus Two

JG: Have we covered everything? Visual? Auditory? Kinesthetic? These are the channels that we know about. These are the channels that are fairly well established. I think everybody will agree that we take in information on the visual channel, the auditory, the kinesthetic.

The quantity of information is another important factor. If you were to glance at this room for one split second and then close your eyes and recite everything that you have seen, you'd probably still be going a week from now. The amount of information is probably in excess of a hundred thousand bits per second. It's an incredible torrent of information. Now, how many items can the conscious mind hold at one time, in conscious awareness?

Ralph: Seven.[1]

BG: Seven. Five to seven.

JG: Seven! Right. So conscious awareness is about seven one hundred thousandths of the information that's coming in.

Ralph: If you're walking around in a group of people—seven other people and you, you can know without counting whether everybody's there, and if there are more than seven people, somebody has to say—''Is everybody here?''—you have to stop and count.

JG: So the magic number seven, plus or minus two—more or less—that's what you can handle consciously in conscious awareness. That's it! Just try. You'll find it rapidly fades out.

But the amount of information that comes in pays no attention to what your conscious capacity is—it comes in anyway, and it goes directly in, unfiltered and unselected, uncensored, goes right in to your brain.

First Day Of Kindergarten

And under appropriate circumstances it can be retrieved again. Unless you actually lose neurons, the probability is that all of that experience from the moment you first opened your eyes on day one, is filed somewhere, and you can get to it. You may be able to remember the shoes that you wore on the first day of kindergarten. You might even be able to remember whether you had a broken shoelace. I very well remember the smell of the oil that was used to oil the floors in that school.

Kay: That brings back something that I've been reading lately, which is how smell is such an underestimated sense and that nothing evokes more memory than smell—

JG: That's exactly right. Because it is the least conscious. It goes directly into your unconscious.

Tasting The World

Kay: Do you think children go through stages where they are pretty much fixed in one area? I mean, I know that all this is happening at once, but it seems like there is a time when they are—eating every bit of fuzz or they are tasting the world or—

JG: They don't hesitate to get unbalanced, and then balance it up next month or next year. You've noticed that!

Kay: Especially because he's eating most of our house!

Knowledge From Way Back

Ralph: A friend of mine has a couple of kids, and he at one point said to me that the kid's job in the first two years is to learn how everything in the world tastes and how it sounds when you bang it against something else!

By way of demonstrating this, he said, ''Well, you know, for example, take that piece of cardboard over there. You know how that tastes, right?'' Almost everybody that he quotes knows the taste of the cardboard—and when was the last time you ate cardboard? It's been probably a long time ago, and it's also true that if you show people two things and say, ''How do they sound if you bang them against each other?'' you know that for almost anything.

JG: Knowledge from way, way back. How many of you remember the taste of the paint on your crib?

Theodore: I remember . . .

Kay: I remember . . .

JG: And the difference between the taste of wood and the taste of cold metal, for example, if your teeth happen to encounter the metal retainer at the corner of the playpen. I used to chew the paint on my playpen. I neatly put teeth marks all the way around my playpen. Those things you remember, and you remember them with that direct impact of primary sensory experience. You remember the taste, you remember the smell, you remember the feel of the wood and the metal.

Left Breast, Right Breast

Now a baby can tell the difference between the left breast and the right breast.

Sally: Yeah, this kid doesn't like my left side!

Raven: With my Jimmy, it's just the opposite. He's in love with my left breast!

JG: They have not been taught to disregard their olfactory experience.

Sally: Even with my two year old, I can tell when he's noticing smells. He doesn't say it yet, but he points out—if I don't catch it when Fred is dirty, he will.

Raven: My older boy smells it from a mile away!

Charlene: You say he can distinguish the left breast from the right breast by smell?

JG: Um-hmmm. The taste of the milk.

Raven: He ordered chocolate!

The Baby Doesn't Like Chlorine

JG: Some babies can, at least. Beth, you had a patient once, didn't you—a breastfeeding mom who was puzzled because her baby started refusing to nurse, making faces and angry smacking noises and then pulling off of the nipple?

BG: Yes, and the problem was that Mom was a swimmer and she had just started going back to the swimming pool again, swimming three times a day, and we figured out that her baby could smell the chlorine from the swimming pool on her breasts, and he didn't like it!

The Smell Of Security

JG: You need to be tuned in on all the channels to pick up things like that. I'm constantly amazed at how Beth does it!

BG: There's a Dad in our practice who always wears Mom's bathrobe when he gets up at night to take care of the baby, because then the baby can smell Mom.

JG: One of the nurses in our office saw her thirteen-year-old daughter fondling the tattered blanket she has had since the age of two, and she asked her, "What does your blanket smell like, Tammy?"

And Tammy replied, "Safe things!"

Smells And Tastes

JG: Now, Gustatory and Olfactory are often better expressed in this area of the face, with the nose and muzzle, rather than the eyes.

So if you saw a child looking like that, with his nose wrinkled, in the high chair with their Filboid Studge in the bowl—

Ralph: It would be a good time to take the food away!

Priscilla: Before it ends up on the floor.

JG: It might be a small hint that you should change brands!

In modern civilization Olfactory and Gustatory are somewhat undeveloped.[2] Do we have any Gustatories here? Any Olfactory-Gustatories?

Esther: I know I'm not!

Theodore: I love to cook, but I have no way of knowing. I'm not the other people—

Morilla: Oh, but you live with me!

Theodore: Oh, that's true, that's true. Yeah. Meat and potatoes is fine with her, but my God, with me it's gotta be every spice off the rack.

Ralph: With me it's the same thing. Kay can remember her spices and everything, and I'll say, "Is this whatever?" and I'm always wrong.

The Smell Of Grandma's House

Olfactory and Gustatory, because they are so neglected and ignored, have the most power to influence you unconsciously. That's why you feel good if it smells like Christmas.

Woman (whispering): Yes!

Arthur: Pine trees!

Mark: I was saying during the break, for maybe the last 10-15 years I've never understood why Christmas didn't feel the same as it did when I was a kid. It finally hit me this year that there was a certain smell in my grandmother's house. Evidently it was the final piece that I'm missing.

Three Thousand Omelettes

JG: I understand in France, for example, where cooking is a fine art, there are three thousand omelette establishments registered with the government. Each and every one makes a different omelette which is registered—and they all taste different.

Arthur: Wow!

Sally: That would make sense, though. Some of my relatives are French. They put all their emphasis on meals—especially breakfast and lunch. Dinner is considered sort of like a lunch for us—it's often skipped. But they put more time into their eating, and they put more into it—they give two hour lunches, minimum. They go home and they sit down and they have these beautiful lunches. They spend all this time on it. When I go over to their house and eat, I can tell if he's cooked because—you notice those things. You notice that he's put so much into it.

JG: It really changes the entire—flavor of your life.

Dewy Mountain Mornings

Raven: My grandmother lived in the mountains in Kentucky, and on the dewy mornings you'd go out and smell this wonderful smell. About once a year, if I'm lucky, I'll get that for just an instant—that smell.

JG: It brings everything back, just really powerful. So this is a very powerful source of information, either conscious or subliminal; but there's a problem, because Olfactory doesn't translate into verbal very well. If you try to describe that smell on that dewy morning, there's no word for it.

Early Memories

You may remember from your childhood the smell of bacon and eggs frying in the morning . . . or the smell and taste of hot cocoa after being out sledding in the snow. A powerful positive experience, right?

But there were certain aunts in my childhood whom I hated to visit. I couldn't stand to be kissed and hugged by them, because they wore cheap, penetrating perfume that created an intense negative response in me—almost a physiological response of revulsion. They thought I was shy—or that I didn't like them!

There were other relatives whose house was always full of the smell of boiling cabbage. How I hated that smell! I always got a migraine! To this day I dislike visiting them, in fact I get nauseous just thinking about them!

OLFACTORY—"It brings everything back, just really powerful."

What I'm suggesting to you is that you have the power to influence your own child's experience of the world by means of smells and tastes.

If you don't do it consciously and deliberately you will still be having an effect, but you won't know what kind of effect you are having.

The Meaning Of A Campfire

How many of you have had the experience of sitting around a campfire? Almost everyone. Whatever your experience has been with a campfire or a bonfire or some similar setting, I'd like you to go back there and reexperience it now.

I'd like you to recapture the excitement, the exhilaration, the thrill you felt then. I'd like you to see again the flames, yellow and red, leaping upward, and the glowing embers of the logs. I'd like you to hear the crackling of the flames and smell the smoke and feel the heat of the fire and as you remember yourself sitting on the sand or on a tree trunk or a log before the fire, I'd like you to feel the roughness of the tree-bark, the texture of the sand, the feel of the earth on your bare feet. I'd like you to smell the tangy smell of the fresh air and feel the coolness of the breeze on your skin as well as the blast of heat from the fire. I'd like you to smell the delicious aroma of the food cooking on the fire or on the grill—the hot dogs or the marshmallows or whatever it was. I'd like you to hear again the voices of your friends talking, laughing, shouting, perhaps even singing old familiar songs. And I'd like you to feel again that wonderful feeling of adventure, of comradeship, of sharing that you felt then. Do it now! Enjoy! Take your time!

And when you are thoroughly satisfied and ready to come back to the present time and place, I'd like you to mentally review your experience with specific attention to each and every sensory channel, and I'd like you to notice how the limited information on each individual channel is integrated into a comprehensive experience of the whole thing. And I'd like you to appreciate what a tremendous complexity of unique individual experience is compressed into that one little word: "campfire". No one else in the whole world has the same reactions, the same memories that you do when you think of the word "campfire".

Now obviously, you all had a different campfire, you all weren't sitting around the same campfire, so your experience of this event for each of you is totally different and yet is fundamentally the same. Anybody care to share their experience of a campfire?

> *Kay: I remember when I was in Girl Scouts and we went out to a lake. It was piney and there were mosquitoes everywhere, and we were standing around the campfire. One of our scout leaders had brought in a flag and we were going to burn the flag because that's what you do when you dispose of old flags. You don't just throw them in the garbage can, you burn them.*
>
> *They tore it up into strips and everybody had to toss a strip into the fire and say something about our country. It was so moving and none of it— hardly any of us could say anything because we were just choked up about the whole thing. That's just one particular campfire—and we said that, you know, standing there and tossing this in—it was red, my strip was red, and . . .*

JG: Powerful experience!

Kay: Yeah!

JG: You were really choked up.

>   *Kay: Yeah! I still get that way.*

JG: Yeah, I saw it, your eyes went down—in the midline, interestingly enough.

>   *Kay: Probably because I had my head down at the time . . . trying to come up with something to say and could not . . . just thinking about a bunch of about ten girls crying.*

JG: A rich experience, and you've kept every detail of it.

>   *Kay: Right down to where I got a mosquito bite!*

JG: Anybody else?

>   *Cora: I went with my best friend and another good friend of ours and—the camp was in three levels, down a lake area and then another midlevel. We were up on a very high area where there really were no activities, where there were mostly just cabins; but, that was a big, huge, gigantic ring where there would be a big bonfire at the end. That was just about the only thing that was done up on this high level.*
>
>   *I remember that. It was a big bonfire, it was really neat. There were all big pine trees, all around and it seemed very dark. It was very cold. Everyone had sweatshirts and bluejeans on and so forth, and—I'm sure there were a lot of marshmallows and somemores and so forth but—I don't remember exactly— the fire was too big for anyone to get close enough with a stick or a fork or anything like that to melt much of anything. But we sang a lot of songs and—it was just a lot of fun. It was really good, there was a lot of camaraderie in that camp and it was a real coming together.*

Using Words To Evoke Experience

I want to remind you that for the past half hour you have been smelling smells and tasting tastes and experiencing early scenes that are not actually happening now. You have been experiencing those delights with such present vividness through the power of words—mere words.

Parallel Accessing

You notice that one person talks about her childhood, and several people access their own childhood, their own experiences, as a result of that.[2] You don't even have to talk about the subject that you want to discuss, you can talk about something parallel and produce an experience. It won't be the same experience.

Each and every one of you has had an experience of being at a campfire—those of you who have—and each one of those experiences was your own personal experience. It was triggered by the word "campfire". The word "campfire" in the dictionary has only one or two meanings, but you understand now that it has as many meanings as there are experiences. For each individual person it has as many meanings as you have experienced campfires.

The Power Of Words

Words have this incredible power to call up experience. I didn't say, "mosquito" right?—but it was there! That's right. And your understanding of the word "campfire" includes mosquitoes.

So, when you speak to another person, you don't know what you are eliciting. You can get clues by noticing their nonverbal responses, but in order to know what it means to them, you have to ask. You have to find out by asking. That's when you begin to get a peek into the other person's Mental Model, when you ask and they tell you.

So you can understand that when you say a word to your child, you conjure up as if by magic a whole world of previous experience. This is one of the ways by which you can get into another person's world. This is not a voluntary choice on your child's part. There is no way that they can refuse to experience those associations, because those associations are what that word means to them.

Mere Words

And you understand what a momentous thing you are doing when you speak words to your child or your spouse or to any other person. You have the power to create their experience, you have the power to shape it, to make it beautiful. You can give them the experience of competence, of comfort, of success.

Chapter 6

Where Have I Seen This Before?

Putting It Together

JG: What we're doing is going from the basic elements, like the alphabet, up to words and then sentences. So we start with the understanding that everything you know about what your baby or your child is doing comes from sensory perceptions to take that information in. Now that may not be strictly true. Some moms, especially, have radar. They have intuition. They're the ones where the child is in the other room, and they call out, "What are you doing and stop it!"

But that might be sensory perception, too. It might be that they are perceiving the unnatural silence. When it gets too quiet, you know something is going on!

Kay: Too loud or too quiet!

JG: So we're going to operate on the assumption that maybe there is such a thing as intuition, but that for practical purposes—for the purposes of this course—the information that you get for dealing with your baby or child comes from sensory perception. You look and you see. You listen and you hear. Believe me, this is not a small matter. This is a big item, because a lot of childrearing is done with an almost total absence of attention to the feedback. If you can learn to do that, you'll be ahead of ninety percent of the human race. Just learn to look, listen, and also pay attention to your own feelings in that situation; because although the way that you feel the feelings of another person is a bit mysterious, we're going to assume that you do it by seeing and hearing—by your own sensory modalities.

Mental Model

Now putting together the sensory awareness into a picture of what's happening is also a bit mysterious; but it's something that all parents do, whether they know it or not. When you get the visual information, the auditory, and the information from the other sensory channels, you put it all together and make an image in your head; a Mental Model of what's going on with the other person.

Mental Model is a very basic concept.[1] Verbal Model is a closely related concept. That's the name you give to your Mental Model. That's the idea that you have in your head about the situation. Those are the words you use for what you think is happening.

It's a great advantage for your Mental Model, your Verbal Model to correspond to what's really happening. It's very easy to overinterpret. It's easy to look at a child and say, ''He's being stubborn again.'' That kind of interpretation is not necessarily useful.

I Used To Think She Was Stubborn But Now I Know She's Just Lazy

We had a mom who brought her child in at six weeks and said, ''I used to think that she was stubborn, but now I know she's just lazy.'' Six weeks old and already labelled!

BG: Right, this was a breast feeding baby, and that was the mother's assessment of this child. I said, ''Wait a minute, hold everything, stop! We're going to discuss this!''

JG: ''Stubborn'' meant that the mother couldn't get the responses that she wanted. Then she was able to change that to the concept ''lazy,'' which meant the child wasn't deliberately frustrating her, it was just a slow responder and was lazy. She probably had one other term in her verbal model and that would have been ''a good baby'' which is one that would spontaneously do what she wanted. That is a verbal model that's too simple. It's got too few distinctions in it.

If you only have three choices in terms of thinking about your baby, either a good baby or a stubborn baby or a lazy baby, then you're going to be hallucinating 97% of the time. You're going to be putting one of those three words, your verbal model, on to this lovely, rich, marvelous reality. So, as we go along what we're trying to do is to increase the richness and precision of our mental model of what's actually happened.

Gina: Does the idea of not having expectations flow from that?

JG: Expectations flowing from your mental model. Yes. If you see ''stubbornness'', then you're naturally going to expect certain things. You're going to act in certain ways, you're going to get an interaction started that assumes this. Within two or three years, the child will be absolutely convinced that you're right and so will you. They will know in their heart that they are ''stubborn'' or ''stupid'' or whatever, and so will you. Don't do this!

So when you see a child doing something, you make a mental model of what it means. For example if the child is producing a sound of 8,000 cycles per second at 80 decibels, you call that crying. Do you see my point? ''Crying'' is the mental model that you use to make sense of that particular piece of behavior. It's very natural, and very practical, for parents to say, ''My baby is crying,'' when they're emitting 8,000 cycles per second at 80 decibels. That's what it is, right? But there are times when it's useful to consider it just as behavior without any interpretation attached to it. Beth and I have learned to do this over a period of years. We have seen babies that are brought in spitting every 15 seconds. Has anybody in this room had that experience?

War On Spit

Man and Woman: You mean spitting up?

JG: Spitting up every 15 seconds, brand new babies, 3 weeks, 3 months, 5 months, and a lot of spitting. Typically Mom and Dad will be standing there with a tissue in their hand, and the instant the baby spits, they lunge forward and wipe the baby's cheek. And guess what's happening?

Mark: It likes having its cheek rubbed!

The Attempted Remedy Now Becomes The Producer Of The Problem

JG: The baby likes having its cheek rubbed! But even if they didn't rub the baby's cheek, simply widening their eyes and moving forward towards the baby is a sufficient response to lock in that behavior.

Anything that a baby does that causes Mom or Dad to pay attention and move a fraction of an inch closer, will be locked in and will happen more frequently . . . so the attempted remedy now becomes the producer of the problem.

It's invariably presented as a problem in the baby, ''My baby has a spitting disease. My baby spits up, there must be something wrong with her stomach.'' If you think of it purely as behavior, the remedy—which can be done right here in this room, and Beth and I have done it many times—is to have Mom or Dad count to ten before they move, defocus their eyes, stare into empty space above the baby's head, and move back a quarter of an inch.

Nonevents

That makes it a nonevent. If the baby does something and it doesn't produce any effect on the outside world, there is less motivation to do it again. They might spit again for some reason or other, but you won't get that conditioned linkage between their spitting and something specific that happens in the outside world.

Then the baby stops spitting for a second because it's puzzled, and Mom widens her eyes, smiles, looks, and comes in close to the baby. The baby doesn't know what's happening, but now he is being conditioned to do that other thing that he's doing when he's not spitting. Then the power of the conditioning takes over again and he gets ready to spit and Mom sees that he is about to spit so she moves back a quarter of an inch, breaks eye contact, looks bored, and that spit is a little less than the one before. When it stops Mom widens her eyes and moves in, and all of this is done on an split-second time scale. The response has to be within, I think, five-eighths of a second. This has all been tested.

BG: You can do this on camera, slow it down.

JG: Right. With a camera you can see that anything that Mother does within a certain fraction of a second will reinforce what the baby is doing at that moment; but if Mother does not respond in any way, then it is not reinforced. Then when she responds, if she has timed her response carefully, it will coincide with the baby relaxing, or smiling, or looking around or being puzzled, or whatever. You can reverse that spitting syndrome in 15 minutes.

But if you go to the emergency room they will regard it as a disease, and they will admit the baby to the hospital and strap the baby to a vertical board and recommend that Mother come in and sit in front of the baby and wipe his cheek every time that he spits. Those babies get a diagnosis of Rumination Syndrome. They are regarded as having some kind of rare disorder of muscle coordination—perhaps incurable, because the mothers will sit there for 24 hours a day, and it just goes on and on and on.

> *Raven: You had us do that reversal with Jimmy when he was crying for no reason and it really worked . We went home and started doing that, and his behavior just switched totally around—*
>
> *Quentin: —instantly.*

> *Raven:* —*and he was always smiling then and since has been the happiest baby.*
>
> *Quentin:* *It's hard to catch each stage. You have to really pay attention to the timing.*
>
> *Woman:* *Giving them negative attention does it too. They'll just keep doing it: "I'm getting some kind of attention here!"*

JG: Right. Even yelling, slapping, or hitting will strengthen the behavior that you don't want.

The Mind's Eye

Now the next step is the big one and you need to get prepared for a shock or at least a big surprise. We've been spending all this time sharpening our awareness of sensory data coming in on all the channels and I've been harping on how important it is to use your eyes and ears and all your sensory equipment to be keenly aware of what's actually going on.

But now we move up one level above that to the level of patterns, and all of a sudden we encounter one of those strange paradoxical reversals that so often happen when you make a big step upwards. Suddenly the important stuff that you need to notice is no longer detectable with eyes or ears or other sensory equipment. The next level is visible only to the mind's eye. It is the level of recurring patterns of sensory data.

Beyond Channels

This is a step beyond channels. The things that you see are not just visual impressions. No matter how keen you may be on the visual channel, seeing a pattern of behavior is quite different from just having your eyes open and looking at a child. The same for the auditory channel. It's one thing to hear sounds, it's a much subtler thing to recognize the sound patterns that tell you your child is getting agitated or sleepy or whatever it may be.

Patterns: Where Have I Seen This Before?

So how do you learn to "see" an invisible pattern? We start with the recognition that we have seen a particular set of sensory cues coming back to us from that child before. We have seen that look and that body language before. In other words, we're building now from the individual sensory data to the synthesis, putting it all together. We have heard the child speak with this tone of voice and vocal register and we have seen this facial expression and this body movement before. We've seen it before and we think we know what it means—or at any rate, we recognize it.

Ego States

Now, the English language or any other language is very deficient with regard to behavioral displays, because we don't identify these transient patterns as such. There is a fundamental language problem here. We don't have names for them; and if there is no name for something, there is a strong tendency to overlook it, to not notice at all that there is something there. You remember George Orwell's book, *1984*. Big Brother—the dictator—deliberately removed from the language all words that could prove troublesome.

But everybody has experienced these states. You may know, for example, when your spouse raises an eyebrow in a certain way, it carries an encyclopedia full of meaning. You've seen it before, you know what this means! You can call it whatever you like. The important thing is to recognize them.

BG: I've heard people say, "I can see the wheels going around in his head."

JG: You see a little baby sitting and tensing and getting red in the face, and you can pretty well guess what's going to happen!

BG: You're going to have to change his diaper pretty soon!

JG: Beth can recognize, for example, what I would regard as an extremely subtle color change around my mustache area, here. She says that when I turn green here, she knows that I'm going to have a migraine within six hours.

Kay: God!

JG: I don't know it! I go and look in the mirror. I can't see it, but she can see it.

The next step in organizing your knowledge is to put these individual sensory perceptions together into something that makes sense . . . into an entity . . . so that when you look at your child you say, "Oh, Resistance coming up!" or Compliance: "This child is now in the Yes Set." They're nodding their head like this, and there's a little smile and a little automaticity to their behavior. That's the Yes Set. Then you can know—you see, this is pragmatic—when you see a child in the Yes Set, you know that you can go directly to asking for what you want—unless it's too big a change—because they are more likely to say Yes than No.

But if they're like this (all tensed up, frowning, chin out) particularly if they get that something around the eyes, then you can guess, "Gee, maybe I ought not to ask that kid to do anything. Maybe I should offer them a cookie or something." You've recognized what I would like to call, for lack of a better phrase, a transitory ego state, a momentary ego state.

Parts

We don't need to get into technicalities about all this. All schools of psychology have their own ways of dividing up the human mind, but they all agree on one thing; that is, the idea that people are made up of different parts and that you can elicit or talk to those parts separately. We're not going to get into questions about which part we're talking to at the moment, we're just going to stay at the simplest level of direct observation and call them behavioral states or ego states, without any further specification.

Sequences: The Next Ego State

You can think of a human being as flowing from one such state to the next. What switches ego states is unknown, but you can tell when a person switches from one ego state to another. I'll give a baby a shot in the examining room. The mother will pick the baby up, the baby will be crying, mother will take one step through the door frame, and the baby will stop crying and instantly start doing something else. That's a shift of ego state. It's dramatic. Once you begin to look for these things, it's really dramatic.

BG: It's almost like seeing a movie—each frame changes a little bit. Three frames down, you've got a whole different thing. I think of it like this.

JG: Yes. You watch actors and actresses—turn off the TV sound and watch those images and you will see the ego states floating by, on the face and in the body of the person that is acting. You can say to yourself, "Oh! Now that looks like an ego state of tender emotion, this one looks like an ego state of warding off emotion, this one looks like anxiety coming on." You can name them according to your own subjective estimate of what they are.

The art of inducing a person to switch from one ego state to another is what this is all about. For now, let's just call it an ego state if it's a pattern that you recognize very well, you have seen it under many circumstances. We are going to talk about ways of inviting or inducing people to switch from one ego state to another. That's the name of the game. If they're in an ego state where things are happening that they, and perhaps you too don't like, you want to have the power to give them an opportunity to switch ego states.

BG: And/or—head 'em off at the pass if you know the early signs—

JG: If you know what the precursors are, you can move in before they get there.

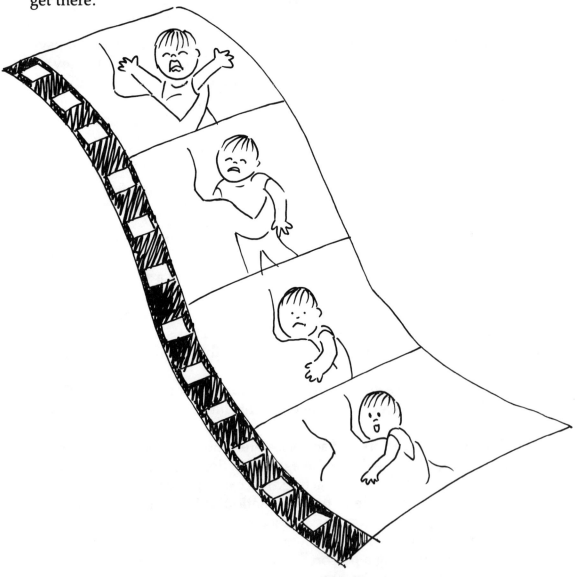

SEQUENCES: THE EGO STATES
"It's almost like seeing a movie—each frame changes a little bit."

Punctuation

BG: Let me say something here, too! When we're talking about a smile in response—or some kind of action in response—the smile or the action is what *we're* marking. This is the signal or the mark or the thing in the sequence that *we're* noticing.[2]

But don't forget, there's a whole lot that's going on all the time that we are not marking—that we may not be noticing, and that may be where the crucial problem is. If you're getting behavior you don't want, what reward is the child getting out of what you're not noticing in the sequence? One of the ways of finding out is in the book, which I think is a good book, entitled *Without Spanking or Spoiling*,[3] and that is to notice what happens just before, just during and just after whatever the behavior is that you don't like—or that you do like.

You really have to have your antennae up to check what's going on, because you may miss it if you're only marking certain things.

Your spouse can also help you if you're puzzled about an interaction that's going on between you and the child. The spouse is a wonderful source of observation and can say, ''I notice this was also going on as you were doing this.''

The Observer Ego State

I think in one of the other psychology schools, there's a part of us that's been called the Observer. This means even while you are in the interaction with somebody else, there's a part of you that's up there looking down and observing both parties to the interaction. What we're talking about here is getting more skill in the observer fraction of our own self; where we can either step aside or go up above and look down to see what's happening.

If you're just observing, it takes away the sense of blame. Then maybe you will be able to change something that will make it more positive if that's the problem.

Over and Over (Loops)

JG: If a great operatic singer came out for an encore and sang the same aria a second time, you might applaud if it was really well done. But if she came out again and sang it a third time, you'd probably get bored. If she kept coming out and singing the same encore again and again, you could imagine the audience walking out or even tearing up the auditorium.

The same thing is true in human relations. If we sing the same song over and over every time the other person triggers us off, it quickly gets boring and then really painful for everyone.

In advanced family interaction problems, violence can be triggered by somebody raising an eyebrow[4] because they all have gone through this loop so many times it is utterly unbearable. They are so tuned in to each other's signals, but they don't know what they're tuned in to—it's out of their control, because they're not consciously marking.[5]

So develop your sensory skills. Practice on all the channels. Practice on your spouse. It's kind of fun.

> *Louise: True for us! Sometimes the day just starts in a bad way. I'm just mean to Kyle as he gets on my nerves, and he's worse and worse. Then I'm worse and soon we're ready to murder each other.*

JG: That's a loop.

> *Louise: It's just awful! His Dad pointed it out to me and said, "Look! If you just stop, say 'I'm not going to do this, I'm going to be nice to him,' then he may get better."*
>
> *That does reverse it. It's amazing. I didn't realize it, but he pointed it out to me.*

How Do You Interrupt The Loop?

JG: People go through these ego states and they come out in a loop—back again at ego state "A". If people didn't go into those repeating sequences of behavior, we'd never be able to understand what was going on . . . because we would never be able to recognize any pattern. Fortunately people do repeat themselves; and if you pay close enough attention, you will quickly realize that you can learn to recognize the repeating sequences.

If you get a painful loop going and you can't get out of it, then you have a problem. That's the definition of a Problem. The definition of a Problem is a locked-in loop, a painful sequence that keeps recurring. In Cybernetics the question is simply: How do you interrupt the loop, or how do you avoid triggering it in the first place.

But first let me just suggest to you that some of the ego states that people get into—when you get into one—you feel like you can never get out.

If you have ever had a long-standing emotional reaction of some sort—where you feel really angry or really depressed—you know how hard it is to get out of it. But if you do get out of it by some means—maybe you don't even know how you got out of it—then you can't imagine being in it!

Morilla: *That's true!*

JG: You know how it is when you're feeling really good and on top of things and you say to yourself, "Boy, was I depressed the other day! Wonder how that happened?"

If you've ever tried the experiment "I wonder if I could make myself depressed right now?", pretty soon you're laughing. You can't do it. You can't get from one ego state to the other by willing it.[6] It's very difficult.

Louise: *So that's why when I'm really sad, I try to think of all the funny jokes I know and all—and it just won't work!*

The Problem With Shaping Up

JG: So when you tell a kid to shape up, you're asking them to voluntarily pull themselves out of one ego state and switch into another. Well, sometimes it works, but by and large that's real hard to do. So you have to have the skills to help them to do that rather than simply demanding, "Do it without any assistance, without my even knowing how you're gonna do it. Just do it!" That's basically the command which is given to a lot of kids. "Not only must you do your homework, I want you to like it!"

So now we've got the idea of what an ego state is. You can call it what you want—make up a word if you don't like that one. That's what that is.

My Mother Told Me
Never To Talk To Strangers

BG: I was over at the discount store at the Mall and I was standing in front of the clock display on the wall. I don't know if you've been down there, they've got clocks all over the wall. This kid—with lots of pimples on his face, wearing a big jacket, looking really husky and strong—comes up to me and says, "Can you tell me what time it is?" I said, "Well, no, I really can't!" He says, "Well, I can see your watch right there! So why can't you?" I looked at him through the bottom of my bifocals and said, "Because my mother told me never to talk to strangers!"

He was trying to rip me off!

Morilla: *Where did this happen?*

BG: At the discount store. There wasn't anybody else nearby. I'm sure he was trying to get my watch or go into my purse while I was looking at my watch. I could tell he was up to something. It was a con, but I really flipped him out. He turned around and went out laughing. He had never been treated like that before.

JG: He didn't know what ego state to land in. You made him stumble in his pitch.

The Message Sent Is Not Necessarily The Message Received

Morilla: The real tough thing here, though, is whether or not the way you say it is the way they receive it.

JG: Exactly! That's exactly right.

BG: That's the crux of it all.

Morilla: We have this problem all the time, the way we react. If you want something, you really have to be able to second-guess how they'll hear it.

JG: Exactly. Virginia Satir said it, many years ago.[7] *It's not enough to send a straight message. The other person has to hear it, and therein lies the art.* Therein lies the art. You have to develop your own repertoire to the point where, by paying attention to the feedback you get, you can decide, "Gee, this approach doesn't do it. I'll try a different one."

So the more repertoire you've got and the more aware you are of your own feedback, the more likely you are to switch to a strategy that will work. It's not just a matter of switching ego states but also strategies. So we're really at a very elementary level here.

We're just getting introduced to the idea that there are ego states, and that you do have this power. You can pull an ego state from another person—six times out of ten—not a hundred percent. There are some people—like John Wayne—who seem to have only one ego state.

BG: It's pretty big!

JG: A man gotta do what a man gotta do!

A Real Quick Switch

Dr. Ray Helfer, who did so much pioneering work with Dr. Henry Kempe on child abuse, tells the story of his visit to London to speak at a conference.

After the conference, he was standing at the curb getting ready to cross the street. Suddenly out of nowhere a total stranger lunged at him and knocked him to the sidewalk. You can guess what ego state he was in when he got up! He was going to knock that guy's block off! But just then one of those big London busses roared by on the left side of the road inches away from the sidewalk. Dr. Helfer had been looking the wrong way and was about to step into the path of the bus. Dr. Helfer realized all this in less time than it takes to tell, and his ego state suddenly switched from rage to gratitude. He thanked the man for saving his life.

Now that's what you call a real quick switch of ego state.

Hyperactivity

Now with a locked-in loop, let's think of it this way. Mom comes in to the doctor's office and says her child is so hyperactive that she spends the whole day trying to calm him down and keep him from destroying himself by his impulsive behavior. At the end of the day she's exhausted and has a headache. What she understands is that the child's hyperactivity is the cause of her chasing him around all day and ending up exhausted and headachey. But it's more useful to think of these two people as caught up and locked into a loop. We can diagram it as a circle with one arrow going from hyperactivity to Mom's chasing, and another arrow going from Mom's chasing towards hyperactivity.

Do Something Else

Once this loop is set up, it doesn't make the slightest difference which is considered cause and which is considered effect, because this is a self-sustaining situation. The only thing that will break it is to interrupt the cycle. You get them to do something else. Almost anything will do. Any change—no matter how small—if it interrupts the sequence, can snowball into a major redirection of their life pattern.

This is where the idea of feedback comes in. The child's behavior feeds back to set off Mom's behavior. Mom's behavior feeds back to set off the child's behavior. To be more exact, it's positive feedback; that is, what Mom does is not diminishing the child's hyperactivity, it's increasing it. Mom wants her behavior to diminish his hyperactivity. She thinks she's acting to diminish it, but in actual fact, she's increasing it. That's where the problem is. If your car is going too fast and you think you are stepping on the brake, but it's really the accelerator, you've got a problem. Until you get your foot off the accelerator, things are just going to get worse and your car is going to go faster.

"It's more useful to think of these two people as caught up and locked into a loop."

Trying Hard To Fall Asleep

A child doesn't fall asleep soon enough and so his mother urges him to try harder to fall asleep. The child tries to obey only to discover that trying hard to fall asleep is a very wakeful activity. The harder he tries, the longer he stays awake until finally, he's lying in bed with his eyes open all night. The parents, meanwhile, are getting desperate. Sometimes they may misinterpret this situation as stubbornness. If they begin to punish their child for staying awake, the situation may escalate. The child may develop secondary behavioral problems. His school work may suffer and eventually he may come to believe that he is a bad person—that there is something wrong with him.

Now those of you who have a really sensitive ear on the auditory channel have probably noticed that this use of the word "feedback" is not exactly the same as the way we used it before when we referred to Sensory Feedback. The feedback we're talking about now is not the mere observation of a change in the other person. What we're talking about now is the actual change in the observer that is produced by the response of the other person. This is the technically correct use of the term feedback. To distinguish it from what we have been calling Sensory Feedback, I'll call it Cybernetic Feedback. That's a scary enough term!

What Mom needs to notice is not so much her child's hyperactive behavior as that part of her own behavior that triggers the hyperactive response in her child. She needs to use her God-given power of contingency-detection to notice what she is doing that feeds back to her child to produce the behavior she doesn't want.

"Please Send More Cylert!"

The worst case of hyperactivity I ever encountered was a girl who was eleven at the time her parents brought her to see me. She was very bright, but she had begun to exhibit signs and symptoms of hyperactivity at a very early age—age two. Her parents were divorced around that time. By age four she was so hyperactive that she was under a psychiatrist's care. The psychiatrist prescribed first dextroamphetamine, then Ritalin, and then Cylert, in ever-increasing dosages.

But the mother didn't believe the diagnosis. She couldn't believe that her child was truly organically hyperactive. So she took her to a second psychiatrist, who agreed with the first one that this was true organic hyperactivity characterized by the quality of organic drivenness—

Kay: You mean chemical imbalance?

JG: And neurological. So they doubled the dose. They doubled the dose again. They went up to the maximum allowable dose for dextroamphetamine sulfate. They switched to Cylert, which was a new drug at the time.

The mother still didn't believe the diagnosis, so she took the child to a team of psychological specialists in another state. The report came back confirming the psychiatrists' diagnosis. The mother then went to another psychiatrist—I think there were three or four psychiatrists and a team of psychologists. They all agreed across the board. There wasn't a single dissenting opinion. This was organic hyperactivity. This was a neurologically damaged child, but with no neurological deficit.

They continued to prescribe Cylert and increased the dosage until finally when she came to see us, the kid was on a dose of Cylert that was so high I think probably it would sedate an elephant.

Louise: Did it sedate her?

Kay: Did you see the toxic side effects?

JG: I did not see any toxic side effects. But the teachers at school were just beside themselves because she was destructive in school as well as at home. She wouldn't do her homework. She would get up and wander around the room. She'd attack the other kids. She'd bite them. She'd generally be a nuisance. The teachers would send home notes, but generally the gist of the notes they sent home was: "Please send more Cylert!"

Louise: Ohhh!

JG: When it would wear off after three hours, she would be totally uncontrollable.

Mother at this time was in the midst of a fight with her husband who had moved away to another state, for custody of the kid. She was determined not to let him have custody of the kid.

She had to sell her house. She got it all fixed up to show so she could sell it. This eleven-year-old girl went up in the attic and trampled through the plaster between the beams, and basically tore the ceiling out of the house. It fell down into the mother's bedroom. They had to stop showing the house while they brought in the repair people. It cost several hundred dollars.

The very next day after it was fixed, the girl went up there and did it all over again. At that point, the mother felt that she was in imminent danger of killing this child. So, she came to see us.

I told her that I would take the case if she would promise to do exactly what I said without asking any questions. She would have to bind herself in advance to do exactly what I said without questioning me. She said she would do it.

I said to her, "I want you to go home. I want you to call up your ex-husband—contact him. During the night, while the child is asleep, I want you to load all of her belongings into the rear of the station wagon. I want you to take all of her medications and flush them down the toilet. The next morning, when it's time to go to school, don't say anything to her. Let her get in the car and then you drive her—first you check with your ex-husband —you drive her out of the state to his house. Leave her there and leave her baggage. Then get in the car and drive back home.

Next I called the ex-husband and asked him if he would contact the local school authorities and ask the school psychologist to give me a report in six weeks. He was not to say anything about hyperactivity or behavior.

Six weeks later I got this very puzzled phone call from the school psychologist. He said, "I've got this note here that says I'm supposed to call you up there in Michigan about this girl. I don't know what this is all about. She's a model student. She's making all 'A's. Her behavior is perfect. What's the problem?"

I said, "No problem."

I heard from Mom a few months later. The girl was writing home once a month. These were very friendly letters, and they were always signed, "With love."

Then the father called. He said, "The girl seems very happy down here. Do you mind if I keep her a while longer?"

I advised the mother to say, "OK."

A year or two later I got another piece of information via the grapevine. The girl was a National Merit Scholar—and well behaved. No Ritalin, no Cylert, no nothing, no hyperactivity.

So the years went by and I forgot about the case. Then an occasion came to present the case at the medical school. I called up the Mom in the city where she lives. She said, "Well, the first thing is, I've remarried. I've found a very nice man, and we've got a very nice relationship. We're doing real well. And oh, yes, Jeannie is back with us. She's in college. She's studying to be—"

Kay: A psychologist?

JG: "—an elementary school teacher!!"

I asked her how this came about and she said, "Well, she stayed with Dad for several years and got along very well. Then Dad got a new girl friend. Jeannie got very upset about that, and she began to misbehave. After a couple of weeks, she realized that she never did like Dad all that much anyway. She really likes Mother best.'' She called up Mom and asked if she could come home, and Mom said yes.

Now that girl had, from the age of four to the age of eleven, seven years of medication under psychiatric auspices. She had medication to the ultimate tolerance limit of the human body. She had the unanimous decision of all the psychiatrists involved—and the psychologists too—that this was a hyperactive child. She was cured in one day. Her cure was: to flush her medicine down the toilet and send her back to Daddy.

> *Louise:* *Why was she so unhappy with her mother?*

JG: Who knows? Who could say?

> *Kay:* *Well, just the change—*
>
> *Cora:* *Was it just the shock of being completely uprooted?*

JG: Why, I think she got what she wanted!

> *Kay:* *You mean she wanted—*
>
> *Cora:* *What? Just to get away from the mother?*

JG: She wanted to be with Dad.

> *Kay:* *But Mom wasn't gonna do that. She wanted custody.*

JG: Mom wasn't gonna do that. But Mom herself was an extremely energetic and active professional woman. I'd call her hyperactive. Adults learn to hide it, you know. It was a case of, ''Like Mother, like daughter.''

You can take this kind of thing and torture it over and over again and get all kinds of elaborate explanations; but to invent an explanation for something that's already happened, you just have to imagine something. The point is, the feedback loop got interrupted and the undesirable behavior was no longer being triggered.

Invisible Webs: The Systems Approach

You get in the habit of noticing these webs of relationship—of seeing a person in their whole-family relationships. You learn to see those invisible systems in your mind's eye—those invisible loops of interaction.

That isn't easy. This is where people get stuck and after a while decide there aren't any solutions. Then begins the whole sad process of looking for some kind of disease inside the child that is generating the unwanted behavior out of nothing. Then the child can be diagnosed as having a disease, and the whole problem can be turned over to the psychiatrists, the mental hospitals, and eventually the police.[8]

One thing is clear. If this is what they call hyperactivity, then somebody is making some serious mistakes.

Reification: The Language Problem

It's worth noticing again how the structure of language itself limits our ways of thinking, and thus, our options. We invent a word like "hyperactivity" when what we really mean is, "I don't know how to cope with what's happening here." It's so easy to take one piece of a complex process of interaction—the piece associated with the child—and turn it into a *thing* by giving it a name. Obviously if it has a name, it must be a thing.

So now we have invented a thing called "hyperactivity" and the next thing we think we know is that hyperactivity is the name of a disease. So now we need to call on the medical profession to find a drug that will cure it, or at least keep it under control.

Do you see how insidious this is? Here we are, hallucinating wildly—creating diseases out of whole cloth—when the essential core of the whole problem can be better expressed in the simple words, "I don't know how to cope with this."

"Hyperactivity"—not the thing, but the word—has become the new problem that prevents a successful approach to the real problem.

The Name Of The Game

It's so strange, when you think about it. Nobody would try to do fencing without learning the elements of how to handle the foil and how to defend himself. Nobody would try to do karate without some basic lessons, but we try to do this marvelously intricate dance of human relations without any training at all—just a set of commands more or less roared into our ears in childhood.

So we don't even know what the name of the game is. We don't know what the ground rules are. The power comes from learning the rules. It comes from learning the repertoire. It comes from learning how to analyze the situation. You don't have to use any particular system. You can use your own mental structures; but somehow, you have to be able to have a schema in your head and to know, "OK, this is situation X and the correct response is either Y, Z, or K,"—or whatever it is. When you have that repertoire, then you can win a few. You don't have to win 'em all. Even if you only win thirty percent, you can feel good about yourself. So that's what this is all about. That's where I hope we can get by the next six or seven sessions.

Chapter 7
A Twenty-First Century Way

The Sine Curve Theory
of Human Communication

JG: How many engineers are there in this group? Two! OK! Engineers know what feedback is, right? And the word, "Cybernetics" is not too awful terrifying. It means control through feedback.[1] You get your feedback. You realize what has happened as a result of your previous communication, and then you adjust your next communication in response to that.[2]

> *Mark: That's the important thing about feedback. You can either get a stable control or an unstable control. You don't want to overreact to your feedback.*

JG: Exactly. Very good point. That's going to bring us back eventually to the famous sine curve of human behavior. Memorize this sine curve! That's the diagram of feedback—of a feedback controlled system. When it goes too far this way, it gets pushed back. If it goes too far that way, it gets pushed back.

> *Mark: Overshoot and undershoot.*

JG: Overshoot and undershoot. Whether you take a course in computers or mechanical engineering or psychology, the fundamental principles are the same. When you're dealing with a system that responds, you have to know the operating characteristics of the system. You have to know what state it's in at the moment—that's your feedback. Then you know whether to push this way or that way—or whether you need to push at all.

Those of you who have an engineering background know that every piece of machinery that moves oscillates in a wavelike motion. An airplane that's on automatic pilot is not flying level. It's going like this—a few feet too high, a few feet too low, and so on. Every engine and every machine that was ever made works like that.

The cybernetic idea here is very simple. It is that you operate by feedback. The plane's altimeter says it's too high, or the sensing device says

"The automatic pilot does not fly the plane level. It's always correcting an error."

the nose is too high, and it brings it down. If it says the nose is too low, it brings it up, and so on. The automatic pilot does not fly the plane level. It's always correcting an error.

Now, what you are trying to do is to get a fix on where your kid is at. Your error correction consists in looking and listening and finding out what is happening. That's the database that you're operating from, and you've got to update it every three seconds, two seconds, every millisecond, depending on how fast your kid is changing states. You have to see that.

A Twenty-First Century Way

It's a different way of thinking about the interaction with your child. I think of it as a twentieth century way—a twenty-first century way—but it's really as old as the hills, as old as Zen, as old as Tao, as old as Yin and Yang.

Pushing On The System

Every human interaction does that also, including the interactions between the members of a family.

A kid will go along and be real fine and will gradually start to be too—whatever, say, "too timid" or "too aggressive". If you don't remember the sine curve; if you only see it as an isolated piece of behavior, you'll say, "Oh my gosh, he's getting to be too X". When the kid is getting up close to the top of the sine curve, the tendency is for mom and dad to push back. And one way they do that is just to push back directly by confrontation and say, "You're too this, you're too that," and try to get them to stop.

But of course the kid is responding to the dynamics of the whole situation, so when you push back against the kid, you're pushing back against the whole power of the machine. In fact, if you let things just follow their own pathway, sometimes you'll find the kid will go only so far. If you hold back and don't do anything, they will then begin to slide back down the sine curve and go in the other direction. So you didn't have to intervene at all.

Pace Them Right Into It

But maybe you're not sure that they would stop. The other method, other than confrontation, is the one called tracking, pacing, and leading. If you've decided they really are going too far in this direction, instead of confronting them—which leads to sort of a collision pattern—what you do is to track them, then pace them . . . actually pace them right into more of the behavior that they're doing.[3] "Oh, you really do like to put your head in the toilet!"[4] You pace them right into it. If necessary you can lead into more and more of it, and at some point they will flip into resistance and start back again in the desired direction.

> *Renee: Are you talking about behavior that you don't like or that you do like— shyness, for example?*

JG: Whatever! As long as it's an observable thing.

> *Renee: How could you do that regarding shyness? If someone's being real shy, how could you pace shyness?*

More Shy Than They Are

JG: You just get more shy than they are.

> *Renee: If a child is having a problem with shyness—not just with you but with other people, too—you get shy?*

JG: You get shy, you say you don't want to. You don't want to go into that room. It's too scary. You don't want to go out today. It's too scary.

Higher and Higher

You just encourage them to go higher and higher on the peak. You just pace them right along until eventually they'll turn around because there's a point at which it's too much even for them.

Positive Connotation

There are two basic methods: One is confrontation. The other is pacing and leading. Pacing starts with something called positive connotation.[5] If you don't learn anything else I want you to memorize that phrase, "positive connotation". You start by accepting what they're doing.

Now I'm not talking about reaching for the electric plug, OK? But in general, whatever it is they're doing, start where they're at because obviously they're accepting their own behavior. In their world view that behavior is the thing they should be doing. So you start with their picture of the world. You start by accepting it, and then you suggest a little more of it. You do some of it yourself, and pretty soon they are not moving away from you. They're moving in parallel with you. Then you move out a little ahead of them. You're leading them. At that point you can lead them down the hill or even farther out, at which point they will often switch and come down the hill by themselves.

Helping Him Bite

BG: There was a mother in one of our groups who did child care in her home. She had four children every day besides her own child who was 18 or 19 months of age. The problem was getting quite severe. This 19-month-old was biting. He bit the mother. He'd bite her on her arms. He was biting the other children to the point where one set of parents took their child out of this home because he had teeth marks on him.

This was a serious problem. The mother was in our class and she asked, "What in the world can I do?" She said, "I don't think biting him back is going to work." We said we would not recommend that.

What we did was have her take a special day or two—in fact, she had a sitter lined up for the rest of the whole week—we suggested that she spend most of her day helping him bite. The way she did this was to get different objects like—one of them was a rubber doggy thing—it smells horrible if you know what it's like. Another one was a piece of rawhide that dogs would chew on, and then I think there were some other objects she made—four tongue blades with some adhesive tape around them in different flavors.

JG: Old pacifiers!

BG: Old pacifiers . . . just a whole array of things. She had this other person manage the daycare and take care of the other children. She spent the entire day bugging him. Every few minutes—especially when he was very engrossed with something he was happy to be playing at—she'd say, "OK, Dustin, it's time to bite again," and she'd come with one of these things. She'd either hand it to him or put it in his mouth. She wasn't to force him, but just—you know—bug him all day long. She was anticipating that this was going to take at least a week. By that same evening, when it was time for him to get ready for bed, he says, "Mommy I don't want to bite anymore." She had her helper come in again the next day and she started in again. He said, "No, Dustin won't bite."

That cured it. He never bit another person.

JG: And you can memorize the following sentence: "I know how much you love to do X, so I'm going to help you." What you do is you stay on their side. You give them what they want, but you give it to them under circumstances where it's just not really satisfying.

Quentin: It's boring!

Mom's Thing

JG: It's boring! Any behavior can become a chore if it's required on a schedule.[6] Especially if Mom takes possession of the behavior, so that it becomes Mom's thing. Mom plops on their perch, and they have to fly over to another branch. The more Mom is in it, the less and less desirable it becomes. It's like the night-time bottle that gets more and more watery, until it just doesn't seem worthwhile to wake up and call for it. That blends into the strategy called The Less and Less Desirable Alternative.

Do you notice how these strategies tend to blend into each other? I think that's because they are really all just special cases of one thing, the cybernetic thing.

> *Samantha: It worked for us when Peter was biting. When he was maybe a little over a year, he was biting his sister and he'd bite me occasionally. It wasn't that much of a problem, but Dr. Gall suggested getting one of the dog chewies and just offering it to him after he had bitten somebody. We did that and his biting disappeared in about three weeks.*

JG: People really won't keep on doing what they thought was fun, if it isn't really any fun for them. You can let them do that thing if it's so much fun for them, but you let them do it in such a way that unnoticed components of the situation are grating.

> *Mark: Would you do the same thing with fighting?*

> *Sally: I was going to say, how can you transfer that to hitting and kicking?*

Keep Switching

JG: Remember to keep switching! There are lots of these strategies, of which this is only one example. The rule is that in any particular situation you try to start with one that's going to work, but if it doesn't, you immediately switch to the next. If that doesn't work, you quickly switch to the next strategy. In other words, you don't ride these things to death. What causes the trouble is the programmatic approach where you've got it all settled in advance in your own mind that this X is the remedy for Y. What you need to know is, "Here's situation Y, now I've got strategies A through X, we'll find out which is the remedy." So, this might work for a certain type of fighting, but it might not. There isn't any one single magic panacea that you do for fighting.

Observe The Sequence!

BG: Also you need to observe the sequence. Your Observer part needs to get up above the situation and figure out what happened just before the fighting started and then what happened right afterwards. Then you may be able to intercept it. For example, if a kid starts to fight at the age when he's being toilet trained; if he's starting to fight when he gets the urge to go to the bathroom and if you figure that out, you immediately take him towards the toilet or help him with that. You may not know what the reason is, why they're doing a certain thing, but you watch the sequence and see if you can pick up what's happening to trigger this.

Say, Poopy! Fifty Times

Samantha: We were having trouble with Peter saying ''poopy'' at the dining table, talking bathroom language. We had sat him on the time-out chair. He had missed half of umpteen suppers. I finally decided, ''OK, when I hear it again I'm going to say, 'I want to hear it fifty times.''' The first time it happened it was great, he went ''Pooey, pooey, pooey.'' The next time it wasn't quite so much fun. Now he doesn't do it any more.

The Punishment Trap

JG: Now it's really important to remember that it must not be considered punishment. Punishment leads to the desire to get back—to get even. You don't want that.[7] The child who has real spirit and defends his freedom the most, is likely to be the guy that gets the most punishment. So, you want to stay out of the punishment trap. What we're aiming for is parenting—skillful parenting.

Sofa Tantrum Or Rug Tantrum?

JG: A mom came in the other day and said, ''When you saw my child back in November, he was having tantrums. I want to tell you that he stopped three weeks after that visit. I asked, ''Well, what did you do?'' She said, ''I don't know. I've forgotten.'' I looked back in the chart and the instructions were, ''When the child is having a tantrum''—this is a little kid, too, 15-18 months—''look down and say, 'Are you comfortable there on the rug, or would you rather have your tantrum on the sofa?''' That was all the intervention. That was all there was to it.

Lie Down For Tummy-Aches

Wendy: Pamela was having stomachaches all the time. When we came in for a physical, I said, "Dr. Gall, we have a big problem here. Her tummy hurts all the time." Dr. Gall said, "I don't know why six-year-olds' tummy aches hurt so much, but I think what you should do is have her lie down for half an hour every time it happens." She even got to the point where she'd say, "Oh mommy, my stomach hurts, I better go lie down." She hasn't had any in the last few weeks!

Linda: Half an hour, every time you have a tummy ache during the day, takes a lot of your time out of your day.

Wendy: But she never considered it punishment. That's what's nice about it.

Kim: That's a good idea. Our five-year-old does that too. She wakes up in the morning saying, "My stomach hurts!"

Anneke: Why do they do that? What are they looking for?

Kim: I don't know. She just says, "My stomach really hurts, my tummy hurts."

"Your tummy hurts?"

"Yeah, my tummy hurts."

"Well, do you want to lie down?"

"No, I don't want to lie down."

"Well, do you want to go back to bed?"

"No, I don't want to go back to bed."

"Well, what do you want to do?

JG: "You poor dear, you better lie down for 30 minutes."

BG: And give her a clock. Can she tell time yet?

Kim: We give her a timer!

Keep Putting Your Hand In The Bucket

Kim: Yeah. It even works with my 11-month-old.

JG: With the 11-month-old?

Kim: I was mopping the floors. We had the bucket with the soap—this real smooth soap, soapy—and she was helping me. I mean she was right there helping *me mop the floor. She kept checking out the bucket as if to ask, ''What's in this bucket and why do you keep putting your hand in the bucket?''*

So, when I finished, I just left the bucket there because she was kind of hanging on to it and looking at it. Then she started putting her hands in it and playing in the soap. So I rolled her sleeves up for her and told her, ''Go ahead and play, just don't get your arm wet.'' She played in it. Then she started putting the water on the floor. I told her that that wasn't a good idea. ''If you want to play in it then just keep the water in the bucket.'' She's excited, as if to say, ''Wow! This is cool!'' and just looking at me. I sat right next to her and she played with it the whole time. About 10 minutes later she indicated, ''I'm tired of this,'' and she left. Then I picked up the bucket and dumped it. She didn't even know it was gone.

JG: That's a real smooth operation! She doesn't even know why she doesn't want to play in the bucket any more. You didn't even raise the issue.

Kim: No, I just rolled her sleeves up for her.

JG: You conditioned her. That's cold-blooded manipulation!

Kim: I told myself I'd never do this to my child!

JG: But you also let her do it until she was satisfied. She wins, you win. I think that's so great. It's wonderful. Once you've got that you've got the whole thing in a nutshell.

''You Really Like Having Your Foot Up On The Table

Wendy: Last Sunday night at dinner Pamela was putting her foot over the arm of the chair, with her leg cocked up on the arm of the chair. We didn't find it that great, but Henry said to her, ''Oh, I can see you really like having your foot up there.'' She said, ''Oh, yes, I do!

He said, ''Do you think you can do it with both feet?'' She put the other foot up. I don't know how she did it. She must be double-jointed. There she is, sitting in this chair with both feet over the side, trying to eat her dinner. I think Henry said something like, ''Oh, I wonder if you can do it for the whole meal.'' She said, ''Oh, sure I can.'' But, by the end of the meal she was saying to her brother, ''Craig, please hurry up, please hurry up!''

That was great! Then just about Tuesday, she kind of slipped. She almost put her foot up, and she said, ''Whoops.'' She stopped herself.

JG: She knows where that will lead, right?

Wendy: That was exactly it. We were just encouraging her to do more. Henry was saying, ''Oh, Pamela, you're doing such a good job keeping your feet up there.'' She was just so funny. She kept slipping down in her chair.

Anneke: How did you not laugh?

Wendy: I had to leave the room once. I couldn't stand it. It was so funny.

JG: So Henry actually wrote it down and memorized the magic words.

Wendy: Right, he really did.

JG: "I know how much you love to do X."

Wendy: That's right. "I know how much you like to put your feet up." She's usually the slowest eater too, but she quick-like gobbled her dinner because she didn't want to have to sit there forever. Plus she didn't want to have to say that she couldn't do it for the whole dinner. It was great.

BG: Don't you have that satisfaction inside of you, knowing that you know what you're doing?

Wendy (laughing): I feel terrible, knowing that I'm manipulating that poor kid!

Let's Bite Your Toy!

Samantha: I took your suggestion with the biting—to find a toy that Erica could bite—because every once in a while she'd get excited and want to bite something. She'd say, "I want to bite." So, I found a toy that was really neat to bite. Every time she says that I say, "Look! I know how much you like to bite. This is your toy, let's bite it." Well, that lasted about two days, and now she wants to lick!

Now when we're holding the dogs, she says they're happy and they like her, because they lick her so much.

A Rag To Chew On

Neil: Angela's got this bad habit sometimes of chewing on her shirt—the whole shirt—till it's wet. So we gave her a rag to chew on instead of ruining her shirts. She has basically stopped it.

JG: Just like that!

Kim: It was like, "Well, here, Angela, since we know that you really want to chew on this, then we have this—actually it was a piece of old material I had. It wasn't stained. It was clean—and I gave it to her and said, "Why don't you just chew on this instead, and then you won't ruin all your shirts and you can still chew."

She said, "I don't want to chew on that, Mom!" "Well, if you don't want to, it's all right. Just put it in your pocket, keep it next to you."

JG: You're being so helpful, so accommodating.

Kim: —and she was saying, "I don't want to chew on this. I don't want to chew any more, that's gross!" Actually it was like, "What a stupid idea!"

So I kept it in the living room where she usually does it when she's watching television. Her sister Margaret got hold of it a couple times, and it was like, "Well this is fun!"—everything goes in her mouth, and she's chewing on it. Then Angela was chewing on her shirt, and so I handed this cloth to Angela. She was appalled. "What? Margaret just chewed all over it. I don't want to chew on it now! Just forget it!"

A Less and Less Desirable Alternative

JG: There's more than one strategy there. You're being helpful, but you're also offering a less and less desirable alternative. By suggesting that she chew on the rag after Angela chewed on it, you introduced a new element that made it just really too much! You didn't even have to offer to sew it on her collar so she'd always have it handy?

Kim: Oh no, because then I'd have to change it!

JG: You batted a thousand on the first try.

Woman: What happens if they say, "Well, I don't want that, I want my shirt." How are you going to do that?

JG: They want their shirt. They want to chew their shirt.

Neil: Well, we'd been trying to get her to stop doing this for a long time. She knows it makes us angry. This is the first time that she's been pleased with the situation. As a matter of fact, once I told her to take her shirt off and throw it away. It just ruined it, and I said, "Take it off and throw it away." It had only been in the laundry a couple of times. Of course this was before we were educated parents!

JG: Power struggle!

Neil: She knows we don't like her chewing on her shirts. Maybe we were lucky.

Kim: We could just give her one shirt—just keep one shirt as her chewing-on shirt, that she would have to chew or suck, or "get juice". That's what she says, "I need juice. That's why I do it."

JG: All right!

Kim: I even asked her, "Why don't you just ask for a drink of water?" "I don't know, I just want juice." It doesn't make any sense; but, well, if it gets that bad, we can give her one shirt.

JG: Is there a good heavy denim or something that you could use as this special shirt? Something that would be a little bit stiff and scratchy, a little uncomfortable?

Kim: I don't know if they have them for her that way.

BG: You could make a terrible sacrifice and sew one especially for her. Just sew a piece of denim in the flap.

Linda: A washcloth sometimes comes in handy.

Samantha: Even if she wanted her regular shirts, you could set up special times every twenty minutes and say, "OK, it's time to suck your shirt!

JG: That would be another approach.

Linda: Would it help if it was one of her favorite shirts and make that her sucking shirt too; or would that make her mad and not want to do it?

Kim: Actually if it was a skirt, I think she'd get more upset, because she loves to wear dresses and skirts. If it was one of her favorite dresses—like one of her good dresses—"Oh, let's go put your good dress on and see where you want to suck, OK?"

JG: Gosh, I think I'm in the advanced class here!

Time To Hop Up and Run Around
The House Three Times

Samantha: We've also been working on conditioned responses this week. I've been reading the book, Don't Shoot The Dog. One particular problem I just started working on last night: Peter loves to get up several times during dinner and run around the house and then come back. So I thought, "Well, why don't I—every time he comes back—why don't I give him a hug, and pretend like I missed him?" Is that enough of a conditioning to change behavior?

JG: Have you tried it?

Samantha: Well, I did it today, at meal times, and I can't say whether it's going to change or not work.

JG: I can imagine a few things that might help. You might start popping up every ten seconds to help him get a hug.

Samantha: OK.

JG: He might gradually shorten the circuit so that he would just hop up and go get a hug, or he might just get completely tired of it.

> *Samantha: Because we're trying to give him a little longer hug, and a little tighter, and a little bit more—you know, more you than him.*

> *Linda: When he's ready to squirm away, then let him go.*

JG: That's right.

> *Sally: "Just one more hug, just one more, here, oh, oh—!"*

JG: It's so simple isn't it, when you get the idea of it?

> *Samantha: I tried setting the timer for a half hour and saying, "OK, dinner is on the table. If you don't eat it by the time the bell rings it goes in the garbage." That doesn't seem to make any difference to him. Sometimes he misses out, sometimes he doesn't.*

JG: Sounds like he's getting enough to eat right now.

BG: What's his age?

> *Samantha: He's almost four.*

JG: And he likes to hop up and run around the house.

> *Mimi: I'd send him outside and see how many times he could go around the house!*

JG: Good idea! Praise him, praise him for it.

> *Mimi: Try fifty! "I think you can go around fifty times."*

> *Samantha: I did try that once.*

> *Mimi: He just did it, right?*

> *Samantha: He said something about eating his french toast. I said, "OK, eat this piece and then go run around the house. Then eat this piece and go run around the house, and then eat this piece and then go run around the house." I was going to run him to death, but he—I guess that did work because he sort of backed down in his chair. I could see he was thinking about it.*

Cigarettes In The Attic

JG: I'm reminded of the overweight lady who went to Dr. Milton Erickson and told him she wanted to reduce. Doctor Erickson said: "Well, that's very easy. I know you're a smoker so put your cigarettes in the attic and put the matches in the basement.'' That took care of it. She lost weight and gave up smoking.[8]

Turn It Off, Turn It On, Turn It Off, Turn It On

Yesterday a little kid was in the office—he might have been two years old—and after a few seconds he realized that he could jump up on the chair and get the light switch. He was doing this sort of thing, flipping the lights on and off. I'm embarrassed to let you know that I've been in practice for more than 35 years, but it was only two days ago that I realized that I could use this method for the light switch! I sidled over and said, ''Oh, I see you like to do the light switch!'' and he goes, ''Yeah,'' with this great grin on his face. I said, ''And you like to turn it on!'' ''Yeah!'' ''And you like to turn it off!'' He said, ''Yeah!'' I said, ''Oh, OK, turn it on!'' So he turned it on. I said, ''Turn it off!'' He turned it off. I said, ''Turn it on!'' He turned it on. I said, ''Turn it off, on, off, on, off, on, off.'' After about 10 seconds he looked at me and said, ''Ecchh!''

He realized that I had hooked him, and he jumped down and ran away. He just left.

The Time Frame For The Sine Curve

Now, I've noticed something about my eating habits. I will go on binges. I will eat potatoes—being part German, I eat potatoes—any Germans here who like potatoes?

Linda: Love that starch!

JG: I'll go on a potato binge or a rice binge or spaghetti binge, something like that, and I can go as long as a year and a half.

BG: I attest to this!

JG: Then one day, I will announce, ''I'm tired of this!''

BG: The end!

JG: Does that sound familiar?

Sabrina: I did that exactly! Then one day you just turn on it. ''I can't stand this stuff!'' Then it takes forever to get to eating it again, but then sure enough . . .

JG: Right! So when you're doing this technique, you've got to check it out. Is your kid a little gourmet who's going to switch in say three days, or is he or she a meat-and-potatoes type that might adopt this for the first five years of life and then switch? You just have to know what is the time frame for the sine curve there. It might take them two years to get to where they really like Spaghettios or Cheerios.

BG: Well, we've had kids that balance their diet over two-week intervals— they eat all peas for two weeks and all eggs for two weeks—

JG: Good example. Just walk right along with them. If they want to go somewhere you walk with them. Pretty soon you're in step with them and they feel so good about that. Then you're making a few little suggestions, naturally designed to increase their enjoyment of whatever it is that they're doing. After a while somehow they begin to lose interest. And you haven't said aye, yay or nay.

Ride The Sine Curve

JG: So, no matter how problematic, even abnormal their behavior seems, remember, it is fluctuating on a sine curve. If you have the courage, you can ride that curve until it hits the peak. You don't have to confront them. You can just let them ride. Then they will know that you actually have faith in them, that you really do trust that their self-regulatory mechanisms work.

Tabitha: That's a good attitude for your own survival, too, as a parent.

Just Wait For The
Next Level Of Development

Sabrina: I think, ''This isn't gonna last. I can hang on a little bit longer.''

JG: With kids you know if you wait long enough, they move to the next higher level of development, so that the old stuff is no longer an issue, because they've just left it behind.

So you just wait. Waiting is a very powerful strategy. If you have a problem that you just can't solve, don't give up. Just wait, and after a certain number of months or years, that problem may be gone—and you will have another one!

RIDE THE SINE CURVE!
"If you have the courage, you can ride that curve until it hits the peak."

Sabrina: *What if it still doesn't go away?*

JG: You may need to ask yourself if it's really a problem. Maybe it's really your own problem. If it's a big problem, you may need to ask an expert for some help. Waiting is just one strategy. It's not suitable for everything.

Chapter 8

Polar Opposites— And The Space Between

Polarities

JG: Every wave has a crest and a trough. Every pendulum swings to the left and then to the right, and back again. And most of real life is lived in the space between the extremes.

Our next key idea here is the idea of Polarities. They're sets of ideas that represent two sides or two polarities. I want to raise these distinctions so that you'll be thinking of them as you go along.

Verbal Versus Nonverbal

The first set is one we've already spent some time with, the Verbal versus the Nonverbal. Most people have been raised, have gone through the school system and have been talked at for 16 years, to the point where they think that reality is a set of words that they have. Well, verbal interaction is very important, but nonverbal interaction is even more so. The proportion of nonverbal to verbal is probably about 100 to 1, or 1,000 to 1. We tend to lose the nonverbal because the school system implicitly and nonverbally tells us that verbal is important and nonverbal isn't important. If you spend 16 years studying verbal models of the universe, you come to believe that that's really important.

All right! Verbal versus nonverbal. When you say to a child, ''Do something!'' or, ''Don't do something!'' if their face changes, the color goes out of their face, their breathing changes, their shoulders slump, and their eyes go down, they're telling you something, right? You could pick up the message. You don't have to wait for them to speak. You already know. That's your nonverbal feedback.

Explicit Versus Implicit

Explicit versus implicit is very similar to that. Certain assumptions are made.

117

If you put a baby in the playpen, you don't have to explain to them verbally that they need to be confined for their own safety. They pick up on that. They understand that they are being restrained. Think about explicit versus implicit.

Conscious Versus Unconscious

Conscious versus unconscious comes very near to the same thing. When you speak to somebody, they take some of your message in consciously. The unspoken implication of what you say, as well as most of your non-verbal communication, goes in at the unconscious level. When you speak to a child, you can see or hear their conscious reaction to you. You can also pick up some of what their unconscious response is. It's really useful to do that, because if you don't have the unconscious part of the person on your side, you're not likely to get very far.

They Split Into Two Pieces
(Compliance Versus Resistance)

OK, and finally the big one, the compliance and the resistance. When you speak to someone, they split into two pieces. This happens all the time, to everybody. It's not just two parts, but for practical purposes you can think of it that way. There is a part that wants to go along with what you say, and then there's a part that wants to defend their individuality . . . they're not going along. There's a part that agrees, and a part that disagrees, simultaneously. Nobody is ever 100% compliant or 100% resistant.

So your job as a communicator is to keep your eyes and ears open and notice whether your child's compliance is stronger or their resistance is stronger, because if the resistance is stronger, you can then jump over to the other side and let them resist you and succeed in resisting you and thus do the thing that you want. That way, you both win.

Coloring With Her Toes (Followup)

Wendy: I just wanted to report that Pamela was making Valentines when we left—very happy. She had six pieces of paper taped together on the floor and she was coloring with her toes!

Last week I gave her the pictures from Beth, painted by handicapped artists using their mouth or their feet to hold the paintbrushes.

POLAR OPPOSITES—AND THE SPACE BETWEEN

> *She had a crayon between her big toe and her second toe and she was just coloring away! I don't get it!*

JG: You've created a strange compulsion!

> ***Wendy:*** *I have!! The other night at dinner Craig was tapping his foot on the end of the chair, he was going, "Tap! Tap! Tap! Tap!" and he was looking at me like, "Oh, is that OK, Mom?" I said, "I kinda like that. You think you could keep it up till I'm done eating?" He was going, "Tap! Tap! Tap!" and just then Pamela put both her feet over the edge of the table again! I guess she got the idea. She said, "Oh, that reminds me!"*

JG: Deep down underground in the realm of the unconscious, where all individual minds flow together, this stuff spreads like a grapevine, and it pops up here and it pops up there. You never know, when you make an intervention, what the long-term effects are going to be.

Taking Possession Of The Symptom By Making It Mom's Or Dad's Thing

What you did was Taking Possession of the Symptom by Making it Mom's Thing or Dad's Thing.[1] Now they're doing it because Mom wants it and requests it and in fact she asks for more. Well, if there's anything a kid is ambivalent about, it's to realize that they have been captured into Mom's system and they're doing what Mom wants—or Dad. So that gives you the power. You now have created a situation where if they're going to resist you, they have to stop doing it.

On the other hand, if they want to go along with you, you know how to handle that. You just keep encouraging them, and what the heck—maybe they can make a living painting with their toes.

This is where you actually ally yourself with the resistant behavior, and from that position you have the power to go this way or that way. You can go yea or nay, you can play the compliance or the resistance. It's your choice, which means that you have that wonderful feeling of being in control of the situation—until the next day—when they start to do Valentines with their toes!

He Didn't Want His Ears Examined

I saw a little kid yesterday who absolutely did not want to have his ears looked at.

"Ally yourself with the resistant behavior."

BG (to the group): Strikes a responsive chord, eh?

JG: It was clear that he was bound and determined to resist me no matter what I did. It was clear that he was going to get a great deal of satisfaction out of resisting me. So, I decided that I would give him an opportunity to resist me, systematically.

As he was sitting there in the chair next to his mom, I said, "Open your eyes." So he started to close his eyes; but he didn't really want to close his eyes, what he wanted to do was to resist me. He was breathing fairly regularly, so as he took another breath, I said, "Now close your eyes." I had just said, ''Open your eyes,'' and they had sort of sagged. I said, ''Close your eyes,'' and he triumphantly raised them wide open. Then I said, ''Open your eyes,'' and they really did close. Then I said, ''Close your eyes,'' and he opened them. Then I said, ''Open your eyes,'' and he closed them. His breathing began to get very regular and deep, and I said, ''Open your eyes, close your eyes,'' and he was very, very satisfied with himself because he was absolutely doing the opposite of what I wanted. Every time I said, ''Close your eyes,'' he opened his eyes. When I said, ''Open your eyes,'' he closed his eyes.

He was so satisfied that his head gradually fell down on his chest and he began to snore, opening and closing his eyes as I continued to instruct him to close and open his eyes. As he did that, I put one hand against one ear and looked in the other ear. I continued to tell him to open and close his eyes. He was so busy resisting me that there was just no resistance left over for the ear exam.

Gina: Isn't that a hypnosis type of thing?

JG: I got more compliance than I had bargained for! He actually went into a trance. You really don't need that much effect for ordinary everyday parenting!

But he was satisfied. He was resisting me, and I was perfectly happy to have him resist me. Now, actually by ordering him to open and close his eyes—and he was closing and opening—he didn't realize that he was doing exactly what I was commanding. He was just one half-wave off, you might say. He just had the switches reversed. So we were all very happy with that arrangement.

BG: If you can stay in Observer Mode while you're doing this, it's OK.

JG: That's right. If you can stay up there where you're watching this rather than getting involved in it. That's the important part.

Compliance, resistance, this is the magic key. If your child is resisting you, if you're aware of that fact, you use the strategies that build upon the polarity.

Too Little To Do ''X''

The little kid is coming into the examining room, and as he glances around I say to him, ''You're too little to get up on my table—''

Cora: —and he'll say, ''Oh, no I'm not!!!''

JG: Exactly!

''Well, you may be able to get on my table, but you sure can't reach that mobile up there.''

The next thing you know, he's standing on the table. He's reaching up like this to pull on the mobile. His mouth falls open. I look in his mouth and I don't even have to ask him to stick out his tongue. He's doing what he wants to do. I'm doing what I want to do. We're both winning.

BG: Crass manipulation!

JG: Crass manipulation! He isn't being frustrated. He's being allowed to do what he wants to do, and the thing that he wants to do most of all at that moment is to prove that I'm wrong. So I let him prove that I'm wrong.

BG: —and then be surprised!

You Let Them Win Once In A While

JG: Then I say: ''Wow! You really can!'' and he says, ''Yeah! I'm big!''

''I'm separate from you.'' That's the assertion of autonomy. That's the way it works, and that's how you foster it. You give them a chance to beat you. You give them a chance to win.

Louise: That's Kyle's dream—to be bigger than his Dad.

Squinching Down
(Let Them Be Bigger)

JG: You can actually do it just by squinching down, so that they look down on you. That act alone conveys everything that needs to be said.

Priscilla: My kids get up on the top bunk. Then they're way up higher than everybody else.

Do You Want To Do This?

Karla: I have a question about this. If we ask Bridget to do something, it's an automatic ''No.'' But if we ask her if she wants to do it, then she's always more than happy to do it. It's like, ''Do you want to go get the tissues for me?'' ''Yes!'' and she's off to get it. So, what's going on there?

JG: It sounds like you've got a situation such that if you ask, ''Do you want?'' she goes into compliance mode. If you say, ''Do it,'' she goes into resistance mode.

Karla: So it's just giving her the option, once again?

JG: ''Do you want to do it?'' She has this choice of saying, ''Yes'' or ''No.'' Now if she says, ''No,'' to be fair, you should stop at that point, because you asked her if she wanted to.

Karla: Oh, I definitely would.

JG: If you were then to go on and coerce the child to do it anyway, you'd really be setting them up. You asked them if they wanted it, and then they gave you a response that's not satisfactory to you. That's not fair, to insist that they guess and read your mind.

Karla: I know she's going to do it. I know that she'll do it if I ask if she wants to, and that she will take help if I ask her if she wants help. But if I say, ''Let me help you,'' she will not.

Tonality

JG: There are certain phrases that she will respond to. It can even be more subtle than that. You can say exactly the same words, and have a slightly different intonation, and then some kids will respond to that. Like—who is it?—Bill Cosby. On his program, you hear him ask his kids to do something and he has a tremendous range of tonality. He can ask a kid in such a way that bombs are going to explode or he can do it in a very gentle way. So you can vary your tonality. That's a powerful way of doing it. If you use exactly the same words and vary your tone, you can get a lot of variety of responses without the other person even knowing.

Bite My Jacket

Vance: I was going to say, Lily is very much into resistance at the moment. Yesterday evening I picked her up at that children's center to bring her home. Of course she doesn't want to be picked up. She just likes to bite my jacket. OK, so I bit her sweater, and that made her laugh. That was a surprise.

Will You Drive Us Home?

When we got to the car, she climbed into the driver's seat. So I climbed into the passenger seat in the back, and fastened my seatbelt up and told her to take me home.

JG: Vance, you are a virtuoso!

Vance: I was in a good mood and able to do that, because I usually go for the directive approach, such as, ''You gotta do it''. ''Sit there!'' But for some reason I thought, ''I'll try that.''

She said, ''Oh, OK,'' and she ''drove'' for a while and I just sat there. Then she answered, ''Well, it's your turn now,'' so we changed positions.

Stay Awake, Please!

Vance: Last night Charlene was putting her to bed and she was very resistant to going to sleep. Almost two hours—one and a half to two hours—and eventually I went up to Lily and I asked her to make sure she didn't go to sleep so she could wake me up in the morning because I was very tired.

And she just went ''Plunk!''

I told her, ''Please make sure I wake up when it's day break, stay awake please. Keep your eyes open, don't let them shut,'' and she just fell over and went to sleep.

JG: ''The heck with you, dad!''

Vance: Well, I was feeling in a good mood yesterday.

Humor

JG: Sometimes that's all it takes. If they pick up that little undercurrent of humor.[2] If they realize that you are playing with communication, quite often that takes all the heaviness out.

Conformity

Gina: My style is manipulation of emotion. I always try to get sympathy. I think my son has a rather empathetic part to him. If it hurts, he'll kiss it. Whenever you're cold , he'll warm you. But I found out that 90• of the time when he resists, it's really when I just want to get it done. I guess I'm communicating the fact that I just need to get it done and can't get it done.

JG: The very fact that there is now a constraint. They sense, ''Now I'm going to be forced to do what I don't want to do.'' If they pick that up at long distance, they start to dig in their heels. That's a realistic situation. That's the existential position of the little kid. All around them are these big people making them do what they don't want to do. I think it behooves us to be able to put ourselves in their position and understand that an awful lot is being required of them.

A Little Time With The Dog

JG: Eleanor was nineteen months old and she fought the car seat. She fought being placed in it and she fought being removed from it. Finally Mom decided to just let her stay in the car seat by herself. She left the family dog in the car, but she herself got out of the car, closed the doors, and went into the house, where she peeked out the window to see what would happen. Eleanor continued to talk happily to the family dog, then looked out the car window and called, "All done!" Then she was quite happy to be removed from the car seat.

If you want to minimize problems, it really does help to minimize the amount of compliance that is required. The amount of just flat-out conformity that is required—or if it has to occur, you can set it in a framework of good humor or compensatory advantages. In some way you can take away the starkness of it.

Keep Switching Strategies

The other thing to remember is this. With any strategy, if you get a 10% success rate you're doing fine. The mandate is for us as the adults to switch strategies rapidly until we get the one that's going to work in a situation. Again, this is just the opposite of your general rule that everybody's taught, which is to keep on trying, try again and again.

In behavioral interactions the best thing is to try something, see what your feedback is, and if it's not satisfactory, quickly move on to another strategy. That's why I keep emphasizing: get that repertoire down so that you can go from one strategy to the next until you get the result that you want.

Flexibility
(Consistency Versus Inconsistency)

Charlene: Where does being consistent fit into this?

JG: I'm glad you brought that up! That's another one of those things that come out of a classical textbook. Why on earth would anybody want to consistently keep repeating a failing strategy? That just locks you into failure. You want the option to be inconsistent in situations where that strategy might be useful. You want to stimulate your child's neurons, so that they will think about what is happening and learn to change their behavior a little bit. The way you do that is by being flexible yourself. Now if you're consistently flexible, they will begin to understand what consistency is.

> *Vance: That's a very interesting point—consistency, in terms of trying to develop moral and ethical values. It seems like you would want consistency there. You want a certain message in terms of how to treat your family first and then the world, and so on. Yet, you're talking about inconsistent behavior.*

JG: The implicit message that they learn if you switch strategies from moment to moment is that you are consistently willing to put yourself out in order to avoid a coercive situation. You are consistently not willing to oppress a fellow human being. That is basic humanity, isn't it? Maybe the word ''flexibility'' conveys that idea a little better.

Now, when you first try this out, it feels kind of artificial. After you've done it three times and have succeeded, believe me it doesn't feel artificial anymore. It feels very natural. Even if it did feel artificial, you would keep on doing it because you are rewarded for doing it.

Distraction

> *Gina: Is it quote, unquote, ''a manipulative trick'' to bring attention to something unrelated to what you wanted them to do?*

JG: That's an absolutely valid strategy, or half a strategy.[3] Distraction. You build on it.

So here we've got Distraction as a specific technique, we've got Playing the Resistance or the Compliance, Sympathy, Plopping On Their Perch, Humor. We have five or six already.

The Ten Thousand Year Old Strategy

JG: Many kids are very much into compliance. They want to please. These are the kids that—you ask them to do something and they do it. That's beautiful. It's just wonderful. When that's happening you don't have a problem, you can use the old standard method . . . the strategy that has been available for at least ten thousand years. Which is, you ask them to do it, and they do it. That's so neat, so simple, but it only works about 40% of the time.

It's when they don't do it that you need more strategies. The purpose of this class is to give you a whole bunch of alternative strategies—because you all know the strategy of asking for what you want; and if you don't get it, escalate: demand it, and if you still don't get it, threaten, and if you still don't get it, throw the atomic bombs. That's one strategy, the whole world is stuck in that including the big nations. What you need is the other strategies. Playing resistance is one of these others. Playing the compliance when you can get it, knowingly, that's—well, I don't know whether that's the original one. When you do a strategy and know it, I think there's a difference, because then it becomes a part of your conscious repertoire.

Tippy-toes

BG: I'll never forget one of the first times I saw John. This was before we were dating or anything. He was a pediatric resident in the well-baby clinic at the public health agency where I was a nurse. I saw him squatting down on the floor, talking to a two-year-old little girl with patent leather shoes on—black patent leather shoes. He said, "I see you've got new shiny shoes. Can you stand on your tippy-toes?" He was looking up at her—a two-year-old, this great big man looking up: "Can you stand on your tippy-toes?" You could just see her beaming, "Oh, I can do that!"

JG: To her, that wasn't part of the neurological assessment! To her it was a moment of triumph and warm satisfaction, a moment to savor her own undeniable worthwhileness and competence as acknowledged by the world around her.

The Yin And The Yang

BG: I remember something David Brinkley once said a long time ago on TV. He was talking about his family and he said, "Togetherness is great, but don't knock getawayness!"

JG: Well, that's part of the Yin and Yang, too. The kids need you to be there and they also need you to be away. They need you to be firm and authoritarian. They need you to be flakey and absent. In other words they need both sides of every equation.[4]

Utilization

That's the secret. Use everything. Wherever you find yourself, use that instead of struggling against it. Use that.

Chapter 9

How To Tie Them Up In Nots

The List Of Things
You're Not Supposed To Do

JG: Now, here is a list of Eleven Things That You're Not Supposed To Do as a parent. That's my idea of poor teaching. That list is too long.

BG (holding up a printed list): It looks like this—yard-long words and two columns of definitions and explanations.

JG: It's hard to memorize a list of eleven things—especially when all of them are abstractions. There's no way to operationalize them specifically except to use your imagination; which means, you may end up thinking that you're doing it or not doing it. The third thing is, it is a list of things that you're not supposed to do.

Not Doing

One of the things that I want to get across right away at the beginning of this class is that it's much harder to NOT DO something than it is to DO something.[1] For example, you're now over Niagara Falls on a tightrope. Now DON'T FALL OFF. See how hard that is to do? It's really hard to NOT DO things. So, my advice, when you are dealing with your child, is, if you see them heading toward danger, say, ''STOP!'' because that's a positive thing that a person can do—they can stop. They know how to stop; but if you say, ''DON'T FALL!'' what does that mean? It means, concentrate on this thing called ''falling'' and try not to do it. But as you concentrate on it, the way you make meaning out of that word ''falling'' is: Since speech is a kind of minimal subliminal action, when you say the word ''fall,'' or the word ''sleepy,'' or ''sneeze,'' the other person makes meaning out of it by actually minimally doing it. So when you tell a person, ''DON'T FALL!'', you're very likely to see them stumble in that moment. If you say, ''DON'T BLINK!''—how many people have to blink?

So this list is absolutely correct but it's pedagogically very ineffective, because it does not produce in the reader the desired behavior. It requires the reader to INVENT the behavior that is the negative of those things and then, whatever they think of, they operate under the belief that that is NOT DOING the bad thing—but they don't have any way of knowing.

> *Kay: It's also hard to know as a parent where you fall, 'cause I was reading and saying to myself, "Yeah, I do that, I do that, and I do that. I do all those terrible things." I'm thinking, "Gosh, I'm gonna have a little basket case on my hands when it's over and done."*

JG: So I would say the correct response to this handout is to tear it up.

> *Bobbi: When we say words to a child like, "Don't do this, don't do that"—is that one of those words we ought to omit from our vocabulary and substitute something else?*

JG: Do you want the long answer or the short?

> *Bobbi: The short!*

JG: The short answer is, "Yes." Now for the long answer!

Well, there's a problem with the Mental Model of the World. We make a model of the universe; and because we are sophisticated adults, a large part of it is a Verbal Model. So we have words like "Good" and "Bad" and things like that, that we use to process the information that we take in from the outside world. Then we decide to act or not act, or to do this or to do that.

The problem with the child is that their mental model is very incomplete, very fragmentary, and their verbal model is extremely crude compared to ours. So when you use language, you are using the weakest way of getting the child to do or not do a piece of behavior. It's far more powerful to use circumstantial methods, nonverbal methods, methods that involve you behaving in a certain way, or moving in a certain way, or responding in a certain way. Language is the weakest—it's like trying to pull the elevator up by twisting the indicator dial—it doesn't work very well. So you can tell the child, "Don't steal!" "Don't lie!" and they'll say, "Yes, Mommy, I won't," and then they'll promptly do it again. You with your sophisticated verbal model, you ask, "Why did you do that?"

The problem is that the verbal section of the human brain that controls speech, is on the lefthand side. If you look at a human brain, there's actually an extra structure on the lefthand side. The two sides are not symmetrical. There's an extra structure on the lefthand side. That's the speech center. In general, people process language with the left side, which is the side that is specialized for logical, rational thinking; that is, for operating through a logical or verbal Mental Model.

The righthand side is the side that makes pictures or patterns. It takes in visual information or auditory information and makes sense of it through a picture or pattern of some sort.

The child operates primarily with the nonverbal components of the brain. When a child has an experience of some kind, there may be a picture or a feeling, but there may or may not be a word associated with it. Now think a minute about the word, "Don't" or the word, "Not." Not only is it a word, and so it ought to correspond to a picture, but it is also a word that corresponds to the absence of a picture.

Make A Picture In Your Mind

I ask you now to make a picture in your own mind of somebody planting a tree. All of you will have your own individual picture. There will be no two pictures that are alike in detail, but they will all show a person planting a tree. That's very easy.

Now try to make a picture of somebody NOT planting a tree. It is utterly impossible, because there are no NONEVENTS in nature. The real world only consists of positive events. It does not consist of negative events.

You see the problem. Our language permits us to make a verbal construct of something that does not correspond to our experience. The child, who operates primarily out of the picture-making, creative right side of the brain, is beginning to make these tieups with the verbal model. They're beginning to understand, "Yes, I vaguely understand what Mom means by 'lying' or 'stealing' or 'whatever'"—the connection is very poor. Then you add this other thing, "NOT" and you really throw them for a loop. At that point they have to think about it, but NOT think about it. They have to think about it, but think about the ABSENCE of it. You are asking them to do something that is actually neurologically really perverse. It's a logical construct. It's not an experience construct.

So when you say to a child, "Don't fall!" the chances are you will see a stumble or a beginning of a fall. You will see them get into a posture that is out of balance, because that is how they make sense out of the world. They make the model out of direct experience, by taking that word, translating, "Oh! What experience do I have of falling?" and in that moment, because of their lack of skill in switching into the verbal model, they are very likely to fall.

Up And Down A Tree, Safely

JG: Beth Gall! You're on! You're looking out the window above the kitchen sink—

BG: Ah, yes!

JG: —off Traver Road, at ten o'clock in the morning.

BG: We were living in a third-floor apartment on a steep hill and our nine-year-old son was in the Webelos, which is the Boy Scouts before they become Scouts, after Cub Scouts. I looked out the window from the third floor level and here is this kid looking in the window at me from the little tree that grew outside the window—

JG: —a little, skinny tree, thirty feet tall.

BG: —and the windows were open. It was summertime—and I really blanched. I remember the feeling of shock and hot prickles and all that. I took a deep breath and I said, ''Ohhh! I see you're working on your Webelos badge!

JG: And he grinned!

BG: The idea is to shinny up a tree that a bear wouldn't want to shinny up, because it's too small. You get up high enough so the bear won't get you. The next trick is, how to get back down. I said, ''Can you show me how you get down now?'' And he did. I was scared. I mean, you know how parents feel.

Cora: Um-humh. That rush—

BG: —and my instinct was to yell, ''Don't fall! Don't fall!''

(Beth's body tilts, her arms and legs move).

JG: You see, you still use—just as we all do—you use the model of falling, right in your body. Did you all see that?

(Several): Um-humh!

JG: OK! This is what this class is about, learning to see these things. If she had said, ''Don't fall!'' there would have been an abortive letting go and it might have been just enough to let him actually fall.

BG: The startle itself might have been enough if I had yelled "Don't fall!"

Tension Is The Enemy!
We Must Conquer Tension!

JG: When Beth and I went to the Milton Erickson conference in Phoenix a few years ago, there was a delegate there who thought that he understood Ericksonian methods. He had worked out a program for teaching his patients who were troubled with tension. He taught them by drilling them in a slogan. The slogan was: TENSION IS THE ENEMY! WE MUST CONQUER TENSION! You could see the audience tense up as he said, TENSION! Then he said, ENEMY! and then he said, CONQUER!

So when you tell a child, "Don't be so jumpy!" or, "Why are you so shy?", you are inadvertently producing more of what you are trying to get rid of. And "STOP YELLING!!" That's another self-contradictory message.

Inadvertent Education:
How To Tie Them Up In NOTS

JG: So when you're dealing with a kid and it's absolutely essential to get the correct response, don't use a "NOT" in it, because that will tie them up in the "NOTS"—N-O-T-S. Don't get them tied up in NOTS. They have to process your communication that much longer to make sense out of it. In the course of that processing, they have to access the picture in the right brain of doing the very thing that you're telling them not to do.

How To Teach Them To Do What
You Don't Want Them To Do

If you do this consistently, year after year, with a kid and if you constantly harp on what it is that they shouldn't do, you'll make them an expert at it. Because every time you say, "Don't do it!", they have to draw it up out of their memory. They have to rehearse the bodily movements subliminally—and the visual images—and then they have to say, "Oh no!" You can make a person an expert at almost anything if you keep harping on them about not doing it. It's not possible for a human being to not do something.

This often happens with real conscientious parents who want their kids, their teenagers, to be so good. They begin a campaign at age three. They tell them, "You must not do this because when you get to be a teenager

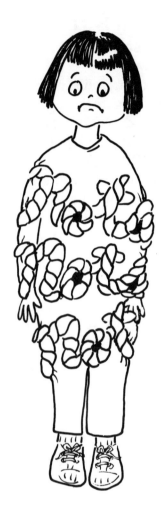

"How to tie them up in nots."

you will be a—blahh!'' and they name this terrible word. After ten years of that the kid is an expert in being a ''Blahh'' because they've been told every detail of how not to be it. The only way they can process that is right through that part of the brain that makes that picture and goes through the motions—and you have taught them how to do what you don't want them to do. So don't talk about it! Replace it with something else.

The Wrong Mental Model

If you don't want it to be in their repertoire, don't talk about it. Don't give them an explicit verbal model of things you don't want them to do. Long lectures about avoiding juvenile delinquency, staying out of trouble—they already know how you feel about this. But you can level with them. When they get to the teen years, you can tell them a few home truths.

Nonverbal Beats Verbal Every Time

I don't think verbal commands are useful when the child doesn't have a well-developed verbal model in their head and when they don't have good impulse control. In general, I think the verbal approaches are overworked. Kids don't have much Verbal Model to work with before about age eight. You may get a few successes at earlier ages.

> *Kay: What about teenage years? Is that when you can start—are they rational enough to talk—use of verbal, you know? I don't think I was very rational at that point. I would just probably—I'm not saying this very well, am I!*

JG: A little problem with the Verbal Model, eh!

I think verbal is real feeble, even for adults. Real feeble. Nonverbal beats verbal every time. You can say what you want to, but if you look sick or angry or excited while you're saying it, that will carry a message that's far more powerful than what you're saying.

On Not Being A Juvenile Delinquent

Or if you're talking to a kid about not being a juvenile delinquent and you've got this half smile on your face—believe me, it happens a lot! Parents will say, "I don't want you getting pregnant," or, "I don't want you beating up on the little kids." But if you look at their face, you will see it's full of animation and enthusiasm. The child gets the nonverbal message twice as loud as they get the verbal message.

Then there are the parents who say, "If you beat up on other kids, I'll whale the living daylights out of you." How do you like that for a double message?

Congruency

So, you learn to be congruent in your messages—to make the verbal message fit with the nonverbal message that you've sent. If that's too hard you might as well just forget the verbal message because it's too weak anyway. Just go with the nonverbal. In fact, probably ninety percent of what we get is from nonverbal.

Nora: Can you give some examples of nonverbal—?

BG: Compare the two TV programs, Bill Cosby and Roseanne Barr. Just look at them with a clear eye and see the nonverbal stuff between Roseanne and her husband and what happens with their kids and then how the Cosbys handle things. The Cosbys do nonverbal really well, really super—as a good model of how to do it with kids.

Nora: I love that man!

JG: They do verbal well, too.

BG: Oh, yes, they're good with verbal too.

Louise: And Roseanne isn't? (Laughs) I've never seen it!

JG: Well, if they've never seen Roseanne, let's not pass judgment, let's let them decide.

BG: I would say, watch Roseanne and see what you can learn, because I think some of it she does real well but some of it has a real paradoxical outcome from what her good intentions are.

Killing It With "But"

JG: Another dangerous word, almost as bad as the word, "Not", is the word, "But." For some reason, many of the childrearing books don't tumble to the destructive effect of this word. They say to tell your child things like, "I love you, BUT I don't like what you're doing." "You did a good job on your homework, BUT you still need to work on your spelling." The trouble is, the two parts of the statement are wildly incongruent. The first is validation, the second is criticism that undercuts the validation. The child begins to feel competent, then suddenly is forced to feel imperfect. Bad conditioning! The child becomes suspicious of validation. It's always a prelude to criticism. It's token validation. Fritz Perls understood this long ago. He said, "With the word, 'But', you can kill anything."[2]

Speaking To Two Parts At Once

JG: This gets us back the idea of multiple messages. Every verbal communication has multiple levels. Every nonverbal communication has multiple messages, plus which, each of those is ambiguous and can be interpreted

"Killing it with 'but'."

in many different ways. So it's worth while to learn to be an actor or an actress and send a few basic messages nonverbally—learn how to do it.

That's the other side of communicating with kids, and that is the part that you communicate that you don't know that you are communicating. You need to become aware of what you really are signalling to them. The more there is of communication that you are not aware of, the more surprises you will experience in your relationships with people, because they will be responding to signals you didn't know you were sending.

But the time will come, when you've had some experience and you have gotten a little awareness of how you come across to the other person, verbally, nonverbally, through your tone of voice—you'll get to the point where you can deliberately send a double message and both of them will be therapeutic and you will have the delight of seeing your signals hit the bullseye. You will have the awareness of your feedback and actually see what happens. That is the Strategy called ''Speaking to two parts at once.''

It Was The Look On My Face
That Saved Him

JG: Did we talk about Fright Face?[3] How to get a kid to stop doing something? It's a useful piece of information! As long as you understand it only lasts about a second or two. This is some research that's being done at the University of Michigan by Marilyn Svejda. There's an angry face, there's a fright face, there's a dull face—and the fright face is the most effective in getting a baby to stop doing whatever they're doing. Even a toddler under one year of age will respond, although as they get older, it gets to be less effective. This is where you go—AAACH!—like this and you put this expression of horror on your face. You jump—you make an intake of breath, and a high percentage of babies—about 60% of babies—will instantly stop what they're doing and look at you—and if no disaster is taking place, then they'll promptly go on doing what they were doing before. But you have interrupted them.

> *Samantha: I have an example of that for you. When Peter was 9 months old, we went to a baby shower held in a meeting room. The hosts had pushed all the tables back in a C-shape by the wall. Then heavy plastic and metal chairs were stacked upside down on top of the tables, and the older kids at some point during the shower had gotten under the tables and were crawling in and out of these chairs. Peter was following them and of course didn't know that as he hit two chairs with his shoulders he would start to push them off the top of the table.*
>
> *We were all standing there frozen, watching this begin to happen as he came to two chairs—and I yelled and I must have had a very frightened look on my face because I knew they were going to fall down on top of him, and everybody else was holding their breath. And he stopped long enough for the chairs to fall down around him and not on top of him. We made eye contact, and it was the look on my face that saved him.*

JG: Right! It's useful information. A lot of early childhood is involved with getting kids to stop doing what they're doing.

> *Henry: This is not news to us!*

JG: And it continues for twenty-one years!

The Command "Stop!"
(Processing A Negative)

JG: It's useful to know that the command STOP, particularly if it's accompanied by this body language, is more effective than an angry face and the word "No" or "Don't!" It's about 50% more effective, which means you're not batting a thousand but you're still getting a little better results. One of the reasons is that babies have a lot of trouble processing a negative. This is also true for adults.

Get Them Started On Something Else

One good rule in dealing with kids or anybody else is to try to decide, if you have the time, whether you can put it in the form of a direct command that they can obey, rather than saying what it is that you don't want them to do and then putting the word "don't" in front of it, because that can lead to problems in compliance.

    The idea is, if you don't want a piece of behavior to take place, initiate a piece of behavior that is incompatible.

Yes Mode

The other problem is that when you talk to a kid, you're using a verbal model of the universe. The child's verbal model is extremely limited. They may be able to say 500 words, or 5,000 words, but they haven't had very much experience, they don't know exactly where those labels apply in the outside world. When you try to change a kid's behavior through the verbal model, you're dealing with a relatively undeveloped resource.

    The resources that they really have well developed from birth on are the modeling resources—the direct modeling of what you do. That is to say, how you move your body and the expressions that you put on your face and the tone of your voice—the stuff that doesn't demand linguistic processing. You can get a kid to feeling good, just by looking like you're dancing. You can start a person to saying yes, by nodding your head like this. And you can put a child into what's called the Yes Mode or the Yes Set[4] by creating things that they spontaneously do, just by your own body movements.

BG: May I tell a story about you?

JG: Sure, why not?

BG: When Dr. Gall is going to call a child into his room, he asks, ''Are you here today?''

JG: And what's the answer to that question? There's no way they can say ''No!'' unless they just want to be contrary, in which case it's very easy then to jump into polarity and play their game. But if the child says ''Yes'', to ''Are you here today?''—

BG: —then John will ask another question like, ''Is your mommy with you today?'' (If the mommy is, then ''Yes'' that's true.) And, ''Did you come to get cookies today?'' ''Yes.''

JG: ''Are you walking towards my room?'' ''Yes.'' ''Are you coming in the door?'' ''Yes.'' ''Are you walking towards the stool?'' ''Yes.'' You see, they really can't say ''No'' because these are absolutely, incontrovertibly ''Yes'' questions. And ''Are you climbing on my table?'' ''Yes.'' And by this time they often have a big grin on their face, because they've psyched out this game I'm playing with them.

But sometimes they will go right into a trance, and you will see their face flatten out and their movements will become semi-automatic and you will hear the ''Yes'' begin before the end of the next question. ''Are you sitting on the table?'' ''Are you sticking out your tongue?'' They'll say ''Yes'' before they even realize, and they will do it directly because all traces of the resistance component have disappeared by that time. Now you can use this but I want to warn you. Don't overuse it. Use it when it is beneficial for you and for the child. If it's used to exploit somebody, it will kick back and they'll get very, very leery.

BG: And it'll break the sense of trust.

JG: That's right.

BG: If you use it for your own benefit.

JG: You don't want to break that sense of trust.

Compliance Versus Resistance

Sally: So to get them to stick out their tongue, you say, ''Are you sticking out your tongue?'' Then, they will say ''Yes'' and then do it?

JG: Because of the momentum of these twenty consecutive ''Yes'' reactions that are in the dance! That's Compliance versus Resistance. It doesn't matter—if they want to be resistant, you just play it the other way. You walk out and you say, "Are you here today?" "NO!," and then you say, "You don't want to come into my room!" "Oh, yes I do!" "You can't get up on my table, you're too little!" "Ohhh, I am so big enough!" "Well, I know you're too little to open your mouth." "Ahhh!" So you can play the resistance. What you have to know is which is uppermost in the child at the time.

He Wouldn't Get Into His Pants

Samantha: Can we take that a little further? The problem that I'm experiencing at home now since I sat in on your class in December—I've been using a little bit of that psychology on Peter. Here's an example that happened the other day. He wouldn't get into his pants. He had three different pairs of pants spread in the living room, and he had tried all of them on. They were too tight so he took them off and he wouldn't get into any of them.

His sister was sitting there watching all this. I was in the kitchen cooking breakfast so I just calmly walked in and I said "Oh, you don't want to wear any of these today."

I picked them all up and I brought them back into the kitchen with me. It wasn't two seconds before he was crying and saying, "Oh, now I want to wear them." He was in there tugging on me to give them back to him.

JG: There you go!

Mother's Little Saboteur

Samantha: I finally said, "Well, you really want these, huh?" I gave him one. He ran into the living room and started putting them on and his sister says, "Peter! Isn't that the one that was too tight?"

JG: Blew it! Blew it!

Samantha: This is the kind of behavior that I'm up against all the time!

JG: That's right, Mother's little saboteur!

Samantha: So we started all over.

JG: These strategies are just the little elementary pieces of behavior control. In order to keep the thing working, you've got to get to the level where you have a whole bunch of these available. Then you can switch from one to the other, even faster than "mother's helper." Because there are some kids, like big sister, who are just sitting there staring at you psyching you out—because they want to be able to break it up. They want the power; and until they learn that Mom and Dad really have far more power at this than they have, they're going to continue that game.

Two Days And Nights Of Wild Free Nakedness

Now little Annie Laurie, four years old, fought being dressed. She wanted to stay undressed. So Mom decided to let her stay undressed. Annie spent two full days and nights being naked. Then she decided she really liked to be dressed. Her Mom didn't say anything, just dressed her. There's been no problem since.

(Baby chirps loudly)

JG: Right! I love it when kids comment.

The Best Interests Of The Child

Renee: Good sales people are trained to do that—

JG: Yes. Many times their motivation may not be the best interests of the person involved. That's really important to remember. If you use these strategies with your own children, it's got to be for their legitimate benefit. Well, you can use it to get an hour of quiet for yourself, but basically you have to be working on their side—with them and for them for their best interest. Otherwise it will quickly become apparent that it's an attempt to exploit the other person.[5]

Renee: This is why with a salesperson who does that, you always end up saying, "I don't think I'm going to go back there!"

JG: Exactly. And there's a pitfall here. You don't want to just assume that the other person's wants and needs are the same as your own. Remember George Bernard Shaw's famous remark about the Golden Rule. He said, "Don't do unto others as you would have them to do you. Their tastes may not be the same."

Proving They're Smarter (Than The Doctor Thinks They Are)

Sally: Even when you put the tongue depressor in his mouth and he doesn't like it, he doesn't consider that exploiting?

JG: Actually what I do at this point with kids where I can initiate this process, is to have them prove to me that they can do three things at once: That they can stick out their tongue, hold their thumbs together without dropping them apart, and roll up their eyes. They are so busy proving they can really do this difficult thing, often they don't know that I have actually looked in their mouth and touched their tonsils with a Q-tip. They literally don't notice that, because what they're doing is proving that they are smarter than the doctor thinks.

And they have succeeded. Now during that time they may have felt a passing touch on their tonsils, but they don't make a picture of that. They don't make a gestalt of that. What they're interested in is achieving their success. So they win, and I win. You can do that with kids. You can be a winner and they can be a winner.

Attributions

BG: Many of us were raised the wrong way. We're doing a lot of things habitually, because "That's just the way you do it". So learning how to do it differently takes a little practice on our part. There's a lot of blaming that goes on with parent-child relations. Have you noticed that? I mean, like, blaming is the thing to do. "This kid has got a real bad feeling about me." Even mothers of little newborns: "He doesn't like me because he cries". They attribute motivations to children and blame them. Most of us were raised in that mode. This is a different way of looking at things.

(The visiting baby shrieks with glee.)

He's Already Been Good To Me

JG: I remember one teenage unwed mother in the hospital who announced to me when I came in the morning after the baby was born, she said, "He's already been good to me!"

"He's already been good to me". At that tender age she was interpreting his behavior in terms of altruism and selfishness—very adult ideas, I guess you would say—or at least ideas that would be more appropriate for a 3-year-old or 4-year-old.

There was that other Mom who told us when her baby was three months old, "I used to think my baby was stubborn, but now I know she's just lazy."

The Language Problem

That opens a whole Pandora's box. It leads into a very fundamental problem about human interactions. That is the language problem. It's hard to believe, but every language that the human race has ever used suffers from a serious flaw. The structure of all languages almost without exception is such that you can make an attribution about the other person. "He is just lazy."

But what does it mean when you say a person is "just lazy?' or "just stubborn?" It really means that you have tried out some of your repertoire of behavioral interventions in order to elicit a desired piece of behavior from the other person and you have failed, because your repertoire was too limited.

What you ought to say under those circumstances is, "I lack sufficient repertoire to elicit this desired behavior X from person Y." Instead of that you say, "He's just stubborn." We put the blame on the other person, rather than recognizing what we should; that it's our lack of repertoire, not the other person's character defect that's involved.

Every language in the world enables you to do this little maneuver that puts the blame on somebody else. If we think a child is doing something called "misbehaving," it's worth remembering that the behavior that a person exhibits is elicited in part by the surroundings. Therefore in theory it should be modifiable by changes in his surroundings. Since we're the most important element in the surroundings for a child, it really means, "Here's a challenge. Our repertoire up till now has not succeeded. Would there be some other items of repertoire that might succeed?"

The common consensus has it that there is only one way to deal with a child; that is to be firm, consistent, nurturing and—what's the rest of it?

BG: Oh, on that list of things to do or not to do to a child.

JG: To be consistent, to be nurturing, to be fair, to be clear, and to explain everything. Then if they still don't do it, send them to the reformatory or the insane asylum, or whatever! Because now they are the ones that are to blame. The fault is in them. But if you have more than one strategy in your repertoire and if you can switch from one strategy to another over a sufficiently wide range, then you'll discover that you can in fact produce amazing changes that you would never have thought possible.

Chapter **10**
A Back Yard To Play In

That Fascinating Electrical Outlet

Neil: I had a question from way back at the beginning. I'm thinking of how I'm going to explain some of this stuff to my wife Kim, and—going back to an earlier example, say an infant or child who sees the cord plugged into the wall. The child somehow gets an idea, "I'm going to go explore this," and they've seen you take the plug out and plug it in, and they want to see what it is that you're doing. So they head on over to it and of course you try the Fright Face and the child stops, but even though you look frightened at what they've done, you still haven't stopped the curosity about what is happening when you keep plugging and unplugging this cord into the wall.

They don't understand why you're frightened. They just want to go over there and see what it is that happens when you plug and unplug. So, even though you can stop them maybe for that instant, sooner or later they're going to get back to the idea. They see that cord in the wall again, and that triggers it. Now can we expand on that, and maybe get back into how you're going to—especially with an infant that can't communicate verbally—how are you going to stop that type of behavior?

Environmental Control

JG: This brings up the point that the very first strategy that I have on my list is called Environmental Control. Why are electrical outlets placed so low on the baseboard that a baby can crawl over and get electrocuted? If all outlets were five feet up on the wall, we would not have this problem at all, or if there was a childproof safety lock on them, we would not have this problem. If Edison hadn't picked 60 cycle, 110 volt alternating current, we would not have this problem. That happens to be exactly right—110 volts, 60 cycles is just perfect for stopping the heart, just by ill chance. Edison picked something that was convenient for him. He was not thinking about little kids when he designed it.

They can get a hundred and ten volts AC out of any one of these sockets. A toddler, who has no conception of electricity, can be electrocuted.

Or, if your appliances are set a little bit apart, they can crawl between them and one of them will be grounded and the other one not, and the current will go right through them. There's basically no attention paid to this kind of thing. The world is built for adults. The assumption is made that everybody knows self-protection in advance, and it's just not true. I think the best solution is to make it impossible for the child to get to those outlets.

Henry: That's what we did. We bought the little blockers, and they are a real pain. When you want to plug something in, they are a real pain.

BG: We've got them all over the office.

Henry: But it eliminates the problem. It becomes a nonissue then and that's just what you want. It works!

JG: But some kids will pick them loose.

Naomi: We bought those little plug-in things and when he was 3-months-old, he was pulling them out. Then we got screw-in wall plates that have a little spring mechanism, and you twist it, and for things that you actually keep plugged in, they've got a plastic thing that you can screw in—

Sally: A little box, that goes over the plugs and everything and they can't get to it—

Naomi: We put those things in and he sort of walked by and poked at them a little bit, and I didn't say a thing, and he doesn't even look at them anymore.

But, I'm at the point now—and I was very comfortable at that point—I thought, we child-proofed our house, all my cupboards are closed, you can't get into these things.

But now I think, "My gosh, what a boring existence for this little kid." I think at some point we ought to be able to pull back on these things a little bit and let him see how things—like you said, they're curious—let him see how things are done, so that he can live in the real world. Everything's not so protected he's not kept from everything so much that his own curiosity can't—

Night Lights

Arthur: That's just what we did with Brett. We bought him some night lights and just stood right there and supervised him. He plugged them in and he goes, "Oh light! neat!" He found out and his curiosity waned down so he doesn't bother it any more.

JG: How old is he?

Arthur: Two and a half.

"That fascinating electrical outlet."

Sally: *We were right there. I mean I was right there for grabbing the hand.*

JG: Yeah, right.

Sally: *But he saw that it was a night light that when you plugged it in, it turned on. He got the definite idea—*

JG: He understood.

Sally: *—that something happened, when you get a—*

Arthur: *—when you plug that thing in.*

Sally: *Sort of like standing there with the light switches for awhile. He's still doing that.*

JG: Still practicing that.

Sally: *On the light switches, yeah.*

BG: —climbs up on a chair and—

JG: I think that's a beautiful solution. It's obviously not an absolutely fail-safe solution, because he still could make a mistake with it.

> *Arthur:* *Oh, no, no. Well, one company has come out with a type of night lights—they have a little plastic guard key between the actual back of the light that sticks out about that far—so if he's plugging it in, he can't get his fingers in there and touch the actual contact. The light itself is run by electric eye so when it gets dark, it comes on by itself. He'll run back and forth turning lights off in the house.*

JG: Ingenious! He gets to do his thing, which is to explore the world, and you are satisfied with the safety aspect so that you both get what you want. Marvelous example. That's the essence of the whole method. The child gets to satisfy whatever is driving him, and you also get whatever it is that you need.

> *Sally:* *He gave us the cue when he was sick and tired of being baby-proofed. We did the boxes under the lights, and he did ignore them. He just now has started getting interested in them again, and I thought to myself, ''I can get a padded lock or I can work this through somehow.'' I would say that I had the house babyproofed for a good year and a half.*

> *Arthur:* *Every time we go to leave the house at evening time, it's, ''Well, we have to go around and turn off all the lights!''*

JG: That can be his contribution to the family.

Change The Environment If You Can

This is Strategy Number One: If it's something in the environment that you can change, then change the environment.

> *Sally:* *Now how do you deal with the people who say, ''No, you've got to teach them their No-No's!''*

JG: I suggest that they can conduct their own classes and see how many people they can get to come to their classes!

Sally: I do that vacant grin and ignore it! Maximum Gaze Aversion!

Bathroom Safety

BG: In this bathroom here, if you'll look, sometime when you're in this class, you'll see that I have a special stool for the toddlers to climb up so they can turn on the water. It's lightweight and very stable. That stool has been a real good thing because the toddlers can reach the water and turn it on and off. That's one of the possible solutions that you could try. Be sure to show 'em how to do it.

Sofa Safety

BG: I spent quite a few days at different times when our kids were growing up, showing them how to do things well so they didn't get hurt. Like: our first born son decided—he was about nine months old—and I had a little step bookcase at the end of the sofa (dutch studio couch) and each shelf farther down was farther out, so it was like a little staircase.

At nine months of age he was crawling and he could climb up and get on the studio couch and then he would inevitably fall down on his head and go "Bonk!" and say, "Ouch!" and cry. So I took a couple of days out between a few other things and I said, "OK, now, we're gonna climb up and then we're gonna climb down and we're gonna do it different ways." Like, he could either come down this little bookcase or he could turn himself around with his feet down over the edge and land. I spent a couple of days doing that and he never fell again.

Crib Safety

BG: Well, the next thing was, he was about fourteen months old and he discovered he could get out of his crib by going up over, putting his waistline on the edge of the crib and then, "Bonk!" right down on his head on the floor, using his head to break the force of the fall.

JG: He thought that was the way you were supposed to do it!

BG: I put sofa cushions around for a few nights and he'd still manage to hurt himself—fall over and bump his other end. So OK! Two more days now we're gonna practice getting in and out of the crib and that's the end of the crib side being up. It was down permanently and when it was time to go to bed he could climb in and when he wanted to get out he could climb out on the chair and get down.

So sometimes you do have to take some time out from your other activities and run it in the ground until they really get it. That saves so much trauma in the long run. I think of it as an investment in parenting.

JG: We finally just put the mattress on the floor and let him sleep on that!

Refrigerator Safety

JG: Now if you'll look over there at the refrigerator in this room, you'll see there is a lock drilled into the door. You don't have to tell the kid to stay out of the refrigerator if there's a lock on it, like this one.

> *Kay:* That's the other problem we have—he's in the refrigerator all the time, doing something.

JG: You don't have to tell him stay out of the refrigerator. You just get a lock.

> *Morilla:* It's a drilled lock?

JG: It's a drilled lock.

BG: That's the most expensive way to go. There are less expensive ways to go.

JG: But if he leaves the refrigerator door open, you're going to lose fifty dollars worth of food.

BG: You can get a chain and put it around. A chain with a plastic around it and put it right around the whole refrigerator with a lock on it, and the kiddie can't get it open.

JG: But he can see a chain, whereas the lock is less conspicuous. This is environmental design—architecture, interior design—whatever you want to call it. This is one of the most neglected ways of creating a safe environment for a child.

BG: All these outlets down low, around the edges of everything.

JG: Just look at this room—obviously designed for the convenience of adults.

BG: The corners of everything are all square and sharp. I was really screaming at the architect. I said, ''I want those windowsills rounded!'' These are the kinds of things that we haven't even thought about in our society for children.

Toilet Safety

JG: So, start looking at everything in your environment, in your household, and you will see the places where a small kid can get into serious trouble—the toilet, for example. How many kids drown in the toilet every year? They don't even tell you. That could easily be controlled by some changes in design.

All that hi-tech video stuff, your nice entertainment center—it's built for the adults. Here are all these glittering knobs and lights and things . . . Well, a stopgap is to put a heavy canvas over it, and then it looks pretty dull. A small child, say nine months, twelve months, fifteen months, will probably not try to get a big heavy canvas off.

BG: When the kid gets older you put a piece of plywood behind the cabinet and fasten the canvas on to it.

> *Cora: For us the refrigerator is the least of our worries. it's everything. Everything is, ''Don't do this; please don't do this.'' But it keeps happening. We said, ''Stop!'' ''Go sit over here for a while.'' He does a time-out and comes right back and does it again. It's relentless.*

JG: Right. Yes. You need high powered strategies for that kind of thing. You can't just ask them.

Video Control

> *Theodore: The other thing that I'm thinking about while I'm hearing this, is that—for instance, we have a VCR and he likes to take the cassettes and put them in. I think that's pretty neat, because it kinda goes, ''Nrowrrr!'' and makes this noise and the lights light up and it's fascinating, right?*

JG: Right!

> *Theodore: I don't really want to stop him having that fascination with the world.*

JG: Right!

> *Morilla: Let me interject, though—*

Theodore: What is this, is this a disagreement?

Morilla: —before we even set up the VCR, we bought a cabinet that has a door on it with a child lock on it, because we dealt with the VCR for two days and we got so angry because of the potential damage that could have been done to it by just touching a couple of buttons, that we said, ''We have to control the environment.''

So the few times that the door is open and he's right there and we're with him, we'll let him do it; but for 95• of the time it's not a problem because we've changed the environment.

Theodore: That's true.

Morilla: 'Cause Luke couldn't handle it.

Louise: Our son was very curious about the tape deck also, so we got him a little tape deck of his own.

BG: Great idea!

Louise: He kept guessing and he figured it out all by himself. He mastered it. He takes the tapes out and puts them in, turns it on, and I was amazed at how he learned it. He just watched it and was just interested.

JG: They probably have more power than you and I have in mastering a new situation.

Hot Water Control

JG: You think about the hot water heaters. They're all set at 145 degrees when you get them. They're so hot that they will scald your child before the child can mobilize his body to get away from that hot water. So just by setting them at 125 degrees, you don't have to lecture them about hot water taps. That's just hot enough that after a few seconds they realize they've got to get away from it.

Balcony Safety

Kay: Well, we live on the fourth floor. We have a balcony with a sliding glass door and we had to ask them to please please—they didn't want to put a lock on it. But I told them we had a two-year-old, and several other things we had to ask them—really twist their arm.

JG: You tell them you understand it's difficult and you'd like them to talk to your lawyer about it!

It took a hundred years to get legislation in New York that you couldn't make apartment windows down to the floor. That's how much attention the child gets.

Priscilla: It's like if you live in an apartment you're not supposed to have any children. You're supposed to get your own house.

Kay: Well, where we are they have a ''family building'', and everybody else is single or married without children. So in a way that's good—and in a way it's not so good—because you're one of many, and your complaints don't get noticed very much.

Decibel Control

JG: Shushing kids. That's another thing. In Sweden, you have to build in such a way that there's an eighty-decibel sound drop between rooms in the same suite. A hundred and twenty decibels between floors. The kids upstairs can play basketball and scream if they want to and you won't hear it. So there are ways to make a civilization in which kids don't have to shush all the time. Then you don't have to use these high-powered strategies, because you can let them be noisy.

Ooopen Doooor!!

Cora: Actually I had an experience yesterday which frustrated me—out in public too. My husband gets season tickets to the basketball games. So the four of us went, my husband and Justin, the baby, and me. We went late so they could take their naps. We felt we had—

BG: How old is Justin?

Cora: He's going to be three and a half this month. We figured we had done everything possible. We fed him and everything before we left. Daddy and Justin at the intermission went and got some popcorn and made bathroom stops and came back. When they came back, I said, ''Well, OK, there's a few minutes left on the intermission, I'll go to the bathroom now.''

So I handed him Conrad—and Justin likes to be with me a lot, which is fine. So Justin said he wanted to come with me to the bathroom. I said, ''Well, have you already been to the bathroom with Dad?''—''Yeah.''—''OK, fine,'' so I thought, well this is like a social thing—

So he came with me. He was fine waiting in line until I could get into one of the stalls. As soon as I went into the stall he didn't want to be in the stall and I said, ''Well, we're in here now, I'm not going to open the door and let you go out,'' because I really don't feel comfortable leaving him in a public bathroom with two entrance doors going out into a huge arena.

JG: Absolutely.

> *Cora: I said, "I'm sorry, I'll be real fast, but you have to wait." He just went nuts! He was pounding, trying to get the door open, and I said, "Well, why do you think I went to the bathroom. You knew you were going to be coming in here with me."*
>
> *"Ooopen doooor!!" He was completely incoherent. Once we got out, he was all right; but—and he's not claustrophobic, 'cause he's been in bathrooms with me before and has not ever done this—but he was like that. Then he had to go to the bathroom again during the game and I took him. They have a little trash dispenser for sanitary napkins and so forth, and he insists on playing with that. I said, "Listen, that's dirty, don't play with that." He'd flip it up and flip it down, and I said, "Don't touch it again!" He just kept doing it so I slapped him on the hand and you know that everybody else in the bathroom can hear this and is going, "Oh! Abusing a little baby!" I didn't know how to handle it.*

JG: Well, he double-crossed you!

> *Cora: Yeah! I felt really put out!*

> *Morilla: Sometimes I'll ask him (my son is almost three) to get the toilet paper off the toilet paper roll for me and that usually—it's often very hard to get toilet paper off the roll—and that occupies him for quite a lot of time. It keeps his hands off things that you generally don't want him to touch. Or else I'll ask him to hold something.*

JG: But you can understand what a setup that is if they decide to crawl under the stall—

> *(Two or three at once): Oh, it's terrible! There's nothing you can do! They started that before and you had them by the ankles . . .*

JG: It's enough to make you want to put one of those little leather harnesses on—

> *Cora: Right.*

Safety Harnesses

BG: We had a harness for our children.

JG: It saved their life more than once.

BG: We were going on trains and planes. It's like a little Lederhosen suspenders and then you just hook a little dog leash on the back cross in the middle, a nice short dog-leash—

JG: It's much nicer than watching people pop out of their seats down the aisle as this creature slithers under their seats—

Louise: How long did you use it?

BG: Until I felt that verbal control was adequate, like when he would mind me—

JG: Maybe next year. He'll be turning thirty-three!

BG: It was quite a long time, like almost till age four. 'Cause the younger one was two years younger and I could manage him in my arms, but this older one was off like a shot—very energetic.

JG: That gets us back to that fundamental safety issue. It may look horrible to have a kid on a leash, but you know he's not going to be kidnapped.

Kay: You see it more and more these days.

BG: Or run over.

Morilla: Maybe that's a good idea for the bathroom situation and places where you know that you may—

Kay: Yes, I was thinking about this as I was driving home and Tony was sleeping—first of all, I didn't know that he was that tired and secondly, I should have had my little harness with me 'cause then he could run around—

Morilla: How do you prevent them from getting strangled? Really caught up in them?

BG: Oh, well, it's in the back.

Priscilla: There's also Velcro around the wrist.

BG: I don't think those are as good as—

Priscilla: They can undo the Velcro.

BG: This is an old-fashioned thing. It's just like suspenders. It has a belt and the belt actually buckles in the back so the child can't unbuckle it. In the back the straps cross, and all you do is hook the dog leash—these snap hooks will go over two pieces of leather and the kid is being held from way back here. You can have it as short as you wish. It goes up to four feet long; and if you need it closer, you just pull it in. That's how I managed when I was carrying the two-year-old. I'd have the leash wrapped around my arm so the older child was almost right next to me. That was very safe on the railroad track especially when the train was coming in.

> *Esther: I wish I'd had that when we were in O'Hare airport last Fall when we had all those suitcases and all that luggage and there she was, going up to talk to every person in the airport.*

A Back Yard To Put Him In

> *Kay: Before I had Tony I told everybody I wasn't going to have a child until I had a back yard to put him in. I really wish I had taken my own advice because now he's old enough and I really do wish I had a back yard to put him in. Where he is now we have to trot down three flights of stairs and I have to watch everything he does because there is the highway right there. There is a small fence, but it's not enough to keep him away from the highway. So it's really restricted for him, and I do feel sorry for him.*

JG: What other large mammal can survive being crowded together so closely? Any other creature our size has to have a range, but we don't pay attention to that. Many of the problems we have with raising kids are due to the fact that our conditions are so highly specialized and they are aimed right for the convenience of the adults. The result is that the kid exhibits the spontaneous behavior that is correct for a hundred thousand years of past history and it's no longer correct. Then we have to correct it.

Well, learning how to do that without actually traumatizing the child— without actually making them feel that they have to give up everything— is what we're trying to do here. Someday maybe we will devise environments that will allow—and even elicit—the spontaneous expression of the child's potential. They will look back on us as a really barbarous age.

Chapter 11
The Flaky Moms' and Dads' Club

Specialty Slots

JG: When you have two, three, four, five people or more in a family unit, there is a tendency for specialty slots[1] to get chosen. One person will be the competent one. Some other person may decide to corner the incompetence market. It doesn't necessarily mean they're really incompetent. It just means they've decided at least temporarily to be in that slot.

Plopping On Their Perch

The strategy to counter that is, if you find somebody occupying a slot and playing one role too hard, you can sometimes help them to move out of it by plopping down on their branch of the tree—by getting more incompetent than they are.[2]

> *Morilla: Interesting!*

JG: Rings a bell, eh?

> *Morilla: Well, actually, we've never tried it, but it certainly is an interesting way to look at it.*

Don't Explain Everything

JG: This is a powerful strategy—and by the way, you don't need to explain everything to kids. You can let them wonder just a little about what's happening.

BG: The children then develop the capacity to figure things out for themselves—

JG and BG (together): —and become competent adults!

"Plopping on their perch."

The Flaky Moms' and Dad's Club

JG: This is to make it happen for them too. If the kid is occupying an incompetency slot, it's really useful to keep this as one of your strategies, that you might be more incompetent than they are. You can try really hard to help but you just can't quite make it.

Separation Anxiety

Many little kids around fifteen to eighteen months go into a certain specialty slot called "scared of the whole world." Stranger anxiety, separation anxiety—it's so common that it's generally regarded as a normal developmental stage. In fact there's a realistic basis for them to feel that way because they have just discovered how little power they really have. After thinking that they control the whole world, they make this awesome discovery and they understand, "Gee, there's an awful lot of stuff I can't do." Then they get scared of everything.

That's a perfectly legitimate position to take. But if it turns into a permanent way of life, one way to cope with that is for one or both parents to become more fearful than the child is. You can become so nervous about doing something new that the child gets disgusted. It's Mom that never wants to go out and play. It's Mom that won't go in the other room. It's Mom that thinks the bathroom is scary. It's Mom that keeps me from doing all the stuff I spontaneously want to do, 'cause she's so timid. You provide the child with an irresistible opportunity to vacate that slot and take on the competency slot.

The child's competency goes up every year. Your competency should go down every year. You should get more and more flaky. That's why the other name for this group is, "The Flaky Moms' and Dads' Club."

Now remember, this is only one strategy. There are many others. But you really ought to be able to lose skill and competency as the child gains it. And if your timing is good, you will turn out to be incompetent at doing something just about the time when the kid is reaching the developmental level where they can master it.

Gravity

You can start this at twelve months of age—fifteen months of age—when you demonstrate to the child that although you love them very much, you can't get across the room in time to catch them before they fall. You know how they toddle and fall on their seat. So you carpet your floors. You make sure that the height is less than about three inches, and then you try to get over there, but you just can't quite make it. You can apologize and say, "I'm so sorry." What they learn is: "Mom and Dad can not protect me against gravity. I have to do this myself."

Kay: School of hard knocks, isn't it?

JG: Very gentle knocks. The idea is to titrate it.

BG: The principle of immunization. Just enough to get the right idea.

JG: How does a kid learn to respect fire? They touch something that's a little bit too hot. You don't let them actually burn themselves. You just want them to find out what it's all about. The same thing with gravity.

You Need A Plan, Don't You?

Esther: I'm wondering about applying this to little children. I've had this sense with my little girl that she needs to feel that I am competent. That there are things that I can do, but also to know that I'm not going to save her from everything. That there are bumps. That there are things that are hot. That if she gets stuck under a chair—one day she was totally stuck and she was saying, ''Mommy, help. Help, help, Dora help.'' I said, ''You need a plan, don't you?'' and I got down on the floor with her but I didn't get her out from under the chair, either.

She eventually got herself out and she was so excited. She felt so competent, and I thought that was—that felt really great for me because she had done it, but I had been there and if it had been something horrible I could have saved her.

JG: Wonderful! You were just incompetent enough. You were available in case of disaster. It's only one of many strategies. You don't ride it to death. Use it when it's useful; and when it's not useful, don't use it.

Let Them Win Once In A While

Eventually—maybe when they are thirty-five—they will realize what you did, and they will feel gratitude towards you for letting them be a winner. Maybe they will even let you win sometimes, too.

The Pattern Of Success

That pattern of success is so important. Unless it's a matter of life or death, you don't interrupt it even if it's not what you had on your own agenda.

Anneke: What do you do when you're starting to become a flaky parent and there's this situation where you really do have to be a competent parent?

JG: Where you have to protect somebody's safety. Then you need to move in in such a way that it is totally obvious that you are in command of the situation—

Anneke: —and then you revert back?

JG: Right.

The thing to avoid is the attempt to be powerful and authoritative and fail. When they're still little, it's better not to ask them to do something that they can refuse and get away with . . . unless for your own strategic purposes, you actually want them to have the delight of successfully refusing you. If you do, they will do it again. It's quite a pleasant experience at first to defy Mom and Dad and win. So don't ask them to do what you cannot enforce. In the case of teenagers who are very independent spirited what you could do is say, "I wish you would do your homework, but of course I can't make you."

Forgot To Make Their Dinner

Anneke: It's been working at our house these last couple of weeks. There's been a big change.

JG: Would you explain that? I'm not sure everybody knows what you mean.

Anneke: I've got a thirteen-year-old and she's going through a stage where she says, "I refuse to do anything that you want." "I'm gonna flunk school." "I'm gonna sit on the phone until three in the afternoon." We fall in that category, where I'm the competent one and my daughter is falling in the incompetency slot. So the last couple of weeks, by me playing Flaky Mom, my daughter has stayed off the phone—

Morilla: When you say "playing Flaky Mom"—

(Two or three people at once): Yes, how—?

Morilla: What exactly did you do? Did you ask for help or something, or say "I just can't figure out what to do about this"? "I need your help in finding a solution," or what? How did you make yourself incompetent and flaky?

Anneke: I sat down one night and made a peanut butter and banana sandwich for dinner for myself. Eva came out and said, "Mom, where's my dinner?" "Oh! I'm sorry, Eva, I forgot. I thought you'd be out playing and I forgot to make your dinner. Would you like part of my sandwich?" She was just flabbergasted. "Never mind!" and she went storming into the kitchen to check out what's there.

I Wish You Would,
But I Can't Make You

Anneke: Another thing . . . with her homework: "Eva, I really wish you would do your homework, but I guess it's no use talking to you." "I really wish that you wouldn't be on the phone so much, but I guess it's no use talking to you." And I've seen her make a drastic change in the last two weeks.

JG: What did she do?

> *Anneke: Oh, she's doing her homework, and she's gotten very considerate. She's come back into social touching contact with me—getting on the sofa and sharing the sofa with me, watching TV. She never used to watch TV. She used to be one of those teens that go straight into the bedroom after school and that's it. ''I need my privacy, good-bye,'' and that's it for the day. Now she's starting to come out, and when the phone rings she's starting to say, ''Mom, just tell 'em I'll talk to 'em tomorrow. Take the message for me. I don't want to talk to 'em now.'' It's not a miracle but it's a definite improvement.*

> *Morilla: Is that simply—is your point that it's not necessarily that you really appear incompetent but you are no longer simply the authority figure, the person that made all the decisions?[3]*

JG: You can put it in those terms, yes.

Use Your Weakness!

This is Carl Whitaker's famous gambit: Use Your Weakness.[4] ''I wish you would do your homework, but I know I can't make you.'' Now when a person says, ''I wish you would do your homework,'' the child is all ready to resist, but they have to agree that it is true that you as the parent do wish that they would do their homework. They have to agree with you about that.

Then when you also say, ''But I know I can't make you,'' they have to agree with you about that. They've agreed with you twice inside of one second. You have forced them to agree with you—twice.

Both parts of that sentence are absolutely, compellingly true. The child has to say, ''Yes'' twice in a row. ''I wish you would do your homework.'' The child says, ''She wishes I would do my homework. I know that's true.'' Then you say, ''But I can't make you.'' She'll say, ''That's right. You can't make me.'' She knows that. That sentence is about all you will ever want to say about homework. Use it sparingly. Say it once a year. That's all it takes.

BG: It's amazing how fast kids learn.

> *Cora: But does that really make them do their homework? A lot of kids would just thumb their nose at you and say, ''You're right! I'm going out bicycling!''*

JG: That's right. ''I can't make you. You can go bicycling.'' They can go bicycling, and all the time they're bicycling they're hearing these words, ''Mom and Dad can't make me do my homework.'' That's an acknowledgement of the truth, isn't it?

The child agrees that it's true. The parent agrees that it's true. They all understand that this is true. So, if there's going to be something happening around homework, it's going to be based on this real truth—that parents cannot make you do it. Which is the truth!

Would You Mind Moving The Car For Me?

Now, using your weakness is not the same thing as negotiating from weakness. Asking a kid to do something is negotiating from weakness.

Ralph: Hummh!

JG: —and it sometimes works and when it works, fine. But if negotiating from weakness doesn't work, then don't keep doing it. A lot of parental frustration comes from negotiating from weakness—asking for the behavior that you want. The older a child gets, if they are basically well-disposed towards their parents, the more likely that strategy is to work. But when you use your weakness as a strategy, you state your request just a little differently and you make sure it's mixed with a little something that appeals to the child. You can ask a teenager, ''Would you mind moving the car?'' or something like that and they're likely to do it.

Anneke: —especially if they're under sixteen!

JG: Now you begin to understand the spirit of it. You tell a fourteen-year-old, ''I've just remembered. I left the car out in the middle of the driveway. It needs to be put into the garage. Do you think you're old enough to handle that job?''

Nora: Roxanne would volunteer at age two and a half!

JG: You've turned it from a horrible command by a hated authority figure into an opportunity for them to demonstrate to you how mature they are—

Cora: The thrill of a lifetime!

JG: That's right! That's what we're aiming at. Just have enough of those strategies so that life for the child can be a series of amazing experiences of achievement and competence. For years and years they may not notice that you're helping them to do what they should be doing to get to the next stage of development.

The Magic Phrase:
"I Wonder If—"

JG: You can make it even stronger. You can deliberately go one down in order to be one up. You can say, "I wonder if—?" You can say, "I wonder if you know how to drive the car into the garage?"

Putting The Critic In Charge

You can carry things even further. Basically, if the person is saying, "Things should be different around here," then you agree with them and let them be in charge of those things. It may take them a long time to realize that now someone else gets to be the critic!

Powerful Katrina

Katrina was eight years old and her IQ was over 140 but she could not get out of bed in the mornings in time to catch the school bus. Mornings were a terrible hassle. Mom had to rouse her up out of bed, argue with her about which clothes to wear and then actually dress her, comb her hair and fix breakfast, nag her to move faster, and then as the school bus approached, she had to shove Katrina out the front door. On many mornings Katrina was just too late. The school bus drove on by and Mom had to drive her to school. And Katrina's IQ was over 140.

Now you can bet they had had plenty of heart-to-heart talks and Katrina agreed that it was unfair that Mom had to do everything for a big strong girl with an IQ over 140. But, things didn't get any better. Mom was getting madder and madder. So she came to see us.

We suggested that Katrina was not getting the opportunity to use that IQ and that resourcefulness in constructive ways to meet her own needs because Mom was too competent. Mom was extremely competent in waking up on time, in rousing Katrina up out of bed, in making breakfast, in combing Katrina's hair, in running outdoors to stop the school bus, in driving Katrina to school. We suggested that Mom very quietly and very gradually begin to lose her marbles, to forget to set the alarm clock, to oversleep, to put too much salt in the eggs and burn the toast.

She could lose her skill at combing Katrina's hair, she could get the part crooked, she could snag and pull with the comb and she could forget to do the laundry when Katrina's clean clothes were used up. She could forget to put gas in the car or she could even leave the headlights on overnight. She could remain the same loving Mom, ever willing to help, but her help would be the kind of help people can gladly do without, the kind you regret ever asking for. In a word, we invited Mom to join our secret society, the Flaky Moms' and Dads' Club.

It was less than two weeks until Katrina decided that her scalp would be healthier if she combed her own hair. Her breakfast would taste better if she made it herself, and she would be more likely to catch the bus and get to school if she set her own alarm clock and got up by herself. Strangest of all, as her fights with Mom became a thing of the past, she found herself admiring and respecting and loving her Flaky old Mom more and more. Katrina is in her teens now and she and her Mom are good friends.

Katrina's problem fundamentally was that she needed to move on to the next higher stage of her development, that stage where she would begin to take responsibility for some of her own behavior. The technical tactic of using the Flaky Moms' and Dads' club strategy works when the problem is one of moving to the next higher level of responsibility. It would not necessarily be appropriate in some other context.

When Katrina's Mom began to lose her marbles and get really flaky, she was only doing to Katrina what Katrina was already doing to Mom. It's a rule in human relations that if all the competency slots are filled, it's easy for someone to start a career in the flakiness department. What Katrina's Mom did was to take over Kristin's flakiness slot and force Katrina to occupy the competency slot. This technique is one that I call plopping down on the other person's branch. There's only room for one person. So the first person who was sitting there—because it was a nice comfortable perch—gets uncomfortable and has to go flying off to look for a better branch. The branch that is available is the one just vacated by party number two.

Grimly Struggling

So many parents are determined that their child is going to have the very best education possible. They fight viciously to get their child admitted into the very best schools. They set up timetables so homework can be done without any interruptions. Mother even becomes a coach for the readiness tests, for mastering fractions and prepositions, for the SAT, the Graduate Record Exam, and the LSAT.

The child struggles and struggles, but just can't get it quite right. There seems to be a subtle learning disability. There is reversal of letters. The child sits and sits and no ideas come. Fidgeting begins. The poor creature has ADD—Attention Deficit Disorder. Minimal brain damage. Maybe a subtle birth injury. It must have been that obstetrician. The OB—that's the one to blame.

It's so unfair because down the street is that neighbor kid whose father goes bowling every night and doesn't even save enough money to put his kid through college. That youngster works at night debugging computer programs and has already been awarded a scholarship to the state college.

Why Grow Up?

The child whose parents are standing on their head to make sure her upbringing is perfect are sending their child two very strong messages at the meta-level. First, they are occupying the Competency Slot, allowing her to have a career as the incompetent one. Second, they are telling her that being adults, and especially being parents, is a grim business in which there really isn't any time for fun—the obligations and difficulties of properly raising a child overshadow everything else.

Grownups Really Do Have Fun!

Such a child may decide childhood is the only real fun time—being an adult is a drag. Why grow up? I'll stay little and irresponsible as long as possible. If you want your child to really want to grow up, show him or her by your example that being adults is what's really fun. You get to play and do what you want.

Chapter 12

Who Has The Problem?

Problem In The Probe

JG: One way of looking at parenting problems, or any type of problem for that matter, is in terms of the logical level—where the problem is. There are three levels. The first is what I call the Problem in the Probe. That's us— we're trying to elicit the behavior from the other person or from the system. We're the Probe. We have to be able to produce a change of behavior in ourselves in order to get the other person or the other system to change.

Problem In The System

The second level is the Problem in the System. That's the situation where the problematic behavior is actually the normal operation of the system. You've set the system up this way. This is the way it functions, and now you are trying to make it change its function, when in fact you designed it to work this way. You probably didn't notice that's what you were doing, but that's what you did.

You Can't Go To Sleep
Until You Stop Trying

A good example of this is when you try to make your child try harder to go to sleep. "Trying hard" is a very wakeful process. The harder you try the less sleepy you're going to be. Here you are, pressuring your child to make him try harder to go to sleep. Every time you turn the screw and escalate that system, what you're getting is less sleep. Until finally, you and the child are both sitting up all night trying real hard to go to sleep. Insomnia is like that, you know. You can't go to sleep until you stop trying.

This is a locked-in cycle. These are the kind that are really hard to figure out because you're already firmly entrenched in the belief that you have found the solution. The other person just stubbornly won't do it. At that point it takes a real shift of viewpoint to realize that it's your own efforts to solve the problem which are making the problem worse.

Problem In The Question

Finally, the third level is the Problem in the Question. That's when you're not seeing it in the right way. You're defining the problem in such a way that you cannot solve it. If we define the problem as, "He's stubborn," then we've defined it in such a way that we can't change it. The implication is if he's stubborn you're going to break his stubbornness or something like that. You tend to think about solutions that are likely to be unproductive. Whereas if you define it in terms of, "Gee, I seem to lack the repertoire needed to produce the desired behavior," then you've defined it as being in yourself, rather than in the other person. Then you can start asking yourself, "What might I do differently to produce a change in the other person?"

He Didn't Know When To Wake Up

BG: We had one little kid who wouldn't go to sleep at night, wouldn't even go to bed at night. This went on for weeks, and the parents were exhausted.

JG: He didn't fit any of the common patterns. He wasn't going to sleep and then waking up and demanding the presence of the parents. He wasn't hungry and he wasn't afraid of his room.

BG: He wasn't afraid of the dark.

JG: He wasn't afraid of the dark. He wasn't afraid of being separated from his parents. But he just wouldn't sleep. He would not put his head down and go to sleep.

BG: We suggested several things, like having the dog sleep in the room. Well, the dog didn't like that. They had trouble with the dog! The dog couldn't sleep!

JG: Ordinarily that's a marvelous solution because the dog is such good company.

BG: Anyway, they had a neighbor in to babysit one night. They were getting pretty exhausted and needed to get out for an evening. The neighbor, who was a grandmother age person, finally figured it out. She said, "Maybe

PROBLEM IN THE SYSTEM: *"You are already firmly entrenched in the belief that you have found the solution. The other person just stubbornly won't do it."*

he doesn't know when he has to get up,''—because the mother worked and everybody had to get out of the house in the morning. ''Maybe he's afraid he isn't going to get up in the morning on time.''

JG: He was afraid that he might be asleep when it was time to go.

BG: So they gave him a windup alarm clock, and they set it so that it would go off at 6:30 in the morning. They showed him how it would work and what it sounded like, and they told him, ''When you hear this bell, then you get up. That's time to get up and get ready for the day.''

That solved the problem completely! He would go in his bed. They'd do the ritual of setting the clock. He'd put his head down and go off to sleep, with great security, knowing that he would be waked up in time. He hadn't told anybody that. He hadn't been able to express that. He was only about three, I guess. The babysitter, from the outside looking in, made one guess and it happened to be a pretty good one.

> *Arthur: It's like the night before vacation or a big test or something. Waking up to look at the clock to make sure you don't oversleep.*

BG: The problem was exactly the opposite of what it seemed to be. He didn't want to go to sleep because he was afraid he wouldn't wake up at the right time.

JG: There's that, ''Ah-ha!'' experience when you realize, ''Oh, this is not that. This is not that, this is this.''

Lying and Stealing

There are a lot of things that are like this, the problem of ''lying'' for example. The problem of ''stealing.'' Those words represent ways of looking at childhood exploration, and childhood fantasy, in a way that is nonproductive. As a parent you actually want that behavior, that you have erroneously defined as lying. You want that fantasy that gets called ''lying'' and you want that exploration of the objects in the material world that gets called ''stealing.'' If you put that label on the child's behavior, the child will be totally unable to shake that label off. They will never be able to be cured, because it is a part of their spontaneous behavior.

Whose Problem?

Here's another way to look at it. The problem can be in the child. It can be in the parent. It can be in the situation or it can be in the definition of the problem again. That's another way. For me these are useful. You might want to write them down and think about them for yourself.

BG: It's like, "Who's got the problem?"

JG: Exactly! who's got the problem? Sometimes the question really is: Is there a problem? Which means: I have a problem because I think there's a problem, when there wouldn't be a problem if I didn't think so. A lot of stuff in childhood is like that. We think that we need to do something about behavior that is perfectly natural, spontaneous behavior for a child.

Sally: By drawing attention to it, you just make it into a problem.

JG: Your attention makes it a problem.

So, one of the first questions to ask is: Does the child really have a problem, or do we have the problem in regard to any particular piece of behavior? We may think that the child has a problem, but in fact, the problem is that we feel uncomfortable about something that the child is doing. We want the child to change so that we will feel comfortable. Not all problems are like that. Sometimes they are real problems, right? But, sometimes we want the child to do something. Yet if we sit back and think about it, it turns out—the reason we want the child to do it differently is because we're feeling uncomfortable. We're asking them to change to keep us comfortable.

Now sometimes that's useful because what they're doing may be dangerous or not good for them, and that's why we're feeling uncomfortable. But sometimes it doesn't have anything to do with that. It has to do with the fact that we just don't feel comfortable. There's a way to tell— by checking your own personal reactions at the moment. If you're trying to get somebody else to change their behavior in order for you to feel comfortable, you may be operating in what's called driver behavior.[1] This is a term from TA—Transactional Analysis. "Driver" is a good word for it because you feel driven to do a certain thing. The mental process involved is, "I can get comfortable again, I can feel OK IF . . ." "I will be feeling all right IF I get there exactly on time." You start with this unspoken "if" business. "I will be OK IF"—one of the following five things: If I am strong. If I try hard. If I hurry up. If I'm perfect. If I please somebody else or if somebody else pleases me. These are the five ways that you can drift out of a sense of being centered in yourself as an OK person. Each of these five drivers is accompanied by a certain internal state.

Number Three is one that I think a lot of us are acquainted with. That's the driver state where you feel like you've got to hurry up and get this done or get on to the next thing on your agenda. The body language that goes with it is a good tipoff because this is the person that's doing this (JG drums fingers rapidly, jiggles foot). If you're talking to somebody and they're looking at their watch and drumming their fingers, that's a tipoff that they are in driver behavior, that they're operating out of an internal state in which they're telling themselves, ''I can be OK IF we just get this finished by three o'clock.''

A lot of the things that we ask of our kids, we're asking them to do it because we're in Hurryup. Does it sound familiar? ''If they'd just get their boots on so they can catch the school bus!'' Meanwhile time is galloping by. Well, they pick that up—the body language, the tone of voice, the rapid speech. They pick that up but they don't care about the school bus or whatever it is that's on your agenda. They're little kids. They go by their own schedule.

Instead of adopting your Hurryup and rushing to get their boots on so they can get on the bus, what they do is push back. Now you've really got a problem, because you've asked them to hurry up and they say, ''No.'' Now you want to know a strategy for making them do what you want when it's really your own personal discomfort that is at stake.

Well, there are lots of times when adults need to hurry, and when they need to have the kids move fast too. So, it's legitimate to use strategies. On the other hand, if a person is more or less permanently in a state of Hurryup, it's going to put a tremendous burden on the child because now they are going to have to adopt your Hurryup and think and feel and react like you in order to please you. It's very likely that a kid who doesn't rebel will go into a Please Me driver and learn to psych out your internal state in order to meet your expectations before you even express them, because you're in such a hurry when you do express them, that they've got to know exactly what to do. Does this sound familar to anybody? Anybody here know what Please Me feels like?

Those who have experienced Please Me know how uncomfortable that is. You can never relax because you have to psych out the other person. You've got to know what they are going to need in the next few minutes. Well, kids don't willingly go into these modes. They are more likely to rebel. In fact maybe rebellion is a little more healthy reaction, so you get dawdling as a rebellion against Hurryup. Or you could get Please Me as a response. In families where there's a lot of high level emotion and acting out, one kid out of the group will often go into Please Me because they feel that they're the only one that is quick enough and keen enough to stave off disaster by figuring out what's likely to happen in the next ten seconds, in the next thirty seconds. It's not a very comfortable state to be in.

If it's the parent who is in Please Me dealing with the child, then you're going to get a parent who is trying to anticipate every possible trauma that the child might experience. This is the mom or the dad who makes real sure that the child is never allowed to experience any danger or discomfort on their own. The unspoken request is, ''Please don't ever do anything spontaneous or dangerous, because I might not be able to psych it out in advance fast enough to protect you.'' You hear the unspoken discount, ''You're just a little kid, you couldn't possibly take care of yourself.''

What do those kids do? Some of them become daredevils. They're the kids who act as if they don't even see the stop light. They just walk right out into the traffic.

I Was Always Trying To Make Me Perfect

OK, Be Perfect, Please Me and get all A's. Perfect attendance and all A's. The kid responding to that kind of a Please Me will then struggle to be absolutely perfect in school. Try never to miss a day, try always to get a perfect score.

Anneke: I can identify with that!

JG: Does that ring a bell?

Anneke: Yeah, especially in junior high. That's when, seventh, eighth grade, it was definitely that.

JG: You felt that yourself?

Anneke: Oh, yeah. I got straight A's in junior high. Inside I'd say, I want to be just perfect. I was working on me, trying to make me perfect.

JG: ''Make me perfect.''

Anneke: Of course that changes when you get into high school, no more straight ''A''s, and it gets real tiring.

JG: These kids get real tired. They try real hard. They just bust a gut trying to be perfect. They are devastated if they get less than a perfect grade. They bring home a 99 on a spelling test, and they have a crying jag.

Anneke: I was doing that to please my parents and they were always pleased that I got straight A's but I didn't get the reaction I expected. I didn't get this ''Wow''—big response from them.

JG: Because after all you might only get a 99 next time. I mean it's too soon to give you the praise. These are the kids that grow up fast, they fly through chemical engineering and they become a great pioneer or something. They get their Nobel prize. Then they have their heart attack and die, because they have been driven, trying to be perfect.

> *Anneke: It's a very frustrating thing.*

JG: It's a very frustrating thing. Parents who are doing this will give you just enough praise to give you the hope that maybe if you really do a super job next year, you'll get a little bit more.

> *Anneke: Well, our parents wouldn't push us real hard to do well. It was something that I felt I needed to do for them.*

> *Linda: The emphasis wasn't always on getting good grades. I know that feeling, because I'm like that too—I still suffer. I grapple with that because I feel like everything that I have to do has to be just right. It can't be in that gray area. It's either I do it right or it's all wrong. Not ''close enough''. It's either right or it's wrong. Never ''close enough.''*

> *Anneke: It's nothing that is really spoken to us.*

JG: You get the message nonverbally. You don't even know you've bought into it until years later.

When you talk to people that are in these drivers, they will give you characteristic descriptions of how they feel, what it is they want, what they're looking for, and what they are trying to achieve. The child will pick this up. If you know about it and can compensate for it, you can avoid driving them into one of the other drivers. Although I must say their radar is incredible. They will psych you out even if you try not to show it.

BG: Even by long distance telephone.

JG: Even by long distance telephone, they will pick it up. So it behooves you as an adult, in order to be a successful practitioner of elegant parenting, to look at your own structure and see where your requests are coming from. When you're asking the child to behave in a certain way, is this really for his benefit or is it for your own. If you feel acute discomfort about certain patterns, is it something that maybe you ought to work out for yourself and deal with in yourself rather than at the level of the child's behavior.

A Trace Of Emotion

> *Neil: Talk about Be Strong but Try Hard.*

JG: Yeah, OK. Be Strong is easy, that's John Wayne. That's the big strong silent person who just doesn't ever seem to have any emotion at all, except a more or less constant low-grade state of irritation. In the final reel at the end of the movie when they go off into the sunset, he kisses the horse instead of the girl. That's so common in America and in many parts of the world that it's really just regarded as the standard, that's the normal way. Did any of you watch television last night?

Have you seen this series called The Lion, the Witch and the Wardrobe? The big conclusion was last night. The lion, Aslan, died—or almost died—and these young British kids almost sniffled. They almost showed a trace of emotion. It was heartrending. I could hardly keep myself from showing an emotion.

That's the Be Strong. Now the Try Hard—this is the one where the kid realizes that you're not so much concerned about them making A's. What you're really concerned about is that they get out their paper and pencil and grunt and groan and strive for three hours every night. The parents' motto is, ''I don't care how poorly you do, just show me that you're really working hard.'' The kids take that literally. These kids often get special assistance, because that really proves they're working hard. They're really trying hard. They'll do remedial work on Saturdays and Sundays and in the summer time, because that proves they're really struggling with it. But they don't actually ever get there and get the payoff.

Is Your Own System Too Rigid?

It really behooves you as a parent to check out your own drivers and make sure you're not putting onto the child something you need to deal with for yourself. In other words, a rigid insistence that the problem must be solved within a specific set of parameters may merely indicate that you as a parent have a problem with rigidity. The child's behavior may be merely an attempt to stay out of your overly rigid system. The child may even be trying to help you to overcome your own rigidity by showing you a wider range of behavior than you had thought possible.

Cora: All the time! All the time!

JG: I don't need to tell you folks about that!

The child's behavior may be really a manifestation of a healthy trend that ought to be encouraged, with maybe just a bit of channelling to keep it from being dangerous or disruptive to family life. A parent who treats every spontaneous piece of behavior as something threatening—that's obviously not the child's problem, that's the parent's problem. Parents who rigidly insist that the problem must be solved within a rigidly defined set of parameters that obviously serve the purpose of keeping themselves comfortable—those parents may have a problem of their own with rigidity, and the correct response is to provide them with some experiences designed to help them feel more at ease in the world.

So maybe the problem is really due to the healthy refusal of the child to internalize and take upon himself what is properly a parent problem or even a social problem. Such things as ''Achievement'', ''Doing Well in School'', ''Manners''. Think about it.

When They Get Around to Feeling Thankful, They'll Say ''Thank You''

BG: Out at the front window at the reception desk, a fifteen month old that can hardly talk yet gets a cookie, and the Mom is all over him, demanding ''Now, what do you say? Say 'Thank you'!'' This poor little kid—

JG: You can practically see the words passing through the little kid's head. He's not even understanding the words—

Nora: You see it in their eyes.

BG: You can see it in their eyes. I think of the robin that takes a drink of water and he tips his head up to swallow, which is the same as saying, ''Thank you, God.'' You don't have to say anything. Anyway, when they get around to feeling thankful, they'll say ''Thank you'', probably—a little later.

Taking Too Much Care Of The Guinea Pig

JG: Once when I was a little kid about four years old, I was playing on the sidewalk in front of our house when another little boy came up the sidewalk carrying a shoebox. He took the lid off the shoebox and inside the box were three little guinea pigs. One was white, one was brown, and one was checkered brown and white.

And I wanted one of those guinea pigs for myself!

And the little boy said he was selling them for a quarter apiece.

I ran into the house and yelled for Mom and begged a quarter so I could buy a guinea pig. She gave me a quarter and I ran out and bought the beautiful little checkered guinea pig.

IS YOUR SYSTEM TOO RIGID?
"Maybe the problem is due to the healthy refusal of the child to internalize
what is properly a parent problem, such as 'Doing well in school'."

I had never had a pet of my own before and this one was my very own. I kept him in a shoebox on the back porch and punched holes in the lid of the box for air. I fed him lettuce and watched him nibble the lettuce. I was very proud, very happy.

But the next day, when I took the lid off the box, the guinea pig jumped out and skidded across the porch and down the steps and began to run away. I chased him as fast as I could run. He kept close to the walls of the house and up under the bushes where I couldn't reach him. I chased him at top speed until I was really out of breath.

Finally I saw him stop running and I ran up to him and kneeled down to pick him up. Then I saw something. . . . The little guinea pig was spreadeagled with his nose in the dirt, his four little paws spread out, and he was panting in total exhaustion. I realized that I had chased him too hard. He looked as if he might die at any moment. The thought flashed through my mind that I had broken my guinea pig. I felt a feeling through my whole body that I had never felt before. A mixture of shame and grief, remorse and fear, a desire to undo what I had done, and a realization that I had unknowingly exceeded the tolerance limits of the little creature that meant so much to me.

I picked him up and gently carried him back to the shoebox and gave him some fresh lettuce and let him rest. Gradually his panting subsided and he returned to normal.

The next day he was fine, but I learned something from that experience. I learned that relating to delicate systems in such a way as to preserve them requires an approach that is just as delicate and just as sensitive as the system itself. I was trying too hard. I was taking too much care of my guinea pig.

If It Gets Under Your Skin, It's Your Complex

JG: Well, I've been really impressed with you folks. I think you've got the essence of it at this point. All I need to do is sit here and ask you what you've done lately, and that turns out to be a new strategy!

It's worthwhile to check your own behavior and see if you can identify Driver behavior—if you can tell when you're in Driver behavior and when you're not in Driver behavior. The reason I say that is that it's quite possible to drift into a pattern of life where you're always in a driver. Where you hardly ever know what it is to be out of a driver. Particularly in early parenthood I think it can easily get like that.

> *Samantha: If I feel irked that Erica's not trying hard enough, chances are I'm in a driver?*

"It's quite possible to drift into a pattern of life where you're always in Driver."

JG: Yes. To quote the great C. G. Jung at this point, what he said was in effect: "If it gets under your skin, it's your complex!"[2]

> *Samantha: Then—at that point it's best to click out of that and pace with the child?*

JG: That would be a reasonable thing to do. Or go get some strokes for yourself. A lot of the time it's just because you're tired, nobody has been taking care of you. Here you are trying to take care of a child and nobody's taking care of you. You reach that point where you're burned out. What do you call it?

BG: Zookeeper burnout.

JG: Zookeeper burnout, right!

Parenting On Empty

JG: I'm glad you brought that up because this is the thing that I always forget to talk about, because I've got this slave driver up here in my own head that says, ''You have to cover all these points.'' I tend to forget that I'm getting tired or that I myself as a human being need to have a little play time for myself.

How can you be a good parent unless you yourself are being properly taken care of? If you're running on empty and nobody is nurturing you, how can you be nurturing to your kids? The answer is, it's hard. It's really hard. It's easy if you've just come back from a wonderful weekend, or you've gone to Florida or something like that. You're feeling great, and for the next two or three minutes? hours? you can be a parent with that real strong sense of your own comfort, your own competence, your own worthwhileness, because you have been taken care of. Now you can take care of your child.

Who Validates Whom?

It is OK for both parties to get validated. But when you're dealing as a parent with a child, it's really important for you to get your validation from your equals and give your child the opportunity to get their own validation from you. The really important point that you get across to them is that they are a worthy human being, worthy of being listened to, and that their experiences are important. *It's not their job to take care of you.*

Chapter 13

The Magic Door

The Magic Door
(Picnic In The Bedroom)

Some of you who have been here with your babies for shots may have noticed that if the baby cries, they will often instantly stop as Mother carries them out through the door frame. It's like just turning off a switch. You've noticed that?

> *Linda: Um-hmm.*

JG: That's because—

> *Arthur: ''—outta here!''*

JG: ''Outta here!'' Right. That's that tendency that we all have—to compartmentalize. When we shift locations, it sometimes induces a shift of ego state. When you're in a different ego state, it's real hard to remember what it felt like in the other ego state. You know how it is. When you feel good, you wonder, ''How could I have been so depressed the other night. I can't even remember.'' Or when you're depressed, ''How could I ever feel good again?'' That's this shifting of ego states, and of course the whole art that we're talking about is based upon shifting ego states. When you go from one to the next, your previous, locked-in pattern of behavior is all interrupted. You can't remember what was happening in the previous one— you usually don't even notice how the shift came about. Simply going through a door or moving the action to a different room will often induce a change. The dining room may be the location where all the bad stuff takes place, where the fights go on; but when the kids are in the bedroom or in the playroom, it's totally different. You just invite a shift of ego state by the simple maneuver of moving the whole scene somewhere else.

BG: Like having a picnic in the bedroom.

JG: Yeah! Or like having blue macaroni for lunch. That's the Magic Door too.

Linda: Or sending the kids outside to play.

JG: Send them out to play. That's one that has worked for you and me. It's also known as Get Out of My Kitchen. I've put it as a subheading of Environmental Control. It's a very subtle one. These strategies blend into each other. Going through a doorway is something that's pretty concrete, but you can shift your body position and cause a shift in the ego states of the people around you (moves into stiff upright sitting position, leaning forward, frowning, finger wagging). If you're in this position with your kid, what can you expect?

Arthur: Trouble!

JG: Trouble! Right!

Linda: "I won't do it!"

JG: Exactly. You haven't even said a word. You just moved your body. You shift back like this, throw 'em a blanket or something like that—whatever you do—it will change things. If it's the right maneuver, it will trigger a switch of ego states. You'll be in a whole different scene and dealing with a different problem from the one that you had before. Hopefully it will be a better one. OK, that's the Magic Door.

How To Condition
B. F. Skinner's Behavior

BG: A little variation on the theme is how B. F. Skinner's students in his class got him to do something. You know B. F. Skinner, I'm sure—the great behaviorist?

JG: I won't vouch for the truth of this one!

Mimi: When I was a teenager, my mother took a college-level psychology class and she was constantly telling me about him. I heard more about him than I wanted to know!

BG: Well, the way the story goes, B. F. Skinner was lecturing his class and they had had it up to here, too, about that time—so they all got together and they figured out how they were gonna change B. F. Skinner's behavior. He had a habit of pacing up and down in front of the class while he was

THE MAGIC DOOR
"Simply going through a door . . . will often induce a change."

lecturing. So what the class planned to do was to look alert and very interested when he would get over to the left side of the stage. Then when he'd pace over to the other side, they'd look down and look away and within a few minutes he was pacing back and forth clear over in the corner of the room. Then they did the reverse without ever saying anything and pretty soon he was pacing back and forth way over in the right hand corner of the room. This was happening only in response to their alert expressions and the interested looks on their faces.

Mark: Was he aware of what he was doing? Was he aware that he had actually limited his movement to one side or the other?

BG: Not until it came out in the laughter that followed.

Linkage

JG: What we're talking about is the linkage of a piece of behavior or an ego state with some other event or situation. It's another name for conditioned response. That's where the bedtime story starts in the bathroom as soon as they begin brushing their teeth. You don't say anything, you just start the story. Let's say by some strange accident the kids are in the bathroom brushing their teeth. You start reading the bedtime story right then and there. In the next day or two you may discover they have this strange compulsion to run into the bathroom and brush their teeth, because the bedtime story might begin. That's Linkage, where the desired behavior becomes a component by what's called Junko Logic or conditioning. The desirable activity is thought to be contingent upon the performance of the desired activity.

Cora: But isn't that close to bribery?

JG: Not if no connection is made between them. In other words, this is just the way things are in the evenings. When the kids are brushing their teeth the bedtime story begins. You haven't asked them to brush their teeth. You haven't told them that you will read them a bedtime story if they brush their teeth—

Kay: Well, what if they don't like to brush their teeth and you have to get them in the bathroom in the first place.

JG: You might need to use another strategy for that. Linkage is this method of moving in and providing a pleasant reinforcement in the course of their performing the desired activity. It's really a form of operant conditioning.

What we're trying to do here is to avoid making a problem out of toothbrushing or whatever it is. We're providing the reinforcement for something that is already happening. It doesn't have to be toothbrushing. It could be any other stage of getting ready for bed. You move in when they are doing it and provide this powerful reinforcement.

BG: Then you're walking down the hall with the book and they have to follow in order to hear.

JG: Right! You don't say anything, you just wait for it to happen again tomorrow. It's more likely to happen tomorrow because you reinforced it today.

> *C: But then you've got this squawking going on, "No, I don't want to hear it now, wait till I get in bed and then I wanna hear it."*

Keep Switching
(Cybernetics Of Cybernetics)

JG: That could happen. Then you switch to another strategy. These are not rigid programs. These are strategies. That means you pick them up and you put them down. You don't try to drive one to the limit if it isn't working. The secret of this method is that you switch from the strategy that is not working to another strategy until you find one that does work.

That's called the Cybernetics of Cybernetics.[1] That is second-order control. It's like the automatic pilot in an airplane. The automatic pilot senses that the nose of the airplane is tilting up and so it pushes the stick forward or does whatever it is that provides the correcting maneuver. But when a plane goes supersonic, the controls reverse and then that same remedy that the automatic pilot has, makes the situation worse rather than better. Now at that point a true second-order control unit would start flipping instruction manuals until it found the manual that said, "Do something different under these circumstances", or even, "Do the opposite of what you did before."

BG: Under these different conditions.

JG: In other words, "No longer do what you were doing. Do a different thing." Then the automatic pilot would start thumbing through directories of instructions to find the set of instructions that would actually keep the plane level, rather than just continuing to do what worked in the past but is no longer working now. When they first began to dive planes at supersonic speeds, the pilots were dying right and left and the first pilot who survived somehow sensed that pulling back on the stick was making his dive worse. So he pushed forward on the stick. What did he have to lose?

This is what we're talking about. This is second-order cybernetics. You are really at a very advanced level of engineering in this course. I mean, you'd have to go to graduate school . . .! But this is human behavior. Elementary human behavior is already more complex than an airplane.

BG: It isn't really that hard. Some people think, ''Oh! I can never do all that many things! I can't come up with that much variety.'' But you can, because it gets exciting and intriguing.

JG: You only have to get one or two successes and then you're off and running.

Bribery

Does everyone have a copy of Karen Pryor's book, ''Don't Shoot the Dog?''[2] The reason a bribe doesn't work very well is because it's a reward for behavior that hasn't happened yet. If you're going to do conditioning, you have to let the behavior happen first, and then reward it. Karen Pryor's classic example is the gorilla that was sitting in the door frame of the sliding steel door of its cage. They wanted to clean the cage and they would offer the gorilla a banana; and of course, the gorilla would take the banana and then immediately sit down again right in the door frame. What they were doing was rewarding sitting in the door frame. That's the problem with a bribe. When you offer it, the behavior that is happening at the moment is the behavior that's going to be reinforced.

So, when you plan to condition someone, you want to be real sure that the person is actually exhibiting the behavior that you want more of. Then you build on that. Once you get a certain amount of it started, then you can begin to shape it by rewarding only the most pronounced examples of it. That's how you get pigeons to dance in circles, and things like that.

Mark: I think you can get a desired response by an appropriate bribe.

JG: What's going to be rewarded is the behavior that's actually happening. Like in the year 900 AD, when the Vikings sailed up the river Seine to Paris, the French got them to go away by offering them an incredible sum of silver. A thousand pounds of silver, or something like that. Sure enough, they went away; but they came back the next Spring, and that time it took a bigger bribe to get them to go away.

So, yes you can condition behavior. You can get behavior with a bribe, but you want to be really sure that you're conditioning what you want, because the bribee may show up again and say, ''This is a real nice arrangement.''

If you want to do this kind of thing, Karen Pryor's book is the one to read. She will give you ten ways to shape the behavior that you want, starting with any example of it no matter how tiny. You can build it, shape it, put it on a schedule, and put it on a reinforcement schedule. Then you put it on intermittent reinforcement. From that point on you've got that behavior under your control. And you know that intermittent reinforcement is far more powerful than 100% reinforcement. You reward only the best examples of it. Then if you want to take down a piece of behavior, she's got eight ways of doing that; the last of which is to shoot the dog—that's where the title of the book comes from—and seven constructive ways. I would recommend that you learn those methods. They'll come in handy some day.

He Just Wanted To Be Put In His Room

BG: I had a friend whose little boy was about five. They moved into a new neighborhood. He's turned out to be the littlest one in the group of kids there, and he got into hitting his mother hard enough so that it really hurt. She didn't know what to do because she couldn't figure out why he had started to hit her. She had noticed that some of the bigger kids were pummeling him and that's what she thought was the connection. She really had a hard time with it because she'd get really angry and put him in his room. He had to stay there a certain length of time, every time he hit her.

Well, finally, one day after this had occurred several days in a row, she observed him coming in crying. He proceeded to head for her and she didn't want him to start hitting her, so she said, ''Go right up to your room right now, go up to your room.'' She was angry. He went up in his room and he was crying. She came up and said, ''What's the matter?'' He said, ''Well, the kids are being really mean to me, and they are hurting me.''

Then it dawned on her that he needed the security and safety of his room and to know that she was in the house, because she hadn't let the other kids in her house. So she said, ''Oh, you don't have to hit me. You can come in and go into your room without hitting me first.'' That was it. That was what his connection was—that if he got put in his room, then he couldn't go out to play any more and he wouldn't be around those bigger kids.

JG: Then he'd be safe. So he was hitting mom in order to get put in his room.

BG: To get put in his room. She had been fending everybody else off, saying, ''Well, he can't come out. He's been bad. He's in his room.'' She broke that sequence by saying, ''Go directly into your room.'' In a sense she was saying, ''I'll protect you.''

Sometimes it's real hard to know what's going on, and it helps to have somebody else look on and see if they can make the connection. You can get other adults to help you or sometimes you can ask the kid. He'll be able to make some kind of connection that you can figure out how he got into that sequence.

JG: What tipped her off? How did she realize—how did she see the picture?

BG: I'm not real sure because this child couldn't express it. He couldn't tell her what the problem was. I don't know what it was she saw or observed that would help her make the connection, but he stopped hitting her at any other time also. She had told him, "It hurts and you can't do that." But these bigger kids were doing it repeatedly to each other and to him. I think he was confused.

JG: He had a kind of a cause and effect in his own mind that this was the way to get put safely into his room. That's how he thought you did that particular thing. That's how the big kids were getting people to do things.

BG: Little children do make erroneous judgments. They'll make erroneous connections and then they hold these for years and years, and you don't know about it. A young unsophisticated child can make the wrong connections for behavior sequences. So think about it if you're in trouble with some kind of behavior. Ask the child, if they're big enough to talk. Some of them can tell you something.

> *Mimi: What other ways can you use when you have a child who won't tell you what the problem is? How else can you approach it other than verbally?*

BG: If it's a smaller child and they can't express it, there's no one real good answer.

The Miscommunication Principle

JG: The principle that applies to all this is the Miscommunication Principle: If something your child is doing seems crazy or off the wall or even downright malicious, that usually means that some kind of major miscommunication has taken place.[3] The responsibility is on the parent to figure out what's really going on.

There was a famous encounter between Paul Watzlawick and Jay Haley's secretary, where Paul walked in (because he had an appointment) and he said, "My name is Watzlawick!" The secretary replied, "I never said it was!'' Then he said, ''But I'm telling you it is!'' She said, ''Then why did you say it wasn't?'' At that point, they both thought the other was crazy or that they were the butt of some sort of malicious practical joke.[1]

That's how fast it works. A simple miscommunication like that creates in the other person—in both persons—the unshakable conviction that the other person is a criminal, or that they are crazy. So if you get that unshakable conviction, by all means go back and review the communication, because this is likely to be where it's at. Does that sound familiar?

Morilla: Yes, because in every one of our fights—

Theodore: She always misunderstands me! Always!

JG: Someday I'll give a lecture on the correct use of ''always'' and ''some''!

Gina: Wait a minute! I must have missed something! I don't get it!

JG: What didn't you get?

Gina: That whole thing about what's-his-name—Watzlawick. What's the point?

JG: Oh! Oh! You and I are doing just what Watzlawick and the secretary did!

Gina: Are you trying to hold out on me? What's the point?

JG: The secretary thought he was saying, ''My name is NOT SLAVIC!'' and so she defended herself. She hadn't said it was!

Gina: Oh!

Learn More Lines!

I don't know any good way of getting into the way of thinking of these answers except to deliberately build your repertoire. You make mental notes of these things. As you build a repertoire, then it will be easier and easier to think of similar things. It will grow by a snowball effect. But there really isn't any substitute for just brute learning—actually learning a bunch of these things.

BG: Like we said on that very first sheet we handed out. It's like a play. You learn more lines. You learn different lines.

JG: Right, you get to where you just automatically say, ''Oh, I see you are

"It's like a play—you learn more lines."

doing X. Wow, and you really like it, don't you? Would you like to do some more?'' Pretty soon you've got that one to where it's automatic.

This habit of thinking about a situation in a flexible way: You could easily say the kid is just stubborn. He won't sleep. But if you think about it and notice the details of it, then you begin to see, well, this is different from the little kid down the street, who wakes up hungry. This is different from the kid who wakes up scared. This is different from the kid that has to have the light in the room. This kid is afraid he won't wake up. That's when you put the definition of the problem into terms that automatically supply the solution.

You Forgot To Set The Timer!

Arthur: We had an interesting experience before we started taking this class. I think we fell into it, by accident, by anger or something. Our four year old, who's now five, liked to read. We'd read to her before she went to bed. She had a light on her bed, so that when she got into bed she had to stay in there—but we let her read her books until she'd go to sleep. We went through the series of, "I've got to go to the bathroom. I need more water"—all of that.

Sally: She'd stay up until eleven o'clock reading her book.

Arthur: 'Cause she wanted to, and then she'd come out to the living room, and say, "I'm not tired, I don't want to go to sleep."

She's in a loft bed. Her bed is about four feet up. We built it with enough space along the side that she could keep books up there, too. She would have a whole library. She'd have thirty books up there. We just went on the assumption, "Well, when she gets tired she'll fall asleep." Finally one night I was just tired of her getting up and coming into the living room and all that—she went through the whole routine.

In anger one night I said, "All right, give me all your books!" I took them all down. We set a timer for her, and I said, "Look, in 15 minutes—from now on you get one book in your bed, and in 15 minutes—we set one of these baking timers—you can read for 15 minutes, and after 15 minutes you can't read any more. You've got to go to sleep."

We've been doing this for what, three months now? She rarely makes it to the 15 minutes. She's usually asleep by then.

Sally: She gets really upset if we forget to take the book from the previous night out of her bed. "You can't leave the room. You forgot to take my book." She's standing there almost ready to fall out of her bed giving us this book. It's very important that we take the book now.

Arthur: I didn't realize till today that the problem was that she didn't have a time to go to sleep.

Sally: She had a time to go to bed.

Arthur: She didn't have a time set to go to sleep.

Sally: She makes sure to remind us, "Did you set the timer?"

Arthur: After we forget to set the timer.

Sally: She'll stand up and scream, "YOU FORGOT TO SET THE TIMER!"

Sally: I have to go into her room and set the timer!

Woman: That sounds like a good Birthday or Christmas present. "Here's this timer, just for you."

Arthur: I think she'd be upset if she thought it was something that we were trying to use to manipulate her. The other thing I've thought about is this. They've got the alarm clocks that you can let the music go for about 10-15 minutes. That could be another stage of advancement. Instead of having a timer, she could listen to the radio for 15 minutes, and when the radio went off then she'd have to go to sleep.

BG: Does she turn her light off then when the timer goes off?

Sally: She is very afraid of the dark.

BG: Oh, so the light is there, and she just falls asleep.

Moms Don't Do That!

Sally: A friend of mine's husband would sit up with the kids and read book after book after book. They finally got to the point where they said, "No more than four books." But then the kids got him into sitting there. So he'd bring a book in with him and sit there for hours and hours and hours. Finally he ended up going out of town. The kids expected the mother to do this. She said, "No way, moms don't do that." And they said "OK!" and went to bed.

JG: There you go! That's great. The learning is highly specific.

Sally: She was expecting a fit, and no fit. When daddy got back, she said, "Eight o'clock, the kids go to bed by themselves." And he said, "Oh!"

The kids wanted to get back into the old routine, but he said, "Nope, since I went on the trip I don't do that anymore."

"OK!"

JG: That's defining reality. Isn't it wonderful?

The Next Thing

It's one of the things that you can do. You try it. If it works, fine. You've won on the first time at bat. If it doesn't work, you go to the next thing, and the next thing, and the next thing.

One More Strategy

If you've got enough repertoire, you'll have a substantial probability of getting a good result. All you need is one more strategy than the kids have.

Chapter 14

Some Babies Are Like That

Some Babies Are Like That

JG (looking at baby): Through it all this guy just keeps checking our faces to make sure this is all just make-believe!

This is a guy who pays attention to his own internal processes, but he does check out others too.

> *Karla: How old is he now?*
>
> *Bobbi: He'll be five months next week.*
>
> *Karla: What makes him so calm like that?*
>
> *Bobbi: I don't know. This wasn't the first time around for us as parents!*
>
> *Karla: I wouldn't know what it would be like to just sit there and have a baby like that.*

JG: It's usually the sibling that does everything that this kid is not doing. It's the sibling that takes the unoccupied position.

> *Bobbi: It makes me wonder what it has to do with me.*

JG: I'm pretty well convinced that babies have an inborn neurological temperament—

> *(Baby is cooing happily)*
>
> *Karla: I think so too.*

JG: Each one is either high up or low down or intermediate, calm—and then they build their personality on that. Of course certain directions are easier because of their temperament. Part of skilled parenting involves recognizing their basic temperament.[1]

> *Spenser: We read somewhere in a book about this couple that had three ideal children—everything ideal—straight A's all through school—just incredible. So naturally everybody agreed that the parents knew what they were doing—*

Jenny: —and they were all the time giving advice—

Spenser: —and then, as the author put it, in their fortieth year the Lord delivered them a tornado!

Jenny: —and then—

Spenser: —and then they quit giving advice! Everything was the opposite! That's gotta be a super shock!

Jenny: Yes! (laughs)

Spenser: Seeing is believing to a large degree. You think, well, it's plain enough that's what we should do. It works every time—

Jenny: —we've had three tornadoes, so the opposite—

Spenser: Well, we're not going for a fourth!

Jenny: Well, they didn't plan on it, either, Spenser, so—

Spenser: True! (laughs)

We Are All Different

JG: One of the things that were left out of nineteenth century childrearing textbooks was an appreciation of the enormous diversity of human beings . . . the tremendous difference between one baby and another. You go through your college education and your psychology courses and you get a schema of a baby as being a little round pudgy thing that lies on a table and maybe has eyes to look and ears to hear but that's about it. That schema is supposed to apply to everybody, but when you get right down to it and start interacting with your own kid, you discover there are a million ways that they are different from anybody else in the world. The extent of that diversity is really limited only by your own skill in seeing differences—by your own powers of discrimination.

Kids Are Different

And some kids—their temperament is different. They actually take on the world in a different way. Some kids are really happy to sit and look and see everything that's happening. Other kids, they haven't experienced it until they've pushed it! Whatever it is, they have to get in there and mix in.

Egg On The Ceiling

BG: Well, we had only two kids and we had I'd say one of each kind.

"Part of skilled parenting involves recognizing their basic temperament."

JG: The funny thing is that our agitator was a very neat eater. He never messed his food; but next door there was a little kid who could get egg on the ceiling. One day Beth took Duane next door—I guess it was feeding time—

BG: I had a part time job. The mother next door also had a nine-month-old son, so she took care of both boys in the mornings while I went to work. The two babies ate breakfast in their high chairs. Duane was so neat that he couldn't stand it to have anything on his lips. Even when he was real little, three months old, and I would be feeding him, he'd fuss if there was any food on the outside of his mouth. I figured out what was the problem. I'd wipe his cheek so he'd have only food in his mouth and not anywhere on his lips.

Well, I can never forget the day that Robbie actually did throw his egg up on the ceiling. It was scrambled eggs and he just took it like this in the palm of his hand and made an underhand pitch and, ''Pow!'' It was stuck up on the ceiling. Duane turned right around in the high chair and looked at Robbie as if to say ''Are you crazy? What's wrong with you?''

JG: I'm convinced a lot of that is spontaneous in the sense that it is just the way their nervous system interacts with the world. One baby will react one way and another another.

Just A Pair Of Eyes

Donald: Some kids have to touch things and others can just look.

JG: A lot of little kids around three, four, five months of age will perch up on Mom's shoulder or Dad's shoulder and they will just look like a pair of eyes, just taking in the whole world with those eyes. They've gotten the degree of visual acuity so they can see across the room and everything is just new and fascinating to them. Other kids, you see them with their eyes closed a lot. They may or may not have their mouth open! You can just see that they are going in a different channel. They are experiencing life in a different way.

Won't Look Back!

Fred: Our daughter Rose, I could not carry her so that she was looking back. She would not let me walk with her if we were walking somewhere. She would have to be turned around looking forward. That was the only way that I could carry her.

Donald: Was that at a certain age or constant throughout her life?

Fred: Even right now, I can't. She's almost two, probably the same age as your son. Even now, it just feels so different when I pick her up and carry her if she stays looking that way. It just feels weird. She doesn't stay that way very long even now. She wants to turn around and see forward.

BG: So you have to carry her on your arm, so she can look forward?

Fred: No, when she sits, her butt is right on my forearm there. I just have my hand around like that and—

BG: She's looking forward, the way you're doing.

Sabrina: Timmy too is position sensitive. He sits like that too.

JG: He's really specific about it?

Sabrina: Oh, yeah! If I start to put him backwards he'll switch.

JG: He wants to be on your left side looking forward? I wonder if these are the kids like me who can't stand to ride backwards on the train.

BG: I always used to get sick to my stomach riding backwards on the train. I had to ride forwards.

Mother-Killer Babies

Karla: The babies that aren't calm like this—do they tend to be the ones that are fussier, or is that a relationship?

JG: They are harder to care for and harder to attach to.

Karla: They obviously come out that way, in my experience.

Jenny: Our first came out screaming!

Karla: It's a lot harder to bond to them. Bridget, too. I yelled, ''Take her!'' ''Take her!''

JG: ''Send this one back!''

Karla: ''Put her in the nursery. When you check me out, I might take her with me, but—''

JG: Now when the nurses put them in isolation, then you know you've got a mother-killer type.[2] They're the real tough ones.

Dawdlers

Charlene: I have a dawdler. I had a thirty-six hour labor because she just didn't want to be born!

Karla: Not in a hurry to get through life, hunh?

Jenny: Our first must have been in a hurry, he came out screaming and then he was calm and passive—

Charlene: Ours was awake all the time when she was an infant. She was calm only if I was holding her—

JG: It's a great advantage if you recognize that you're dealing with a certain inborn trend, and instead of fighting it, you go with it, even if it isn't your own style.

> *Jenny: You blame yourself for so much of it; whereas if you could just realize that you just go with the flow, you wouldn't be so stressed out over it.*

JG: People are different, right from the start.

> *Bobbi: Well, about this bonding. When Aaron was first born, for the first week—I'd gone through so much hard labor and then had a C-section—I just was not with it. I didn't have the strength to hold him unless they'd bring him to me and hold him to my breast. I would feed him and my Mother was there and she'd take him. She spent the whole time with me.*
>
> *Then a few days after I went home my mother left. The night she left I had to take over this child. That's where Aaron and I have been ever since.*
>
> *But with this one, I went in for a C-section and didn't have a hard labor. So I was a lot better after the surgery and I had him right away. He was in my arms—and it was just a better bonding experience.*

Cuddlers And Noncuddlers

JG: Well, some babies are more cuddly. The great secret is not to have a fixed rule in advance but to check it out and find out. What is this baby like? If this is a noncuddler then we're gonna have a noncuddling child here.

BG: Duane at ten days of age already was pushing against my shoulder, pushing like this, looking away, he wants to see what's going on. I would have loved to cuddle with him and the only time he came close it was to nurse and he gobbled it down. Then he was up and away. He had to see what else was happening.

JG: He turned himself off from nursing at six months, just suddenly one morning.

BG: —too busy to lie there with nothing to look at but Mom!

> *Jenny: —the same old thing!*

> *Karla: Bridget would cry whether you held her or not. She was just gonna cry and that was it. But she also didn't seem to be able to handle stimulation— touching and lights and noise. All those things kinda go together to make a certain—*

JG: Right! Low threshold, has trouble keeping it together when the stimuli get above a certain point. Those babies are harder to parent because they don't give you that nice feedback.

(Baby grins broadly)

BG: This baby over here says you're right!

JG: Right! He just loves this. He's the center of the whole circle. You can see how a baby who moves gently and has cuddly movements like this, just naturally gets talked about.

> **Karla:** *Everybody loves them. But the one that's jerking around and screaming and you can't hold them because they're so stiff—*

JG: They have their own destiny and if you parent them according to their need rather than according to some predecided program, then they will find their destiny.

I've got several kids in my practice who are not at all person oriented. They're simply not interested in people, not even in their own mother. They're interested in things. On the examining table they turn away from Mom and they look at the equipment. Maybe they catch my eye and they'll look away. They'll look at the instrument, and things like that. They're just not interested.

A Born Student Of Natural History

JG: This one little kiddy was a preschooler and somebody was trying to label the child as antisocial. The real reason was that she was a born student of natural history. At age three years what she wanted to do was go out and collect snails and frogs. One day she ran all the way down to the edge of the pond and petted a duck and she came charging back to Mom, saying, "Mom! I petted a duck! I petted a duck!"

That was something great for her. Now she's seven or eight years old and she knows all these scientific Latin and Greek names for animals and plants—

> **Jenny:** *Oh! Gee!*

JG: Does that sound familiar?

> **Spenser:** *Oh, yeah! Very much.*

JG: Right! But just try to engage her in a conversation—Mom to Kid!

Spenser: It won't work.

Jenny: I think I was like that somewhat—

JG: There you go! Example!

Jenny: I remember setting worms in a row—having the one worm tell the other, "Now you stay here, Mommy's gotta go to the store!"

JG: So the right kind of childrearing lets the child be who they are—even if it seems rather bizarre.

Won't Talk!

Karla: Is that why a child that can talk very well would not talk to just anyone?

JG: I would think so.

Karla: Bridget won't talk to just anybody, but some people will go out of their way, just determined to carry on a conversation with that child. She makes it very clear that she wants nothing to do with them, but they just persist with it.

JG: They persist and they persist and they persist—because that's "normal", right?

Karla: They think something's wrong with her because she won't talk. But I say, "She can talk, she just doesn't want to talk to you. So just leave her alone!"

JG: Just cool it! Right! Exactly!

Karla: They just come on so strong with her. If they would only just back off, she might walk up to them next week and talk to them.

JG: If adults would learn to read the body language—to read the signals—they would know. They would not have to go through this, because it's quite clear when a person doesn't want to talk to you.

Jenny: You wouldn't do that to an adult—"I want to hear you talk, come on now, talk!"

Karla: Yeah, that's pretty much what they do—or they'll try to change the subject or something. This girl came to babysit yesterday and was just determined to win Bridget over. She kept putting something on her tray. Finally Bridget just picked it up and whipped it across the room. This was a very friendly outgoing twelve year old. She just doesn't understand that you don't just run in the house and talk to Bridget.

JG: You might try it once; but if you've got your antennae tuned in, you're certainly not going to do it again.

Just Back Off

Bobbi: A man rode by my house one day. He had his little boy on the back of his bike on the seat and he stopped to chat. I'd never met him before, and when I started talking to his little boy he wouldn't answer me back.

The father spoke up and said, ''He doesn't talk a lot, but when he does, he has something important to say.'' I could tell he felt very uncomfortable and was probably having a very hard time dealing with it, so I said, ''You're probably right.'' I was uncomfortable, I didn't know how to handle it. I had never met anyone who had had a child that did not talk because they didn't want to.

Karla: They look at you in a certain way, as if to say, ''Just back off.'' They have a certain look on their face and you know you had just better leave them alone!

JG: Life is so much easier if you can pick up those signals and let yourself realize that you're getting a signal that says, ''More distance!'' or ''Less distance!'' or whatever the signal is. That way you're using feedback to adjust your reactions to the other person's reactions instead of operating out of some program in your head.

When you do that, you've got the dance down, and the other person appreciates that you are allowing them the distance. Sometimes they do a quick reversal at that point.

Karla: People just tend to shy away from her. Whereas the other kids that are running around, they're smiling and run up to you and start talking to you. People will just grab such a kid and absorb them. But they don't know how to handle one that challenges them.

What Kind Of A Plant Is She?

Nora: My three-year-old and I are just at odds so much of the time. I don't know how to deal with her.

JG: What kind of a plant is she? Is she a cactus, is she a creeping vine—? Where does the life force flow? In what direction does it flow with this child? If you can find that and tap into it, your task then will just be to sit back and avoid getting in the way.

Nora: Oh, she loves adventures! She's constantly saying, ''Tell me''—

JG: ''Tell me where we're going.''

Nora: Oh, yes!

JG: ''We're going on an adventure! You'll see something you never saw before.'' Have you ever read ''Tom Sawyer'' or ''Huckleberry Finn''? From our standpoint, with our safety orientation, we would never allow a kid to do the things that they did—to go into the cave, to go down to the Mississippi River by themselves. Those things are just utterly terrifying to us, but kids read those stories with fascination and delight. So how can we give them that spirit of pioneering?

Nora: Good question!

JG: It's still possible to let them experience that without imminent physical danger. Sometimes if you can set it up so that they can even feel the danger without actually being in danger, so that they can have the thrill of knowing that they met and conquered something a little scary. Believe me, if there's a little scare in the situation, there's a lot less hyperactivity. As Samuel Johnson used to say, it focusses your attention wonderfully.

Nora: Well, she's telling me proudly, ''I'm holding your hand, Mom. See how I've learned to hold hands?'' This was last night, going to the movies.

JG: She's being taught to hold hands. Actually, probably the best way to learn that is to get separated on a long walk, a nature walk, in a park, and have her desperately clutch for your hand and say, ''Mom, I need to hold on to you.'' That's the lesson you want her to learn.

Won't Eat Peas

JG: Our son still won't eat peas, and he's thirty-three years old. He didn't like them the first time and he still doesn't like them. And that's his prerogative.

BG: He was three months old and I tried him on peas and he just went, ''Poo!'' I think it was partly the consistency and partly the taste. Recently he came home on a visit and I said, ''Duane, I'm just curious. Do you ever eat peas, or do you like peas?'' He said, ''No, I hate them. I can't stand them. I don't know why.'' He couldn't explain it. But he eats other green vegetables. It's no big deal.

JG: And it's his constitutional right as a free citizen to eat what he wishes and to not eat what he doesn't wish.

Donald: Even President Bush didn't eat broccoli.

JG: Right. This issue is so fundamental and the nutritionists just seem to walk right over it. There is an issue of autonomy. Who decides? And there can only be one answer. The person decides—but there's nothing to prevent you from putting some squash in the cookies.

Infant Preferences

Now the textbooks say little or nothing about infant preferences, but once you begin to tune in to what your infant is signalling, once you begin to actually notice the feedback you are getting, then you will realize that the infant is registering preferences all the time. Some infants are happy just to be warm and dry and fed. Some don't even care very much about being dry. Some are even indifferent to hunger for long periods when they're interested in something.

But for other babies it makes a great deal of difference whether a thing is done in one way or another. Some hate the taste of Brand X vitamins and love Brand Y, or vice versa. Some babies hate shampoos and love baths. Some hate baths and love shampoos. Some hate both. Some love both. Some babies won't take mother's milk out of a bottle, but they will take cows' milk out of a bottle. Others won't take anything but juice from a bottle. They have a strong sense of what's proper in this world and they want things their way. It's not a Freudian thing, it's just their sense of what's proper.

My heartfelt recommendation is: If it doesn't matter, if it's not a life and death issue, let babies have their preference. Babies very quickly learn that you are willing to do that, and you thereby avoid the early onset of power struggles.[3] They really know you are on their side when you let them have their choice. As they get older, they will repay you by exhibiting the same kind of behavior towards you. Why not let infants learn that they can get a significant fraction of those preferences satisfied?

Chapter 15

The Bear In The Bathroom

What Is Discipline, Really?

JG: Now this whole question of discipline: The word "discipline" can have two meanings. It can mean submitting to external control. It can mean internal control. The kind of discipline we are concerned with here is internal control. Some parents want to force the child to exercise internal control. That's a contradiction in terms. Outside pressure to coerce internal control. If the child yields to the outside pressure, it's not internal control. So the child resists the outside pressure in order to preserve his internal control. The parents then escalate the outside pressure and the child becomes panicky, thinking he is going to be forced to give up his internal control of his own life. He is fighting desperately to preserve what the parents say they want him to exercise, but when he exercises it they put more pressure on him to give it up. A double bind—the child loses either way.[1] He has to make a choice but both choices are wrong. If a child is brought up in this way it's not surprising that as an adult he or she may be seriously confused about what discipline and internal control are really all about.

Let Them Make Some Mistakes

Mothers sometimes ask me, when their little babies are only a few weeks or months old, whether they should let their babies have two ounces or three ounces or four ounces of formula at each feeding. They are thinking in terms of calories. They have heard something about the number of fat cells or whatever the latest theory of obesity is, and they want to prevent their child from becoming obese or predisposed to obesity. I tell them to be sure to put more in the bottle than their child can possibly take and to let them work on that bottle until they stop drinking and press their lips together and shake their head "No." In that way the child learns that they are in charge of their own intake. No one is holding out on them or rationing them. There is plenty available, and they must consult with their own internal appetite standards

207

to find out when to stop. They learn to pay attention to their own internal regulatory mechanisms, which after all are far more precise and far more sophisticated than the most advanced nutrition theories; and which further-more are specifically tailored to the needs of this particular person at this particular time and under these particular circumstances. That internal reference standard is always available. And the habit of listening to that inner voice, that inner standard, that's the true meaning of discipline—self-regulation, self-control.

You teach a child internal control by allowing them to make wrong decisions. You set it up so that their wrong decisions don't result in loss of life or limb, but you allow them to make those decisions for themselves.

Natural Consequences

BG: I think we need to keep the discrimination between discipline and punishment. Discipline means, ''Like a disciple''—to learn and do it better—whereas punishment is often what actually occurs when people say ''I had to discipline my child.'' They use the word ''discipline'' but they are actually punishing their child. Then there is a third way, which is to just let consequences help the child learn. This is the kind of discipline where they just get the natural consequences.

To Stay In The Lines Or Not (Options)

> *Sally: I was going to say: There are people that do go in the lines and they have their uses, and then there are people that aren't in the lines and they have their uses.*

JG: Who's got the most freedom? It's the person who can stay in the lines or move out of the lines—in other words, the person who's got the most options.[2] What we're talking about is providing the kind of experiences for our kids that will enable them to have the largest range of options[3] so that they can pick the option that is most appropriate for the particular situation.

How To Change
Someone Else's Behavior

That means we ourselves have to have a lot of options because it's kind of hard to foster variety and creativity in someone if you yourself don't have the variety necessary to elicit it. So that's what this is all about. The way you get somebody to change their behavior is to change your own behavior.[4]

REALITY TESTING
"If a child tells you there is a bear in the bathroom,
then there is a bear in the bathroom."

You've got to have the repertoire, you've got to know what to change, and you've got to have a list of things you can do.

Respect The Developmental Level

Now you obviously don't ask for internal control that is beyond the developmental level of the child. That merely sets the child up for a repeated series of failures which will eventually teach him that he is an inadequate human being.

You don't ask a toddler to keep his hands off the new baby. You just keep your body between the two of them at all times. You know a toddler just doesn't have impulse control. Why set him up to fail?

If there's a bear in the bathroom or a dragon under the bed, you don't start a sermon on lying. You help the child deal with the dragon. Can he help it if you as an adult have lost touch with your own primary process thinking and don't notice the monsters in the room?

Sphincter Control

The general principle is: Respect the Developmental Level of the Child. There are several areas where this is really fundamental. One is in the area of Sphincter Control—wetting, stooling. That control doesn't come in until a certain age. It's utterly useless to try to get sphincter control if the kid is not developmentally up to the level of having sphincter control. That's probably self-evident to this group, but not all adults are aware of the fact that it's very difficult to train an eight weeker, or an eleven monther, or even maybe a fifteen monther to be toilet trained either for bladder or for bowels. So, if you find that you are trying to do something, trying to achieve a result and the child is consistently failing even though the child seems to be willing, ask yourself, ''Are they really developmentally up to the point where they can do it?''

Impulse Control

This applies also to Impulse Control. There's a tradition in this country that everything is done by will power; that if you just put your mind to it, you can do it. But a child at the age of two does not have full impulse control. You may tell them that they will be severely punished if they do X but if they get the impulse to do X, it may just pop right out, even though they know they are going to be severely punished. So it obviously doesn't make sense to demand impulse control from a little person that doesn't have it.

This is particularly important in regard to sibling rivalry, jealousy. The new baby comes along, and the two-year-old toddler—some friends told us of their experience with their second child. The first day they brought the new baby home, the older child toddled right up to the bassinet and in the flash of an eye he had two fingers out and aimed straight for the baby's eyes. And he had never even seen a baby before!! Something put that impulse there, and whammo! They just barely pushed him out of the way

"I demand impulse control!"

in time. Now, to scold a kid for that is utterly useless. He can't stop that impulse; or if he does, it will be at the cost of a really traumatic prohibition. Still the impulse will come through, because at two years of age they don't have that control. So the way you handle that is with a modified form of Environmental Control. You keep your body between them at all times. If they are in the same room together, you are in that room and you are close enough that if the impulse pops out, you can just bump them, interrupt the movement so that they get pushed aside. You don't scold them, you don't punish them, you just bump 'em and they understand that one hundred percent. They know that you trust them completely, but you also trust that they don't have impulse control and therefore they don't have to take upon themselves the impossible burden of trying to give you a behavioral sequence that they can't control.

BG: It's real important to maintain that environmental control even if you are sleeping or otherwise occupied. We believe in putting hooks and eyes at the tops of doors in order to protect a small infant from an older child or from pets. For many parents I've recommended that they put a screen door in the doorway of the bedroom of the newborn, with a hook on it, so that sound and air can get through but dogs and cats or children can't get to that infant when you're not physically present. The newborn infant has to be protected.

JG: Impulse Control is very unreliable. Some kids, after the first time they burn themselves, will have pretty good impulse control about fire, because they can see that it is hot. That's one of the first things. With a kid at age three, I wouldn't count on that very much. At age four, maybe a few simple things. Again, what I'm suggesting is, you titrate it to the level of your own child's abilities, because if you ask them to perform at a level where they can't, it's just like that college course that was a little too tough for you. They're going to feel like a failure. So you stay at their level and take away from them that terrible burden of trying to perform above their ability.

Providing A Secure Reality

BG: The child gets a sense of security from knowing that the parents are in charge.

JG: They know!! They know you're doing that for them. They know that nonverbally. You don't have to say a word.

BG: —and that a parent won't let them do something that's bad. A lot of parents that we talk to figure they'll traumatize their kid if they prevent them from doing something, but it's just the opposite. The child feels secure if they have the confidence that their parents will not let them do something out of bounds.

JG: That they will physically protect them.

The Bear In The Bathroom
(Reality Testing)

JG: Item Three is the so-called Reality Testing. If the child tells you there is a bear in the bathroom, then there is a bear in the bathroom! You enter their world and you don't give them a sermon on lying, you help to protect them from the bear. You join them in fighting off the bear.

BG: I remember in one of our recent classes there was a father that had had six children, and the little one was scared about something that had to do with a hole in the bathroom wall and the father had just gotten all through the whole routine about, ''Well, I'll protect you. Nothing is going to come out of that hole there in the bathroom wall''—and the older sibling butted in and said, ''Yes, but Daddy, snakes can come out of that hole in the wall!''

JG: Now, that was an impulse! Impulses pop out like snakes from a hole—and that's why kids have that anxiety about snakes and holes. OK, so Item One is: Respect the Developmental Level of the Child, particularly around these four things: Sphincter Control, Impulse Control, Reality Testing and Sharing. If the child is inhabiting a world where there are bears and monsters and dinosaurs, you join them in that world and you will find that you have much greater power to help them than if you try to tell them it's not real. Actually—I don't know how many of you are aware of this, but some time you can try this out and find out how many adults actually still—they don't see monsters but they know that there are such things as monsters. That world of childhood never totally disappears. It only goes underground. Just watch a program on TV!

It's there! So instead of trying to get rid of that, which is a normal part of human development and is the basis for creativity, you join it. Just join it and work with it and you can explain, ''Yes, that bear in the bathroom is willing to stay in there when it's daytime, and the child might say, ''Well, he's gonna come in my bed when I'm in the bedroom,'' and you can say something like, ''Yes, but bears don't like cookies and cream and they're scared of bedclothes—''[5] You can work with the child. There's a certain delight in manipulating reality. You can actually make it fun and detoxify the situation.

What The Monster Is

Kim: My daughter's really afraid of monsters. She's so scared of them—and not only before Hallowe'en—and we talk about bad monsters and good monsters because Sesame Street has Cookie Monster—and that we have a rule that no monsters are allowed in our house because they have dirty feet.

JG: Now you're talking! That's right!

Kim: We'll talk about it, that there's no monsters allowed in our house because Mommy won't let 'em in, because they have dirty feet. She still gets frightened about monsters every once in a while, but she knows that once she goes in the house, there's no monsters there. Cookie Monsters, things like that, but no bad monsters.

JG: Well, we all know what the monster is.[6] (Pause) You mean you don't know what the monster is!

(Child vocalizes loudly)

JG: You really don't know what the monster is!

Woman: The unknown?

JG: It's the child's fear of being destroyed because of the rage they feel at being asked to curb their spontaneous impulses in order to adapt to the world. I thought everybody knew that!!

(Baby is yelling loudly and indignantly)

JG: That's what the authorities say it is. But maybe it's just a monster! There ya go! The baby picked it up. Their radar is incredible.

Neil: We used monster spray! The reason we bought this house is, it's in a neighborhood where there's no monsters. We checked things out real carefully.

Kim: There's no monsters there so we thought we would buy the house.

May I Borrow Your Ferrari?

JG: In regard to the fourth item, sharing. First comes sole possession, then comes sharing, then comes the state beyond sharing, for which there is no name because there is no issue at all. In most households the telephone doesn't "belong" to anyone, it's just there to use. This is actually the original state of the infant before the origin of the idea of property and possession. When they are in the peak of possessiveness, asking them to share their toys or their ice cream is a lot like having your neighbor ask if they can borrow your sports car. No way!

Stretching The Little Old Umbilical Cord
(Autonomy Versus Dependency)

JG: Stretching the Little Old Umbilical Cord.[7] That's a strategy that's useful at fifteen months of age, age eighteen months, at three years, four years, sometimes even a little longer than that. That's using physical separation from the child.

> *Karla: Well, can you give an example?*

JG: Well, there's a situation in the office where the little kid has taken off his shoes and socks and he's finished with the exam and he's gotten quite comfortable and now he doesn't want to go home. He doesn't want to put his shoes and socks on.

At that point sometimes I will suggest, "Why don't you just leave your shoes and socks off because you don't have to go home with Mom and Dad. Let them go home by themselves."

> *Cora: We use that all the time!*

JG: When you say, "Mom and Dad can leave. You can stay here. You don't want to put your shoes and socks on and go with Mom and Dad," then with every step that the parents take towards that door, the umbilical cord is being stretched and pretty soon it pulls the little kid. That's Stretching the Little Old Umbilical Cord. With older kids you may have to put them on a transatlantic plane to get that effect.

BG: One other little kid wouldn't do it. He wouldn't put his shoes and socks on—this was in January—and so Mom says, "Well, OK, that's all right, you just come along anyway. I'll carry your shoes in my bag." On they went, out the front door, and it wasn't too long before they were all back in real quick. He wanted his shoes and socks on.

JG: A different strategy and a good one: The Less and Less Desirable Alternative, or maybe Consequences.

> *Morilla: That is interesting, though. I think it's the same idea, but—sometimes if you simply do let an older child exist on their own somewhere where there is no mother or father influence, they suddenly become wonderful human beings.*

> *Karla: College!*

> *Kay: Really! I live in the same town where I went to college and I stayed home one semester and it was horrible, because there would be nights when I didn't*

have homework and I'd watch TV and they were saying, ''Well, why aren't you doing your homework?'' I didn't have any homework!

Then—I was probably doing something that was driving them nuts, too— then my Dad said, ''Well, why don't you just go get a dorm and live on campus?'' And it was great. We got along really really well then, once I got out.

Louise: *With little kids too—Kyle is wonderful at other people's houses!*

JG: Yeah!

Louise: *He's wonderful in school. The problem is just in our own house.*

JG: So you know that he's not bad, that he's good.

Louise: *Teacher loves him, everyone—all of the kids like him. He's always with the neighbors, behaves very well, never fights.*

JG: You can shrink down the amount of time you spend at home.

Louise: *Now, it's wonderful when he can play outside all day.*

BG: Especially in summertime, you can do that.

Louise: *Yeah, winter is worse—closing up.*

BG: When we first came up with this idea about stretching the umbilical cord, I had a dream that same night about it. I dreamed that the umbilical cord was mine and I was swinging it like a lariat—we mean the one on the kid, that's the one.

JG: There is an invisible umbilical cord that connects the kid to the parents and you've probably all had this experience if you've had toddlers, that toddlers like to dart away—they like to run away. They'll even get out of sight. They could be kidnapped. You say, ''Come back, come back!'' Then you scold them for not coming back. You argue with them about it. They have not come to the end of their umbilical cord yet. So what you do is, you give them the opportunity to find out where the end of the umbilical cord is. And the best place to do this is—Sleeping Bear Dunes!

Lost In The Dunes

You post your lookout, which is either the spouse or a relative or a friend, far enough down the beach so that you know that there will be an adult nearby so that we're not talking about physical danger, OK? Then you take a nice walk on the beach. At twilight. You let them run ahead or lag behind and you let that distance increase.

There will come a point at which the umbilical cord tenses up. That's the length of the umbilical cord. It may be five hundred yards and the child may be a mere speck, but of course you have your lookouts located nearby. Maybe just a speck on the horizon, but at some point the child is gonna realize, "I'm two years old. I'm alone on this huge beach. I can't see my parents, and I don't know where I am. It's getting dark and I want my supper." This brings home to them in a very basic way—in a nonverbal way—some of the basic existential elements of being a child. "I really am dependent for my life on my mother and father. If I get too far away from them, I really am in danger of losing my life." A child has to know this, just as they have to know that the parents are more powerful than they are. They must know this. Otherwise they will engage in daredevil behavior.

Leaving The Scene

Now it doesn't have to be Sleeping Bear Dunes. It can be the supermarket.

Henry: I was just thinking, a grocery aisle or something like that—that in fact, as they get separated, you can go around the aisles and keep track of them and know where they are and everything and there will be a period of time when they don't realize that they've lost contact but then they will realize that they have lost contact and, "God! Let's get out of here and find Mom and Dad."

JG: You know where they are but they don't know where you are.

Sally: Brett had gone around the end of the building—he always was assuming that I would follow him and I thought he was behind me. I went through the house—and it was just because that was the way I was going—I went through the house and I saw him out the window. He looked back over his shoulder and then just completely fell apart—screaming. For about three months after that he never let me out of his sight.

Nobody Move!

Mimi: I made a scene at the department store once. Heidi just kinda wandered and went under the clothes rack. The shirts were hanging to the ground—and I said, "NOBODY MOVE!!" "NOW I'M SERIOUS!!!"

JG: It's an elemental fear, isn't it? Parents know what that is. The child has to experience it under your tutelage in a titrated form so that it's manageable.

Woman: Otherwise it's play.

JG: Exactly. You can also use Leaving The Scene for your own mental health, if another responsible person is available to take over.

Chapter 16
Meaning Of A Tantrum
(A Higher Level Of Control)

I'm Outlasting Her, Thanks!
(Natural Consequences)

Esther: Before I had a child, I always used to be very disturbed whenever I was in a shopping center or a restaurant and somebody's kid was screaming and throwing a fit—

Theodore: "Can't they control that kid?"

Morilla: "You can't control that child?"

Esther: One day I had Dora with me at a store where I needed to get something and she was determined she was gonna play "Peeks" with the clothes racks. She would go into the clothes racks and then stand in one of them and yell, "Peek!" I was supposed to come find her. Great place to play. I got tired of the game real fast and I said, "You have to stay with me," and she started just screaming and I thought, "Well, OK, if you want to scream, that'll be fine, you still have to stay right here." People started gathering around and staring at her—

Priscilla: —and they stared at you!

Esther: Yeah. They stared at me and I just smiled and said, "I'm buying socks today," and—"I'm outlasting her, thanks!"

She sat on the floor and she lay there and she kicked and screamed and had a fit. Finally she noticed that there was this group of people around us that were all staring. She looked up and her face changed. I think she suddenly became embarrassed or something—I don't know if small children feel it—but she quit and she's never done it again.

It was really interesting and I wondered if a lot of the things that had happened before were because I was uncomfortable with her being noisy.

JG: Well, you just let her experience the natural consequences of what she did. A titrated experience of—not gravity, but social reality.

219

Motherrr! You Shouldn't Do That!

JG: There was another Mom who handled that situation where the child was having a tantrum in the supermarket—this had happened several times—you remember this one, Mimi.

Mimi: Yes, and I'm starting to see in the stores now that they've stopped putting candy at the checkout counter.

Priscilla: Which stores are those?

Mimi: Quite a few of them. Most of the supermarkets now are stopping that—

JG: Of course, if the kid is really into it, they'll do it with the canned spinach. It doesn't make any difference. They throw their tantrum right on the floor anyway.

This Mom decided, "OK, this is it. I am going to use a strategy that really works." Actually I think she just thought of it on the spur of the moment. She stood over the child and looked down—because people were gathering and whispering, "Child abuse," and that kind of thing—

Priscilla: "They shouldn't bring them shopping—"

JG: You know how it is. She looked down and she said, "Gosh, that looks like so much fun, I think I'll do it myself!" She was a good-sized lady, too— and she got down on the floor in front of all these people and began kicking and screaming. The kid leaped up in utter horror—

Cora: Mortified!

JG: —and looked down at her mother and said, "Motherrr! You shouldn't do that!"[1]

Plopping On Their Perch
(Providing A More Horrible Example)

JG: Now that's Plopping on their Perch. That's taking over their turf. It's also Providing a More Horrible Example. Believe me, that's powerful.

BG: I think all the people around them in the store were laughing.

JG: The kid was utterly horrified that her mother lacked all self-restraint. From then on, that kid kept a very close eye on her Mom.

Cora: You don't know when she might do it again!

Be Unpredictable!

JG: You never know! She'll be careful about that in the future. OK! So the general principle here is: Be Unpredictable!

> *Cora: You always hear that you should be predictable so the child can be secure—*

JG: It's the flexibility to be predictable when that's useful and to be unpredictable when that's useful—that's what we're aiming at.

> *Theodore: Well, I hear what you're saying about control, but that's only one objective in raising a child. Another is, helping them learn, and things like that, and so I guess I'm getting concerned. There's a lot of emphasis on control here. That's not exactly what I was interested in in this course. That's just one aspect, so I hope you're gonna emphasize those aspects too.*

A Smooth Dance Rather Than A Confrontation

JG: I think as you go along you will see that in fact there is a method in this madness. But most parents who come to the class—some come just because they want to learn something. But many are experiencing that panicky feeling, "How can I ever control my child? How can I teach him or her how to be a civilized human being?"—which is basically what's meant by the idea of control. Just as a matter of my own strategy, I want to convey to you that you can in fact get some of what you want.

I hope to show you that a lot of what you want really isn't in the best interests of the child, so you can give up trying for those things, and that means a lot less effort and struggle. Then we'll get to the point where the whole thing will be more like a smooth dance than a confrontation.

Cognitive Dissonance

BG: It's like a fish doesn't know it's in water because that's all it's ever known. Maybe some of them will leap out into the air, but they fall right back in and they don't really know that this is the way their world is. We have all been raised in a similar way in that we don't know that there's any different way to do things, so we can't see it. We feel frustrated or we feel conflicted when somebody starts telling us, "There really are different ways to do this." You may be experiencing some of that cognitive dissonance.

JG: Cognitive Dissonance! Because here we are saying things that are so foreign to what you have always known and been taught.

Esther: Right! For instance, you're saying punishment is the fifty-first strategy, but I would imagine that most of us were raised—maybe I'm assuming too much—

Cora: The first! Number One!

Esther: —that that is the first—or only!

Priscilla: The only one!

Esther: And it's hard to go against that saying in that way.

"The aim is NOT to force the child to do exactly what you want."

A Higher Level Of Control

JG: This is a method of giving you some control, so that you can get comfortable with using methods that are not coercive. We're not aiming at coercion of the child, but rather being able to control the situation in the larger sense. I hope I will get that across as we go along, because the aim is not to force the child to do exactly what you want.

These are strategies that in effect open the door for the child to grow and develop according to their own spontaneous inner impulses. They begin to understand that you're not going to let them get into real bad trouble, because you have these undecipherable ways of helping them stay on course. That's a higher level of control than simply saying, "Do what I say! Do it because I say it—or else!"

Dolphins That Have Tantrums

But first I want to tell you about the dolphins that have tantrums.[2] Are you aware of this?

> *Mimi: Is this another story?*

JG: Right! Karen Pryor, twenty years ago, wrote a breastfeeding book. This is THE Karen Pryor. She quit that career and became a dolphin trainer. She became an animal trainer and developed a series of strategies for dealing with animals and eventually became a trainer of animal trainers. She would show them how to do the things that she had learned.

One of the things that she mentions in this book of hers entitled *Don't Shoot The Dog* is that the moment before you have learned something new is a moment of extreme frustration. She has seen this repeatedly with the dolphins. They just have a tantrum, literally leaping out of the water, splashing their whole body, throwing water all around, getting the trainer wet, and then it dawns on them, "Oh! That's what's wanted. That's what I'm supposed to do."

In that moment they have moved up one step. They have gone from a stage of not knowing to a stage of knowing. They have gone from not knowing how to do this particular performance up to the level of knowing how to do it. This is true for kids too. If you see a kid being really frustrated in their homework or something like that, just tell yourself, "That's the learning tantrum, the Prelearning Dip."

> *Morilla: So the idea is—the only way that you can really learn something new is . . . sort of . . . to accept the fact that this leap that you have to go over is, that part of the old can't be true any more.*

JG: And that's real rough—

> *Louise: —especially for little children who are learning something new every day.*

Having A Comfortable Tantrum
(Making It Mom's Thing)

JG: —and a tantrum is a legitimate power tactic for a little kid to use. After all, they don't have so many tactics that they can use. A tantrum is a very straight expression of their frustration. But you can point out that they haven't got it down quite right. They need a little more practice. They could pound a little more with their fists, yell a little louder. In fact, maybe it would be a good idea to have a little regular tantrum practice two or three times a day.[3]

Some of their tantrums are probably a part of learning and if you look at them positively that way, your response will be quite different to a child's tantrum. Instead of saying, "Don't be such a stinker, don't lie there screaming and crying," you can say, "Oh, you're having a tantrum, aren't you? Are you really comfortable there on the floor? Can I get you anything?

BG: "Would you like a pillow to kick against instead?"

JG: Amazingly enough, if you can get them through a few of those tantrums without actually reinforcing the tantrum behavior, they will move to that next level where they understand—

> *Kay: It works. I took your advice sometime about three weeks ago, when Tony was having lots of tantrums. When I got down on the floor with him he looked at me and rolled his eyes like I was the craziest person in the whole world. Now, he's gotten used to me doing that sort of thing where I scream louder, so now I'm having to be creative and come up with something else. 'Cause now he'll get mad at me and he'll say, "Don't say that. That's a bad word." If I say, "You can't do this," he'll get mad at me and start cussing, so I need to come up with something else now.*

The Sweetest Thing

JG: What does a person hate more than anything else?

> *Kay: Well, being told "No."*

JG: Being told they can't do something must rank right up there on anybody's list. And what does a person like more than anything else? To feel free to do their own sweet will. At least it's right up there near the top of the list. So, you try to build your interventions on the child being allowed to do their own sweet will and then guide that behavior so you can get some of what you want, too.

Checkout Line Tantrums

Kay: I don't get a chance to go shopping very much and usually I have to take Tony with me. I had to pay the bill yesterday. I had my check already made out because I knew that we weren't going to be able to stand in line very long, but we weren't even able to stand in line that long. He ran off and he was gone. I managed to find him and drag him back and still we had to wait in line. Then he ran off again and I got him back, and this happened about three times. Finally, I just got frustrated and I gave him a spanking and then it just went downhill from there. He just lost it.

I managed to pay my bill and just left. I was angry and he fell asleep in the car. I knew he was tired, but there was nothing I could do about it at the time. How could I have prevented it or calmed him down long enough for me to get the bill paid, so he could get to the car without being a total wreck?

JG: You might not have been able to do that. There are some situations where the cards are stacked against you, and where you might run through all of your strategies and still not come up with something that works. Taking a toddler to the supermarket takes a certain amount of courage. It's a bit of a setup.

Knock Them Out With Novelty
(Be Unpredictable)

BG: How old is he?

Kay: He's two and a half.

BG: Sometimes when they're in that kind of a boxed-in situation and if you can introduce something that's so novel that he'll be completely blotto from the novelty—for example say, ''Tony, I'm gonna put you in my Jerry-carrier and carry you on my back while we go pay this bill. You can be way up high and see other people and look down on the other people.'' That would be so different that he would probably be able to get through that period of time without . . .

Kay: I thought I had taken care of all the bases. I knew he was going to be hungry so I fed him first, and then we did some things that he wanted to. He had to get his hair cut and he had to sit still for a little bit, and then we did something fun and managed to get through that. But then there was this one last thing that had to be done, and we just couldn't make it. He just lost it.

JG: That'll happen a lot. Sounds like you pushed your luck!

It's Time For Your Tantrum (Anticipation, Or Messing Up The Sequence)

Vance: There's a certain unconventional quality to your interventions. I can imagine doing things more at home, in the privacy of my own back yard than at a supermarket. I didn't feel too bad that you knew that I was biting my child's sweater. I would be more inhibited doing that in a supermarket.

Jill: That's when the kids really test you, though—but I just couldn't bring myself to lie down on the floor.

Dan: You must shop at the supermarket near our house. The floor's pretty dirty.

Jill: I would be afraid that they'd call the police.

BG: I think if you lie down and act out, I think most grownups could kinda figure that out.

Charlene: I won't go down that aisle!

Jenny: I'll get along without that cereal!

JG: There are ways you can vary this. For example, as you go in the store, you can say, ''Oh, I think you're ready—this is where we have our tantrums, isn't it? Would you like to get on the floor now and have your tantrum?''

BG: ''We can do it right here!''

JG: It messes up their sequence. Often that's just enough to prevent the tantrum from happening. Who wants to have a tantrum on command, at Mother's pleasure?
But if they do have a tantrum, then they've had it right there at the beginning and you can take them home and start over.

Spenser: Or maybe at home you can say, ''Well, we're getting ready to go to the supermarket, let's practice!''

JG: That's it! That's how you use the strategy called Anticipation. That's the thing I love about this group, you folks generate the solutions, I don't have to do anything!

> *Sally: What you do is take advantage of the 24-hour supermarket. You go at 3:00 in the morning, when everybody's asleep. You go in and give them a banana—*

JG: —you wake them up at 3 AM and tell them it's time to go to the supermarket! Do that three times and I guarantee you won't have any problems!

BG: Say, "This is a safe time to have a tantrum,"—three in the morning. Right?

JG: It's kind of like with pants-wetting. As the little kid runs to the front door to go out and play, you say, "Oh, wait a minute! I just remembered you wet your pants when you go outside, you better stay in." Then you let them assure you they won't wet their pants if they go out.

The Worst Tantrum In The World

JG: Beth, do you remember the story about the little girl that confided in her grandmother? She said, "Tomorrow, I'm gonna throw the worst tantrum in the world for Mommy."

BG: This couple were coming to our parenting class, one winter a few years ago. We were having classes in the evenings in those days. They were coming because they had a four year old who was a true holy terror. I mean she calculated how to get her mother's goat, how to get everybody's goat.

The grandmother was babysitting for them while they were coming to this class. One night the girl told the grandmother, "Tomorrow I'm gonna throw the biggest tantrum in the world. I'm really gonna fix mother tomorrow." She was mad because Mother was going out to the class.

The parents picked their kids up after the class and went home. After the grandmother was sure the kids had gone to sleep, she called the parents on the phone and told the mother that this is what the kid had said, that she was gonna have a big tantrum the next day and really mess up and fix her Mom. So the Mom and the Dad knew this might be coming and they had had enough help with us in the class that they figured out several different strategies.

Well, this four-year-old had a habit of not getting dressed to get on the bus for morning kindergarten and then Mom would have to drive her in the car or there was generally a hassle. The next morning this kid started pulling this trick. She wasn't dressed when the bus came, so the mother just waved out the door, "Sorry, she's not ready! It's OK!" and didn't say anything. The kid was quite surprised that there wasn't a big fuss. She was running around nude in the house, just being obnoxious. So the mother very calmly went and turned the thermostat down to sixty—

JG: Without telling the child about it—

BG: —without saying anything! She acted as though nothing had happened. She asked, "Are you going to have your breakfast?" "No!" "Oh, OK."

So then she went about her day's tasks and put a sweater on herself and on the other child and proceeded through her morning routine. She responded socially to the kid but did not get in any way upset or berate her in any way for not having her clothes on, acting as if this was perfectly normal, to run around all day without your clothes.

She noticed the child's skin getting a little mottled and blue, and goose bumps all over, and shivering. In fact, she did a few things that would exacerbate this. She took the younger child and went down into the basement and spent a good bit of time down there where it was a lot colder and did some laundry and a few things like that so the four year old was even more uncomfortable. Not a word, no berating or complaining. Around eleven thirty or so, the kid went upstairs and got her clothes on. The mother didn't say, "Boo!" she just went and turned the thermostat up again to a comfortable temperature.

They had also had hassles around lunch and a few other things. Mother forgot to fix lunch. Nobody had any lunch and pretty soon the little girl said very politely, "Mother, I believe I'm ready for lunch now." "Oh! Is that right? Well, OK. We're going to have such and such and such." Not a complaint, nothing was said. They all had their lunch and it was very pleasant. This went on for the rest of the day. That kid quit doing any of those tantrums.

The next morning she got up and got dressed, got on the bus, with no fuss about what she was going to eat or what she was going to wear or anything, and it was a one-time cure. They couldn't believe it. Then they came to the next week's class, and we told them there was bound to be a relapse, not to get too high about this, because she was going to test it again.

JG: Usually the relapse is very brief.

Kids Who Won't Eat

Louise: I like this forgetting about lunch and dinner. Maybe we should do that. Kyle has a terrible time and we really have to make him eat.

Kay: Oh! really? We don't have to ask our kid to come at all.

JG: They don't have to eat if they don't want to. Just tell them, ''You don't have to eat if you don't want to.''

Louise: But he wakes up in the middle of the night and he tells us he's hungry.

JG: Right! And you can wake him up twenty minutes earlier and offer him some food. He'll know what it feels like to be waked out of deep sleep and offered food?

Louise: I need sleep myself!

Grady: If we woke him up twenty minutes early he'd leap out of bed and say, ''Yeah! What's cooking?''

Cora: ''Let's turn on the TV and how about some records!''

JG: After the sixth time of being wakened forty-five minutes after falling asleep, which is that moment when it's most painful, something will begin to click. I can guarantee you.

BG: You're taking charge of the behavior instead of being the victim.

JG: Now Mom is in charge. It's one thing to wake up hungry and call for Mom to feed you. It's quite another thing to have Mom wake you up out of a sound sleep and say, ''Time to eat.''

Eating Versus Control

JG: Nothing is ever just one thing. In regard to children's eating patterns, in America it's almost always contaminated with the control issue. Who's going to be in charge of my sphincters? There's only one possible answer to that. The kid has to be in charge of their own sphincters. They have to be the ones to decide what they eat and how much; but you can determine such things as when the food appears and when it disappears. That's your prerogative. You can put the food on the table four times a day, six times a day, whatever it is. Then after twelve minutes you can make it disappear, and there can't be any argument about that because you're in control of that.

Liver And Peas

Donald: I think if you do try and force the peas or whatever, I mean my—one of my childhood memories is liver!!

Sabrina: Liver!!

Donald: I would have to sit at the table and eat my liver. Every time we had liver, I would chew it up and put it in the back of my mouth and ask to be excused. I would run into the bathroom and spit it out.

Sabrina: (laughs)

JG: Yes!!

Donald: To this day, I won't go near liver and I'm sure it probably still tastes just as bad as it did then. I won't go near it!! There's no way!! I think that's the kind of thing that can happen with—"You gotta eat your peas"—or whatever. I can remember a lot of foods I hated when I was growing up because there was a control issue at our table. "You need to eat this or else you're not going to get any dessert," and all that. It's like—I rediscovered a lot of those foods. I used to hate peas, and I love peas now—and vegetables. I used to hate vegetables, absolutely hated them and I love vegetables now. I think part of that process was because of the forcing issue. I really do.

JG: You've gotten past the control issue and now you can actually enjoy what you like.

Donald: Right! I still won't touch lima beans. I don't care. That one wasn't a control issue!

Self-Service

BG: One family that we knew had the kids pass the bowls around and serve themselves. They started out with paper plates with three or four sections in the plate. The child had to strain a point to serve up more food than would fit in one of those sections. The kid would dole out a few carrots that would fit into this one place and that was enough carrots. When the next bowl came around, they'd put that item in the next little compartment. It was amazing how much those kids really put away. They would ask for second and third servings of food. I couldn't believe my eyes. I didn't say anything while we were eating but I said afterwards, "You should have your mealtimes televised as models of how to do it." There was no fuss, no discussion, just, "Pass the peas, please!"

Wrinkly Chicken

JG: Now Susanna's mother had a slightly different problem. Her two girls, who were named Susanna and Leora and were just two years apart in age, worked as a team to frustrate Mom. They just didn't like the way their food was served at mealtime.

Louise: Hmm!

JG: They wouldn't eat their sandwich because it wasn't cut just exactly in the middle.

Cora: Ohhh!

JG: They wouldn't drink their juice because the two glasses weren't just exactly equally full. They even refused delicious fried chicken because the skin was all wrinkly.

The Real Value Of A Tape-Recording

BG: I had previously suggested that the parents tape-record their mealtimes and then just listen to the tape—in the privacy of their own home, of course—after the kids had gone to bed. They reported back in class that it was even more horrible than they remembered—constant bickering and arguing about food and eating. By the way, that's the real value of a tape recording—it gives you feedback about how you really sound to the kids, about how you really are interacting with them.

JG: To Mom's consternation, I agreed with the girls that they really ought not to eat such food. I suggested to Mom that she continue to prepare it as she always had done, but at the last moment of offering it she was to jerk it back and discover the flaw for herself: "Oh! I'm sorry, this sandwich isn't cut right. You won't want this. I'm going to throw it away." "Oh! I'm sorry, this chicken is all wrinkly. You don't want this. I'll put it away." And what happened? The girls cried out together, "I'll eat it, I'll eat it." And that was the end of that problem.

BG: After they changed to this new technique, their mealtime conversations became interesting and pleasant.

Family Career Slots

JG: What happened there? Very simple. The function of criticizing and refusing food had been taken over by Mom. So the kids were free to flop down on the other perch, the career slot of being really hungry and let's not nitpick about good food.

So when a child repeatedly exhibits behavior you'd rather they didn't, consider that they may be stuck in an unfortunate family career slot. You can help them out of it by quietly moving in and taking over that slot for yourself. Later on, if you wish, you can find another career for yourself.

Chapter 17

Sigmund Freud's Little Brother

Just A Pain In The Neck

Ray: Well, Shelby's absolutely no problem at all, so far. As of about one month of age he slept through the night pretty well. He goes down any time, you just lay him down and he goes to sleep.

JG: Good Heavens!

Bobbi: I don't know why we didn't have him first! Would have been a lot easier!

JG: Come and sit up here! You deserve to teach this class!

Bobbi: It's been easier for us because he's the second. I'm sure we're a lot more relaxed than we were with our first baby, cause we were pretty young then. Now we feel a lot older, at least!

But the reason that we're in this class is because of our firstborn. He's almost two and a half. I hate to say it, but he's just a pain in the neck a lot of the time.

Rotten Parents

Bobbi: Since he's not here, I'll say it. I wouldn't say it in his presence, but he does pretty much whatever he can to disrupt our life, particularly when we're doing something with the baby. It got worse when we brought the baby home in September, but it was there before as well.

Ray: Aaron and his Mom used to do lots and lots of things together and now they can't do that any more and I'm sure that's one reason he's a little bit jealous.

Bobbi: We moved in April into a new house in a new community. Then we took him out of his crib and put him into the twin bed. Then we brought Shelby home. So we've done a lot of things that—(laughs)

JG: You're just rotten parents!

Discipline

Ray: That's why we're here in this class!

Bobbi: And discipline is a major factor for me. I'm having a very hard time dealing with Aaron. With anything I do, he laughs at me. I have no control over the situation. He has all the control and he knows it.

JG: You ask and he says, "No!"

Ray: Right! Discipline is just the main problem we have right now. How to discipline effectively, what we shouldn't do, what we should do.

Bobbi: On the positive side, he's wonderful around Shelby. He's only tried once to pick him up and dropped him, but—(laughs) he learned his lesson from that—I didn't yell or scream or get mad at him, I just said, "Well, he's just too heavy for you to pick up." And he said, "Yes." And that was as far as it went.

JG: What a beautiful remark. "He's just too heavy for you to pick up." That says everything that needs to be said.

He Forgot How To Breastfeed

Bobbi: He comes up and talks to me. He loves to be petted and he loves to breastfeed Shelby because I breastfeed him so he thinks he can do it.

JG: Does Shelby cooperate?

Bobbi: Well, he doesn't really grab on or anything but he kind of stares at Aaron, and Aaron thinks he's breast feeding him. He'll do that at least once a day, and he's happy with that. It doesn't bother me and it doesn't bother Shelby. Aaron asked me once if he could do that—try breastfeeding again. I always told Ray before we had Shelby that if Aaron asked I'd let him try it. But when the actual situation came up I couldn't do it. I thought of all those teeth and how he had forgotten—I couldn't do it. So I just said, "No, just baby Shelby could do it."

JG: Once more your rottenness comes out! Right? Depriving Mother!

Bobbi: He doesn't like it when I spend a lot of time feeding the baby.

JG: How many months did you nurse him?

Bobbi: Aaron?

JG: Yes.

Bobbi: Till he was about fifteen months old. But then that was just a morning and an evening feeding. He doesn't really remember it though. He thinks it's fine to do it with Shelby and his dolls—

JG: Why is it that kids forget that they breast fed?

Woman: Rotten kids!

JG: You take care of them so tenderly for so many months and then they utterly forget it! Strange mechanism!

Jill: I breast fed Val until just five months before the baby was born and in just that five months he forgot. Then when I brought the baby home and started breastfeeding the baby, he wanted to try. He'd try, but he couldn't coordinate.

JG: He forgot how to breastfeed.

Jill: He forgot the mechanics of it.

JG: It's incredible. It's as if there's a program and this drops out of the program—and that's it.

(Baby coos)

JG: I hear a coo of satisfaction!

He Hit The Baby Again

Louise: Our three year old has hit the baby again, and he seems really malicious when he does that. He's been hitting her really often in the last month or so.

Grady: He's only been really bad the past few days.

Louise: Well, when you were away he was especially bad, too, so he's been bad for the last couple of weeks. He just can't stand to look at her any more. He was fine for a long time but just now, I don't know what it is. He hits her especially in the face, the eyes. He'll push her, if she's sitting and playing nicely he'll go and push her real hard. Then I put him in his room alone.

But we soon let him out of his room, we didn't keep him there long. Luckily I wasn't in a bad mood so I let him out. He only stayed there ten minutes.

Morilla: How old is he?

Louise: Three and a half. And she's ten months. Maybe that's what it is— her age—able to get around into his territory?

Sigmund Freud's Little Brother

JG: Sigmund Freud's little brother died at eight months of age, when little Sigmund was nineteen months old. It was shortly after that when Sigmund had his famous accident.[1] He injured himself rather severely. He fell against a piece of furniture and cut his jaw so badly that it had to be sutured. I think eight to ten months after the birth of the sibling is the time of the real peak of sibling resentment. They realize the sib is really here to stay. That's when they really do have fantasies about murdering, doing in that hated rival. Sigmund wrote about it later, about how guilty he felt because he had hated little Julius so much.

Kay: It's really hate, right? It's really hate.

JG: It's really hate.

Louise: That's what he seems to feel, exactly.

JG: That's right. They will hurt the baby if they're given the opportunity.

He Stole My Bottle

Priscilla: There were three of us in the one bedroom. My mother said that she would forever hear my older brother when he would he would climb out of his bunk bed on to the side of my crib, reach in and grab my bottle and fall back in his bed. They'd hear him fall back in his bed. He'd just take my bottle away.

Ralph: Compared to what I used to do to my sister, that's benign! I used to scale up over the side of the crib and then whack her on the head with one of those soft plastic hammers.

Louise: Oh, God!

Ralph: Eventually, she learned and she stayed awake—she woke up early and she had one of those little wooden mallets for the peg sets—and I came up over the side and she whacked me!

Cora: Was that the last time?

Ralph: It was!

He Couldn't Cry At The Funeral

BG: There was a story in the *New Yorker* magazine some years ago about a man who couldn't cry at his older sister's funeral. He wondered what was wrong and he went to a therapist for several years. Finally he was able to recapture the experience of being smothered with a pillow and it was his sister who had done it.

Louise: Ohh!

BG: Children do these things to their littler sibs, so you have to be careful, you have to protect them when they're little.

The Kind Of Obedience You'll Get

Louise: Grady asked him to take care of her, right?

Grady: I just said I was going out of the room for a second and asked him to watch her so she didn't get into the fireplace.

Louise: Oh, so—he pushed her head back—

Grady: —I was out of the room and I heard her scream and she had fallen down and hit her head on the side of the piano bench.

JG: So he literally obeyed you. He took care that she didn't get into the fireplace. That's the kind of obedience you'll get.

Louise: He does love her, though. If we say, "Maybe we should just go and let her stay with someone else or give her to someone who will take care of her—"
"Oh, no, no, I want her, I do love her!" He'll say that, but every chance he gets—

JG: It's really hard to understand about this shift of ego states—the idea that at one moment the person can love someone and the next moment can be a cold-blooded killer.

Louise: So it's really normal, right? He's not strange or anything?

JG: This is a rough patch in the childrearing period, where you have to get them over that without instilling some kind of sense of utter worthlessness on their part.

Louise: Is that right to say, "Just don't touch her. Just don't go near her."?

JG: That's what you're doing now, isn't it? But it isn't working, is it? You can ask, but you can't rely on them obeying. They just don't have that internal impulse control. So don't depend on impulse control, don't depend on the child obeying.

Nora: —*and don't depend on the child taking care of the little one while you go out for a second. That's what we learned. It doesn't work for even a second.*

JG: The child cannot be depended on. Basically that's what it amounts to—and that's normal. So you relieve them of that burden and then they understand at a nonverbal level that you know what they can handle and what they just can't handle yet. You just relieve them of that burden of trying to be good.

They Will Tell You

Cora: Actually we had a very concrete example of that with Justin about three or four months ago. This was when Conrad was at his ten-month stage. In the morning it's a little upsetting getting both of them ready myself sometimes—dashing to get clothes for somebody—and at one point, I can't remember when exactly it was, the three of us were together without Dad. I went out of the room to get something from the kitchen and Justin started crying. I came back and asked, "What's wrong?" He said, "I don't like having to look after Conrad when you're leaving the room!" I said, "That's fine." Conrad was just wiggling in his seat and was fine, and I said, "You don't have to worry about looking after Conrad. I'll look after him."

Since then I've been careful not to try and put him in a position where I say "Just watch him while I run and get this or whatever."

He really said it—and this was completely without me having set that up. Somehow he had taken it on himself—

JG: They will tell you. They will tell you. All you have to do is listen. Allow enough of a gap in the conversation so they can think their thought and say it. It's as straight as an arrow. They will tell you exactly. Even how they do it.

The Fantasies They Don't
Like To Talk About

JG: Yesterday we saw a marvelous videotape by Carl Whitaker—does that ring any bells? He was a pioneering psychotherapist, a psychiatrist at the University of Wisconsin for forty years. Pioneered in family therapy.

Louise: Oh, he wrote a book together with another author—

BG: Napier, I believe.

Louise: Oh, I read that! I read the book, The Family Crucible.

JG: Right. Now he's got another one with another co-author, called *Dancing with the Family*. Even better.

Kay: So what did he have to say?

JG: What he said was that one of the first things that he does when he deals with the family is to get them to bring out the fantasies they don't like to talk about.[2] He will say, "How many days was it after you married your husband that you decided you'd like to kill him? How did you think you would do it? Were you gonna put ground glass in his soup?" If you have rapport you can get people to actually tell you, "Oh, well, yes, I did think about it, yeah, that's right!" And—

BG: "—and what did you say or do?"

JG: "—and when did you decide?"—This was a Wisconsin farm couple, a Wisconsin farmer who had run a dairy herd for forty years. They had come to family therapy because their grown children were having trouble.

"How many years was it before you realized he loved the cows more than he loved you?" And she said, "Five years!" The same thing is true of a little two year old. They will tell you, "Yes, I would like to push out those eyes!" You can bring this out and keep it light, because after all it is fantasy. It's not acting out. You can keep it light by saying, "How about frying the baby in the frying pan?" Or, "Would you like to flush the baby down the toilet?"

Arthur: Fred would volunteer for that—

Louise: He wouldn't really do it!

JG: There you go!

Louise: He would say, "No, I love her, I don't wanna do it."

JG: Exactly. You take these fantasies, you bring them out, you face them, and you detoxify them.

Louise: So you're not encouraging aggressive behavior by saying that? Because he will have a fight with his friends and he will come back and say, "I will go get a stick and poke their eyes out!" or, "I will kill them!" I say, "No, I don't know if you should do that." He says all these horrible things, but he doesn't do them.

JG: Exactly!

Louise: So what should I say?

JG: Help them a little. You can exaggerate, even be a little bit outrageous. Say, ''Maybe you'd like to hang them up by their ankles until their eyes fall out.'' You keep it light, you encourage a little creativity. You get their sense of humor involved. If it is too dangerous to talk about, then it festers inside the person. ''This is too horrible for me even to say out loud.''

That's what Whitaker does. He comes right out and says it. At one point the coauthor was reviewing a segment of that tape, and he says, ''But Whitaker, when you say these weird things, aren't you afraid that they will think that you're a little bit unhealthy?'' And Whitaker replies, ''Of course! I want them to understand that this is in all of us. That there isn't this 'healthy-unhealthy' dichotomy, I want to get away from that. I want them to know that I have thoughts and feelings like that too.''

BG: In fact, one of the things he brought out was, speaking directly to one of the daughters who was attached to the father, he said, ''When did Dad stop letting you sit on his lap and cuddling you?'' and she wasn't about to answer. Whitaker said, ''Well, now, I remember when I was thirteen, boy, that was the end, I never sat on my mother's lap or cuddled her, that was too dangerous.'' Then right away, the girl, ''Yeah, up till—I remember that.'' Like, it was there and available, but they never talked about it.

How Do You Deal With The Second Child?

> *Nora:* *What about the younger sibling? You try to keep the other child away from the younger sibling, but what is happening to that younger sibling—Is she or he too young to understand what's going on? How do you deal with the second child?*

JG: The second sibling by the age of fifteen months has often learned how to subversively provoke the older kid into hitting them. Then when Mom runs into the room, the older kid is hitting the younger and Mom never sees what the younger one did to make that happen.

> *Grady:* *Well, even now, when he comes near her; if she's in a bad mood, she starts screaming. Either she knows what's going to happen or she just wants to make sure that we know.*

Keep Them Apart If You Can

JG: Sometimes you can just physically separate them. Especially when you are caring for the younger one. Especially breastfeeding. The older sib shouldn't have to watch that. That's just rubbing it in.

> *Louise: She really loved him, but now she's afraid of him, since he started being so vicious. For a long time they got along really, really well, but just in the last few weeks, she looks at him as if to say, "I don't want you near me!"*

BG: There's also jealousy by the younger one of the older one. That happens about ten to twelve months. The younger one sees Mom paying attention to the older one and starts the same jealousy—

> *Louise: If I take him and hold him, she'll get real jealous. She wants me to hold her.*

BG: Yes.

> *Louise: Then if I hold her, he says, "You always hold her!"*

JG: When you don't know what else to do, you pace. You say, "Yes, I'm just a rotten Mother—"

> *Louise: He says, "Bad Mommy, I'm gonna kill you!"*

JG: "Bad Mommy. You feel like killing me!"

> *Louise: "Get rid of you!"*

JG: So you say, "How do you think you'd like to do that?" Just carry it along until it's defused. That way it doesn't get pushed down into a hard lump down in the psyche.

Some Things Are Final

> *Charlene: We had an experience at home that I'd like to report. Lily—she'd been doing a lot of baby-talk and wetting her pants. I thought she was feeling ambivalent about being a big girl, so to give her big-girl privileges, I bought her some children's scissors. She promptly used them to cut up a doll quilt my mother had made for her. I just was sick about it. Nice straight lines, she cut right along the lines!—and it was all over the rug and over the floor. There it was all in pieces. I just started crying. And she put her arm around me. She was real upset that I was upset. She put her arm around me and said, "Never mind, Mom! I have other blankets to keep my dolls warm!"*
>
> *Then I told her, "Well, honey, this was special because Grandma made it. This was something special. You don't want to cut up things like this, this was real special." And she said, "Ohh!"—she still had her arm around*

*me—"Ohh!"—she's patting my back—"I didn't know Grandma made this!
I thought YOU made that, Mom!"*

Ahh! Then I was speechless. I didn't know what else to say.

JG: She was ambivalent, all right!

Charlene: Yeah!

*I put the scissors away anyway in a nice safe place. I'm keeping them
safe for her, now.*

JG: Very good idea! So now she knows that scissors can do certain things,
doesn't she?

*Charlene: Yeah. Yeah! She'd never ever used them like that before. It just
didn't cross my mind. I just missed that.*

JG: Well, now she knows, after you cut something up, you don't have
it any more.

*Charlene: Yes. Well, she did like that doll quilt, even though she has other
blankets to keep her dolls warm. She has thought that everything could be
fixed. "Well, we'll just fix it!"*

JG: Good basic piece of information.

Broken Records

BG: I remember when our kids were about two and four, we had a little
record player with little tiny yellow plastic records. They played 'em and
played 'em and played 'em. One morning we came in and there were the
kids, just kinda messing 'em all up and cracking them and making little
pieces out of them.

I said, "Ohh! They won't play any more." But they kept right on.
It was great fun, making a big pile of yellow pieces all over. Next time
they wanted to play them again, we tried to put them back together again
and it just didn't work. I said, "I'm real sorry but there are some things
that you can't put back together." They learned it from real experience.

Rest In Peace

BG: Then their guinea pig died. I guess that's when you really learn that
there are some things that you can't put back together again. They had
a little funeral and buried him out in the back yard and put up a little sign
that said, "Checkers".

Siblings Without Rivalry

Nora: I've seen this book, Siblings Without Rivalry.[3] *Can you have that? Can you have siblings without rivalry or without that sort of thing going on?*

JG: It's a wonderful book, full of excellent suggestions for dealing with sibling rivalry. But as far as having siblings without rivalry—well, I think Whitaker would say, ''Love and hate are always roped together.'' There's no such thing as one without the other. You can't have only one end to a stick.

Morilla: Darn!

JG: The real question is simply how to deal with it in a constructive way. For that you need strategies.

Chapter 18
Lemmings Are Consistent

Who's In Charge Around Here?

Bobbi: Aaron, my two year old, just drives me up a wall sometimes. He knows he can do it. He knows my limits. He knows that he can push me and I'm gonna let him do it.

JG: He takes full advantage. He knows where that line is.

We Don't Spank In This House!

Bobbi: I have spanked him once, because I just lost total control and I couldn't help it—I had to do it. It wasn't that hard and it didn't hurt him and it—hurt me more than it hurt him and now he says, "Don't spank me. We don't spank in this house." I had told him that before and here I went and spanked him. Now when he sees it coming, he says, "Don't spank me. We don't spank in this house."

I just don't know what to do any more. I have no control over this child. He has control over me. Well, that was fine until I had Shelby. Now I need a little order and discipline in my life. I just can't get up and do whatever he wants all the time. I'm just—lost, I just have no idea what to do any more. I don't know what discipline to use, I don't—it's not consistent, and I try these things and he just plays me, and I just don't know what to do any more.

JG: He has a bit more repertoire for manipulating others than you do.

Bobbi: I just go crazy. I was telling Ray the other night when we were lying in bed talking—the only times we get to talk—and I said, "I feel like my head's about to explode. I don't know which direction to go. I feel like screaming, just screaming at the top of my lungs." Ray said, "Well, do it!" I said, "I don't want to do it." I'm afraid to scare him. I just don't know what to do.

JG: You'd like to have something else that is not spanking that would draw a line equally as strong.

Bobbi: Yes! I've tried time out on the steps, and in the bed, and—

Is Mom About To Crack Up?

JG: Most parents that I've talked to, have about three strategies in this respect. They know about time-outs. They know about actual spanking, and then—what's the other one? There might be one other—gold stars, maybe—but it's a very limited repertoire for dealing with a kid's behavior.

A child's behavior is predicated upon the certainty and the faith that their parents are the secure ones who are firm and unwavering in their dedication to each other, to civilized behavior, reasonableness, etc. The idea that their parents might freak out, disappear, or split from each other is hard for a child to handle.

One reason kids push so hard to find where the parents are going to finally take a stand, is that they have to know, ''My God! Am I the one who is really in charge around here, and I don't even have impulse control!'' They push and they push, ''Where are they gonna stop? Where are they going to draw the line and make me straighten out?''

So, you can learn some techniques that will suggest to the child the possibility that you might be getting close to the edge, that you might be getting ready to crack.

Bobbi: (laughs) I feel like I am gonna crack some day!

JG: All right! Now, how old is Aaron?

Bobbi: Two and a half. He'll be three in April.

JG: For a kid this age to see a parent have a tantrum is a very scary experience. Of course you have to discuss this with Dad in advance so that Dad doesn't think you're really cracking!

Karla: That's all right. You can scare Dads, too!

BG: The voice of experience, it sounds like!

The Sound Of Splintering Wood

JG: One of the Moms in our practice had a boy who was oversleeping and skipping school at one point. One morning, while he was oversleeping upstairs, she went down in the basement and began kicking orange crates to bits, trampling on them. The sound of splintering wood went through the house. The boy came downstairs, almost in tears, and he said, ''Mom! Don't do that!! I'll go! I'll go!''

BG: It seemed to hit the sonic barrier for him.

JG: She had found something that was not child abuse but that the child could not tolerate, and that was the idea that an adult would become a raging, rampaging, unpredictable, uncontrollable, lawless creature.

BG: Well she was, just about, at that point for real.

JG: Well, we recommend that you do it before you get desperate. You do it as a deliberate strategy. Once you've done something like that, then you can actually convey that kind of signal to a kid by just the arch of your eyebrow that indicates, ''Gee, Mom is thinking about breaking up crates again!''

They will think very seriously about that, and there is nothing wrong with setting limits, because if you don't set them, the kid pushes further and further to find where the limits are. But just announcing limits verbally, that rarely cuts any ice.

> *Bobbi: Well, Aaron has the power, he does with me anyway.*

JG: Mom and Dad can suddenly become angry at each other and have a fight with each other. If a child thinks that their behavior precipitated that fight between the parents, believe me, that's going to have consequences.

> *Louise: Kyle just hates it when we argue. He says, ''Don't argue!'' right away. Even if we are talking and our voices are raised, he gets real nervous.*

JG: You could rehearse it.

> *Cora: ''Momma's right!''*

> *Louise: Oh, yeah, Kyle's on my side, always! Always!*

Making A U-Turn

JG: You can throw a twist in it. You can rehearse it and pick out a theme in which it's totally obvious that Dad is right and by no stretch of the imagination could it be otherwise. Then, when the child commits himself, then you do a U-turn.[1] Say, ''No, I think Mommy's right.'' ''No, I think Daddy's right.''

Louise: I did something like that. They were both crying—Grady was away—and I just didn't know what to do with them any more. They were both crying to be helped, so I sat on the floor with them and I started crying, too! I wasn't really crying hard. I was pretending more than anything—they both stopped! Kyle looked at me as if to say, "Don't be silly!"

Become Unpredictable

JG: Another possibility is that you become unpredictable.

Karla: Or that you should forget things? They always think that you should have everything perfect, like you could never forget lunch or something. Even if you just postpone it a half an hour and just throw your hand on your face and then say, "I forgot lunch!" they'll look at you real strangely, "How could you possibly—?" and then they start to think that maybe you're not all there. It's hard to explain, but I know it works, 'cause I have done it.

JG: You don't have to make any verbal connection. You don't have to say to the kid, "You made me so upset I forgot lunch." What you do is, you let their behavior go on at the time while you are forgetting to make lunch. That's all you have to do.

Talk Is Cheap

Bobbi: Well, I have told him that he's made me angry. I've told him why he made me angry, and I've told him that we don't want to make me angry. He understands when I tell him, but an hour later it's totally out of his head. He's repeating it again and he's just forgotten.

JG: I'd like to make a suggestion. This is a situation for nonverbal communication. Long discussions and negotiations with a toddler just don't usually work. By talking you just give away your power. Then he knows what you're doing. If he knows what you're doing, then he can counteract it. As the parent, you should be obscure, inscrutable, unpredictable. He has to be on his toes to figure out, "Gee! How do I make Mom and Dad work properly? How do I make Mom and Dad be nice? How to I make them fix lunch on time?" —whatever it is. Keep him occupied, trying to meet the expectations which you are not spelling out. That's how we get to be human. That's what being civilized is all about. Civilized means being tuned in to the other person, finding out what the other person needs and wants. You can't do that if you spell it out in English all the time. Then there's no incentive for them to learn.

Bobbi: I've always thought I was supposed to do that!

Incongruity

JG: You should not necessarily explain stuff to a kid. What you should do is learn how to use nonverbal language, because the nonverbal message is usually much more potent than the verbal. As you are sitting there talking to your child you are quietly conveying to him the nonverbal message that things must be all right. You're saying, ''I'm real upset,'' but you're sitting there quietly. That's a double message. That's conflicting messages. What he needs to experience is something real, the kind of thing Beth calls, ''Behavior behavior.'' Our slogan is, ''Nonverbal beats verbal every time.''

Consequences

Charlene: Lily doesn't care if she has breakfast or not or if she gets dressed or not. She would just go through the day like that—she just doesn't care!

BG: She's uncouth!

JG: She would be quite comfortable with that? OK. So maybe she could be allowed to have some experience of consequences along that line.

BG: Is she four now?

Charlene: Yeah. She's always been like this, though. I mean she's always been like this.

BG: What kind of thing would you do where she'd have to be different, I mean, would you be going out to the store, or going to a friend's house—

Charlene: ''Well, we'll go to a friend's house.'' Well, all right. She'll do something else. ''Oh! Oh, we forgot.'' ''Yeah we did, Oh, well!''

Spenser: Would she go to the friend's house in her pajamas, then?

Charlene: Yeah! She would! She wouldn't mind going to her friend's house in pajamas.

Spenser: Our boys get a little scared when we talk about going somewhere in their jammies or naked. They don't like that at all. Our youngest gets pretty upset—he's three and a half now, so—

BG: So he has some sense of social expectations somewhere.

Spenser: Yeah, he has a serious side!

Jenny: (laughs) Serious!

Dan: My sister has trouble getting her kid dressed in the morning. So twice, within about two weeks, he went off in his pajamas to day care because he didn't care. The closer they got to day care, the more he started to care!

(Several people in unison): Oh-ho!

Dan: He got dressed in the car outside day care, twice, and none since then.

JG: They do start to care after a while!

Charlene: Yeah, maybe if I got her close enough to day care, maybe she would—

BG: It makes you feel humble—but it's true. Other people's opinions often have more weight than yours.

A Very Strange Kind Of Helpfulness

JG: You can be very helpful. You stay on their side, you understand. You are just so helpful. You say, "Would you like to leave your clothes in the car, or would you like to take them with you?" You're helping them, but it's a very strange kind of helpfulness. You're letting the child's failure to learn the desired responses get in his way, not yours. It becomes a problem for him but not for you.

Kitty Too Young

Maybe they really shouldn't be going to daycare, or wherever it is you're taking them. You need to think of that. Little Kitty was five years old and Mom and Dad brought her in to see me because Kitty wanted to talk to me about First Grade. She had started in the Fall even though she was a little young for First Grade. After a few days she told her teacher that she didn't want to attend all day. She explained that she was only a little girl and a half day was just fine, but a whole day was too long for her. The teacher told her it was the law. She had to go all day. Kitty asked to talk to the principal. She repeated her request to the principal. The principal said it was the law and she had to go all day. Then Kitty told her mother what had happened and her mother didn't know what to do. Then Kitty said, "I want to talk to Doctor Gall." Her mother agreed and Kitty told me the whole story. I replied, "Little girls and boys ought not to have to work all day long, even if it's just First Grade and supposed to be fun.

"A very strange kind of helpfulness."

If it's not fun, if it's just tiring, they shouldn't have to do it." I told her Mom and Dad, "If they can't accommodate her request, let her stay in Kindergarten till next year, or whenever she feels she's old enough."

Kitty stayed in Kindergarten. The next year she went to First Grade all day and had a wonderful time.

Kitty knew that a full day was just too long for her and she said so. She kept on appealing to higher authorities until she reached someone who would listen.

This is supposed to be a free country, where the individual needs of citizens are respected. How can we teach children what freedom is if we don't respect their individual situations, and if we coerce them all into the same patterns?

"I Know How Much You Love A Bottle At Night . . ."

JG: You wake up a kid who's insisting on having the bottle two or three times a night—and he's three years old—and you begin waking him up, say, forty-five minutes before he wakes up and you say to him, "I know how much you love to have a bottle at night, so I thought I'd bring you a bottle," and he's trying to prop his eyes open.

You let him go back to sleep and an hour and a half later you come back again with another bottle and say, "I know how much you love that bottle, so I'm bringing you another bottle." You're giving them what they want. You're giving it to them as a friend, but in such a way that it's not quite as pleasant as it once was. It's that mixture, you see.

You do that again 45 minutes after he has fallen asleep again, and again 45 minutes after that, and in a very short time he will not call for a bottle in the night. You have given him what he wants. You are on his side, but he discovers he doesn't like it as much as he thought.

"How much you like a bottle at night". That's his own verbal model. He can't deny it, and you are giving him just that. But the words now correspond to getting waked out of a comfortable sleep when he just isn't all that hungry.

Nonissues

The issue simply fades away. It's not a matter of either doing or not doing. It's just not an issue any more. Since there isn't any issue any more, you really ought not to bring it up. Just let it be.

Let Them Make Some Mistakes

JG: As part of that strategy, you learn to ignore unimportant stuff. Don't treat everything as equally important. In other words, you let them misbehave quite a bit. You let them make a lot of mistakes. If it isn't a matter of life and death or fundamentals, you let them do it and find out for themselves what the consequences might be.

BG: —like when they're learning to dress themselves. If they get the buttons wrong, like one off—just don't say a word, let 'em go around all day with their buttons wrong—

Praise The Achievement, Don't Criticize The Shortcoming

JG: You always praise the achievement! You praise the achievement. You don't criticize the shortcoming. You can say, ''Wow, you really know how to button your jacket!'' You can also say, ''What's this extra buttonhole?'' You're not criticizing. You're just curious and he can have the satisfaction of telling you about it. You can learn from him, and he can teach you.

Who's In Charge Here?

Louise: Now that Kyle puts his shoes on or boots on, they're always the wrong way. It should be fifty-fifty at least!

JG: It's not even fifty-fifty!

Louise: We just let him walk around the neighborhood—

JG: Exactly. If he comes up and stands in front of you with a pained expression on his face, then you can say, ''Is something wrong?'' Now he is the initiator and has the tremendous sense of gratification that he tells you, rather than the other way around.

Cora: But what if he can't figure out why he's uncomfortable? He just notices that he can't really relax?

JG: That's when it's OK to be a nurturing parent.

Cora: Say, ''Maybe if you switch your shoes you may be more comfortable?'' ''Put 'em on backwards and see how they fit?''

Louise: We told him! He likes the other way better.

JG: ''You prefer this way, don't you? You like them that way.'' This is how you get to the real issue. Is it really a question of the shoes, or is it an issue of who's going to be in charge?

You Want To Do It Your Own Way (Verbal Pacing)

Louise: But he's like that in everything. In school art projects, they're making a caterpillar. He doesn't connect the circles so it looks like a caterpillar. He likes to have the parts all disjointed. In everything, he has to have his own way.

Nora: He's a Picasso!

Verbal Pacing

JG: Right! That could be a theme by which you could pace into his model. ''You want to do it your own way.'' Verbal Pacing. ''You don't want to do X. You want to go out and play.'' You have validated their position, you have given them something of great value to them, and they will know that you really understand.

You Don't Want To Get Down, Do You?

JG: I'm thinking of one little kid that was just raising Cain in the waiting room. Mom was carrying him. He was maybe 18 months, maybe 2 years old. I walked out into the waiting room and said, ''You don't want to get down, do you? You don't want to go into the doctor's office, do you?'' I saw the double take. Then there was this big grin, and the kid jumped down out of his mother's arms and ran into my examining room. Somebody understood him. Somebody agreed with his position. That's when they're willing to walk with you. You pace them, and then you lead.

That's the mark of a really good strategy, where it happens out of nowhere and nobody gets any credit for being the one who made anything happen. It's just totally woven into the web. It's not an intervention. It's just a spontaneous response.

Thirty-Three Patches
(Nonverbal Pacing)

Mimi: Heidi had a lazy eye and came home from the eye doctor with a patch over her good eye. Then we had to take her back to the daycare. She was really upset about having to go to daycare with this patch. We went to the doctor and came back that afternoon to the daycare. And lo and behold here's thirty-three kids running around with patches on their eyes, and she's the happiest girl in the world!

JG: Who did that?

Mimi: The university's center for working families. The teachers did it. When they saw that she was upset—and she's kind of shy anyway—they proceeded to cut out patches and have every kid at the daycare wear a patch. She was as happy as can be and wore that patch for the next 6 months.

They only did it for the day, but they never needed to do it again.

JG: Now that's a truly elegant example of nonverbal pacing.

Model Automobiles

Louise: Do you have any suggestions? The other day we went to this expensive gallery. They had model automobiles and I told him about them—he loves them—and they had these really beautiful model automobiles which were a thousand dollars or so each—and we were looking, everything he touched there, if he broke it, I'd die!!

He looked at the automobiles. He started touching everything and I said, "OK, Kyle, let's go. We've seen everything, let's go!" He didn't want to go! He just threw a fit there in the store. I picked him up—everyone is looking at us—and I just wanted to die! I knew what was going on. I understand him, but I couldn't start jumping together with him in the gallery. So I pick him up and walked him to the car. He's just crying so hard, everyone is looking, and it's just so awful!

JG: Child abuser!!

Louise: Yeah! Really!

Kay: That's the feeling you get. You could bite a hole in your lip, because I nearly did—

BG: But you controlled the situation, though. You got him out of there and didn't wreck a thousand-dollar model car—

Louise: Right.

BG: So congratulate yourself.

Louise: I didn't look at it that way.

BG: OK? All right!

Louise: That's true! It could have been a lot worse.

Limits And Control

JG: Limit setting is important, but I'd like to approach it from another angle as we move along because, if you don't have any repertoire, then limit-setting often involves using physical force to control the child. If that's done gently and in a non-punitive way, it's OK to do that. It's all right to control your child physically when they are out of control.

Louise: It's hard for me to do it gently, and that's a problem.

JG: It should be done gently. It should be done without punitiveness. But it is a message. It is a powerful nonverbal message that the adults are stronger, and that certain behaviors will be controlled by the physical strength of adults. It's really important for kids to learn that, but we want to reach a point where it is understood as one more strategy in a whole repertoire of strategies. It has its appropriate times and then there are other times when it's rather crude and there would be better ways of doing it.

Morilla: This is almost something that's—almost like a hug in some ways.

JG: It's a loving hug that has control in it.

BG: Right!

Providing A Secure Reality

JG: This is the strategy called: Providing a Secure Reality. When it becomes necessary to physically restrain a child, you just firmly and gently enfold them. You're not mad at them. You're not hurting them, but you are sending a very strong message to them that they do not have the power that belongs to adults.[2]

BG: Remember I showed you how to hold them so you won't hurt them and they can't hurt you.

I Just Stopped Trying To Change Her

Karla: I have a seven-year-old, a-five-year old, and a two-year-old. I took this class last time for the sake of my two year old, and I don't know what has happened. Either she hasn't changed and I have changed my outlook on how to deal with her, or else she has changed. She's been a problem since the day we brought her home from the hospital. Right now she is the most delightful, happy child, so I'm just praying this is going to continue.

JG: Are you talking about Bridget?

Karla: Yes!!

JG: The same Bridget?

Karla: THE Bridget. I have finally found out after two years and three months what this child needs and wants, and you wouldn't believe the change in her.

JG: What was it?

Karla: What I was doing before was constantly telling her what she could and could not do. Now I give her a choice. For two years now putting her to bed was sheer hell, and now I just tell her, "It's time for bed. You can go to bed anywhere you want." So she starts sleeping in the living room and then she starts sleeping on the stairs. What's most interesting is now she's at the top floor of the house, so she's working her way up to her room! But this is all happening on her terms—she's doing it.

JG: On her terms.

Karla: Right. I just tell her, at nine o'clock, "This is my time to watch TV. Good-bye. Go make yourself a bed." She drags the blankets and pillow. I say, "I don't care. You can sleep on the kitchen floor. You can sleep in the cupboards. Anywhere in this house. You just go." So she's working her way upstairs—

Woman: Does she go to sleep?

Karla: Sure. It's just, "Goodnight!" I've realized that if you just give her the choice to do what she's supposed to do, on her terms, there's no fight. She will do it, as long as you let her do it. But if you try and tell her what to do, you're gonna lose every time. I just won't fight with her any more. I know some people really believe that at nine o'clock you put your kid in the bed. It's just never worked and I just let her go.

JG: She wasn't objecting to sleeping at a certain time. She was objecting to being told and not being given a choice about some part of it.

Karla: I have day care in my home, and we were having some problems with her behavior with the other kids. I have solved those problems in that I have discovered that she is very creative with art materials. I give them to her and she just sits at an art table for an hour. She doesn't care what else is going on around her as long as she can do certain things. As long as I keep her doing certain things, she does much better with the other kids being in the house. She needed more than what I was allowing her to do. There's no more mood swings—

JG: No more mood swings?

Karla: No. It's vanished.

JG: I can't believe this! A few months ago you were talking about real severe mood swings.

Karla: Yeah. Like—really bad. They're gone. I don't know what happened but I am allowing her to do things that I never have before. Maybe that's what did it.

BG: Are you getting any flak from the relatives about it? I remember when you were worried about that.

Karla: I'm kinda steering clear! I'm not strong enough to face them yet, so I'm backing off. She did go to Grandma's to spend the night last weekend, I've never been away from her like that before, but she was fine.

BG: Ohh!

Karla: I showed up the next morning and she said, "Hi."

JG: Gee! This is not the kid that you introduced me to.

Karla: I don't really know if this is permanent or what, but I'm just taking every day—it's really nice.

JG: Well, that's neat.

Karla: Well, if you just let her do what she wants to do she is really just fine.

JG: A lot of us are like that!

Karla: She's just so independent that she doesn't want you touching her or telling her what to do or anything.

JG: I guess sometimes we forget that what we like most of all in the world is to do exactly what we want to do . . . to have our own sweet will.

Karla: Somewhere in this class I discovered that. I had to stop trying to change her, because that's just the way she was. I could not take this person and change her into being what I wanted her to be. What I had to change was my attitude towards her, and somewhere in the class that's what hit me.

JG: That's beautiful.

Karla: That's really nice. We'll see how long it lasts!

JG: Until the next challenge! The next problem.

Karla: Right!

JG: Now, of course, the relatives want you to achieve a certain desired result and be successful with your child, but they want you to do it exactly the way they think you should do it. They lock you in. You've gotta succeed but you have to succeed their way.

BG: But Karla wants to do it the way she wants to do it!!!

JG: That's right!! Exactly!

Karla: But I can fight with them instead of with her. More fair.

JG: Right! It's much better to fight from a winner's position.

Car Seats

Karla: We have no more problems with the car seat either. As a matter of fact she got in her car seat today for the first time in months. I said, "If you sit in this car seat you're going to be higher. You can see out the window, and maybe you'll see something." So we're back to the car seat.

Gina: We used that same strategy; because she would be able to see.

Karla: It happened with the Christmas lights. "I can't see the Christmas lights, I want out of my belt." I said, "If you use the car seat it makes you high, you can see the Christmas lights." Now we're back to the car seat.

Routines Don't Work With Her

Karla: This thing about the bed time—from everything I keep reading you're supposed to make this routine. You're supposed to do this, and then you do this, and then you do this and then you finally do this. Routines have never worked with her because she's got it all figured out. So the second time you use the routine she knows what's going to happen an hour before you even start the routine, so it never works. Every couple of days I've got to change what I do, and it works fine.

BG: Keep her guessing!

Karla: Well, that's what seems to work, because if I'm consistent and I use routines she knows too soon.

JG: Unpredictability. Powerful method, right.

Karla: Dad, when he puts her to bed, he starts telling her two hours before that, "Well, it's almost bedtime." "After dinner we go to bed." By the time bedtime comes the kid is just in tears. She's so worked up. I said, "Never tell her. Just pick her up and carry her upstairs, she doesn't know what she's going up there for."

JG: Yeah, be a little bit interesting. A little unpredictable.

Lemmings Are Consistent

Karla: Forget these routines, they don't work for her.

JG: Most of the books say, "Be consistent." That's regarded as a great virtue. But it is not a virtue if you have a kid who doesn't like consistency.

Karla: Apparently there are some kids that need that routine and consistency.

JG: Some kids need it, and some don't.

Karla: It does work very well. It took me two years and three months to figure out my kid doesn't need routines. Forget them.

JG: Fantastic.

Sally: The difficult thing about consistency is that life is inconsistent. You can't be consistent in the form of discipline. Your mood is never the same from day to day, and the situation is never the same. It's very hard. I always think, do these people ever have children?

Gina: The ones that write the books?

Sally: Yeah, the ones that tell you to be consistent in your form of discipline—

JG: It's what they wish would have happened—right?

Sally: —because—because, clearly, you can't be consistent because nothing else is consistent.

JG: Lemmings are consistent!

Chapter 19

Toying With The Reality

Toying With The Reality

JG: When a little kid grabs something, at two years or three years of age, and you redefine it as "stealing", what have you done? You've turned a spontaneous behavior into a sin. I don't think that's very useful.

Or if a four-year-old tells you about the monster under the bed and you redefine it as "lying", what you've done is to create a character defect. You've done it by your choice of words.

But if a kid falls down, and looks up at you startled, you say, "Ka-boom!" with that upward lilt in your voice and a bit of a smile. Or if they are a little older, you say, "A-ha! studying gravity again, eh?" You've redefined the situation in a really constructive way.[1]

This is a technique that has a very wide spectrum of application. It's very useful, but it also has some pitfalls because redefining a situation involves toying with the reality. If you're going to do it, you need to know what you're doing.

The power to put a name on something is the power to make it a destructive negative experience, or the power to make it a positive experience. Do we have any English scholars here? Any literature majors? Anybody read John Milton? Paradise Lost? "The mind is its own place and in itself, can make a heaven of hell, a hell of heaven?" When you call something by a really powerful name, you have had a powerful influence on the other person. If a kid at age three or four is told that what he does is stealing and lying, he will have a problem with stealing and lying and will be struggling—all his life maybe—to deal with stealing and lying. But if you use a constructive term for it, they may understand that they have this wonderful spontaneous impulse to explore the world, and to pick things up and look at them and study them. All they need to do is to learn that it's socially acceptable to give it back after they've studied it. You don't even use the word "stealing" at all. You don't use the word "lying" when you talk about monsters.

BG: "What a great story you told."

JG: "Isn't that wonderful, what a great story you told."

Sally: I do that with my Angela and she comes up with the most incredible stories. They go on for 20 minutes! I have to tell her, "I really like your story, but—!"

JG: You can write it down or have her say it into a tape recorder and send it to a TV producer. Encourage it and you get more.

Sally: Oh yeah!

Rita: Sasha did this, telling the story into a tape recorder, because my sister did that when she was living away and she sent it to my mom. My mom still has those tapes and she treasures them. The kids hate them! Mom loved it. "It's Christmas time, let's play those tapes for everybody to hear!"

The Value Of Money

Cora: Justin has discovered the value of money. He will take my husband's wallet. My husband puts his wallet in a particular place in a bookcase when he comes home from work. Justin for some reason thinks that the people I work with are especially poor and so he will take all of Daddy's money out of his wallet—he's being taught now that the bills are off limits—but he will fish in Daddy's pockets while Daddy's making dinner and take out the change. He will give it to me to give to the people at work. I guess it's fine when it's passed among the family, but we're trying to teach him, "It's not so cool to take money from other people—it's noble to want to give it to people who don't have as much, but what's in Daddy's wallet needs to stay in Daddy's wallet." How do we teach him not to do that?

JG: How old is he?

Cora: Three and a half.

JG: So he knows what he wants.

Cora: Oh, he's always known what he wants!

JG: But he doesn't have a very good idea of what other people want.

Cora: Right.

JG: Right. You give him this verbal stuff about "I want it" and that goes into this puny little verbal model that's not capable of controlling this human being.

"'Why' is a very sophisticated concept."

Cora: Well, I ask him why and he can't give me any reason.

JG: Right! "Why" is a very sophisticated concept.

When I was a kid, I discovered that nickels were the things you could buy ice cream with. I would go into my mother's wallet—

Cora: —take all the nickels?

JG: —take the nickels, and go up—it was two blocks away to the corner grocery store where they sold the ice cream. My Mom rather quickly discovered this. She didn't say anything about lying or stealing. She said,

''I want you to keep out of my wallet!'' Very clear instruction! I could do that!

> *Cora: Well, we've done that with Daddy's wallet and it doesn't work.*

JG: So you need a next strategy, right?

> *Cora: Right!*

''It's Not 'Stealing'; It's 'Discovery'!'' (Redefinition)

JG: So you just redefine it. ''Oh, wow! I see you're really interested in coins!'' ''You're really interested in exploring things!'' ''You really like to find stuff in wallets!''

> *Cora: Yep!*

BG: So what do you do? You get another wallet—

JG: Be careful, you might start him on a career of some kind!

BG: —and have Daddy put his wallet where the child cannot get it.

> *Cora: Well, then he knows and asks for it. We've done that too.*

BG: Oh, well, just substitute the new wallet or whatever, his own wallet—

A Wallet Of His Own

> *Cora: We've been thinking of getting him a wallet of his own.*

JG: That's an excellent idea. Let him have a wallet of his own.

BG: He wants the power. He wants the symbol of power.

> *Cora: We can give him old expired charge cards and all that—he likes those too!*

JG: Not only that, but—why don't you get one of those packages of foreign coins and secretly put a different one—

> *Louise: Ohhhh!*

JG: —in his wallet every morning. You'll turn this into a totally different experience. It's no longer stealing, now it's—

Cora: Discovery!

JG: Discovery!

Lying

Louise: We have a problem with lying. Kyle lies—

JG: How old is he?

Louise: Three and a half. It's nothing vicious or anything. He just—when he knows that what he did was not right—he'll lie and say, ''No, I didn't do it.''

Cora: Right.

JG: Correct!

Morilla: At that age, is it lying, or is it just—

Louise: —wishing it were different—wishing that he had done it differently.

JG: Yes. This is kind of like telling an eighteen-monther not to wet the bed.

Louise: His teacher in school was horrified that he lied, but it didn't seem—I mean I knew, I know I lied when I was a kid, and it didn't strike me as anything strange. But he walked out with half the kids out of his classroom and they're not supposed to go out. He didn't really know he wasn't supposed to do it. I'm sure no one told him, ''Don't walk out,'' so he thought it was fine to go look for me. Then she asked him, ''Kyle, is that what you did? Did you lead half the children out of the classroom?'' and he said, ''No.'' She knew he did and she says, ''He lied!'' I thought, ''Well, he didn't really know what he did was wrong, but I guess he was afraid of being punished.''

He'll do that. What we do is say, ''Well, your nose will grow bigger.''

JG: Then he starts checking—

Louise: He says, ''No it won't! It's the same!'' But I don't know what else to do.

JG: I would suggest that you not ask him. Don't set him up to tell an untruth.

Set Them Up To Succeed

JG: Don't set him up for that, because he will fall into it, just the same way that an eighteen monther is going to wet the bed. You say, ''Don't wet the bed!'' and he's going to fall right into it. He's gonna do it.

> *Louise: So you shouldn't say, ''Don't lie!'' ''Did you lie?'' ''Did you just lie?''*

JG: If you ask those questions, the child will fail a second time. The first time he failed you was when he did whatever it was he did. The second time is when he lies about it. That's setting him up.

> *Louise: That's terrible.*

JG: You want to set kids up to succeed.

> *Louise: We ask him, like, 'Did you just hit your sister?'' He did, you know. ''Why did you just hit your sister?'' Both questions seem terrible, because just like you say—*

BG: He doesn't know.

> *Louise: —he says, ''I don't know why I hit her, but I did.'' Or he says, ''No, I didn't hit her,'' and you know he's lying.*

Double Messages

JG: Now some people come in and they say, ''I really want to lose some weight. I really want to lose some weight.'' (Shakes his head from side to side slowly).

You can see them shaking their head, ''No.'' Their conscious mind wants to lose weight but inside, in their unconscious mind, they don't want to lose that weight. No way!

And a good doctor will do this [shaking head from side to side], and say, ''I see that you really want to lose some weight.'' That's a double message. You're sending one message verbally, another message nonverbally. Both parts are satisfied. ''You really want to lose some weight.'' [Head shakes from side to side.] This is to get it to the light stage where you can handle it. Take the heavy away from it.

> *Louise: Then you shouldn't make a big deal out of it?*

JG: It depends. I think at three years of age, three and a half, you're still at a stage where these things are very reversible. You probably will have faster success if you take a light approach to it and don't try to lock it in to an adult definition.

BG: It's the name that we adults put on it that's the problem, because one of the richest times of the child's life is in the age around three to four to five when they're very creative. At the same time they are busy learning the social rules and so in order to stay comfortable they have this creativity to say something that will please whoever is asking for something. This is a very positive thing for a child to be able to do. You don't want to squelch it, but you need to help them to get through it.

JG: The more you think about redefining, the more applications you'll find. It literally encompasses the entire range of human behavior and the entire spectrum of language. You can learn to do it automatically and effortlessly in regard to your child's behavior. You can redefine it so that it's practically identical with what the child thought it was, but it's more constructive. In that way the child will feel that their own spontaneous impulses are wonderful, creative, constructive. They feel, ''Gee, I've really got the right stuff because everything that I do is a success with Mom and Dad.''

Gee, You're Wonderful

This is closely related to the strategy called ''Gee, You're Wonderful,'' or the Bellac Ploy.[2] Giraudoux was a French playwright who wrote a play called, ''L'Appollon de Bellac,'' about a woman who whenever she met somebody would be immediately under the delusion that this was the most wonderful person in the world. It's also called, ''Gee, You're Wonderful.'' The subtitle is, ''When you say that (or when you do that) I feel good all over.'' You can use that with kids.

Nonevents (Selective Blindness)

JG: Now, you can carry this all the way to where something is a non-event. Where you don't put any name at all on it. It's the strategy called Selective Blindness. If the parent does not notice that the child has fallen down, but goes on talking as if nothing had happened, the kid—you can see this for yourself—they will sit there with this puzzled look on their face. They will look at mom and dad. They will look for that shocked expression that tells them something awful has happened and they should cry. Sometimes they'll start to cry and then stop because Mom and Dad don't even seem to notice. You can make something into a nonevent. Again, this is a very powerful technique. You want to be careful, of course.

Rita: That works with older people, too.

JG: Sure does!

BG: If a tree falls in the forest with no one around to hear it, is there a sound?

She Hexed Him

Rita: I can remember being in an art class when a kid cut himself on a paper cutter. I think he ended up having to have about 30 stitches in his hand. He didn't see it. He didn't respond to it. The person that was closest to him, the teacher's assistant grabbed his hand, put it behind his back and would not let him look at his hand. She got him to the infirmary, and the nurse freaked out and ruined it because the kid was not reacting. Bleeding all over the place, not reacting at all. The nurse goes, "Ahhh, look how terrible that is!" showed it to him, he passed out.

JG: That's exactly how you do it. If you want to put a hex on somebody, that's how you do it. If you want to avoid the hex, that's how you do it. A beautiful example. Do you see how that's under the control of the people involved? The nurse actually had great power there. She didn't realize that she had power, but she had the power to turn this into a disaster. It wasn't a disaster until she defined it that way.

Rita: Especially her being a nurse, I think that even added to it.

JG: When the authority figure tells you things like that, you tend to believe them. It takes a lot of power to decide that the authority figure has it wrong and is using wrong words.

The Dark Side Of Reframing
(Contaminating The Metaphor)

JG: Another name for this is: Contaminating the Metaphor. Remember the story about little Giulio and the pasta?[3] Little Giulio was an anorexic.

Louise: I don't think I've heard it.

Bring Me Pasta!

JG: It's such a wonderful story! Everybody knows that the grand Pooh-Bah's of the medical establishment have decided that anorexia nervosa is a disease of metabolism with biological causes. But Giulio was a twelve-year-old Italian boy—little boys get anorexia, too. It usually masquerades as overtraining for track, gymnastics, etc. Giulio at age twelve had gotten down to about fifty-seven pounds. He had been to several psychiatrists, and he had had several hospitalizations. None of that had worked.

Finally his parents took him all two hundred miles to Milan to the famous Milan therapy team. Mara Selvini Palazzoli saw him and at the end of the hour of interviewing the family, she said that she had to agree that Giulio's behavior was quite appropriate to the situation in which he found himself. That she couldn't see anything wrong with what he was doing. That it was obvious that there had been some mistake in the family, that evidently his mother and father had expected a little Giulia or Giulietta. They had accidentally gotten a little Giulio and she, the therapist, did not understand the reasons why Giulio had chosen to become sick around this and that, but she had to respect his decision. In particular she couldn't understand why it was he had chosen a female disease but since he had done so, she had to respect the decision. Her advice to the family was that everybody should continue to do just exactly what they were doing.

The family left the room—this was one hour of therapy—and as they began to drive through the city back to their hotel, the boy demanded that they stop the car at a restaurant. He marched in to the restaurant and said to the waiter, "Bring me pasta!" and then he proceeded to eat a pound of pasta. He gained his weight back and never again was anorexic.

Louise: Because she allowed him—?

JG: The therapist contaminated his metaphor. She told him it was a female disease, and that was utterly incompatible with what he was trying to do—whatever it was.

Accidental Witches

You can do that. You can contaminate a person's metaphor. You should be really careful when you do it, because there are born witches amongst us who do this all the time to contaminate real good metaphors by things that they say. You don't want to be an accidental witch. It's the dark side of the reframing that we talked about earlier. "You really like to explore the water in the toilet!" That's turning the metaphor into something good. Obviously the little kid doesn't think it's something bad to put his head into the toilet bowl. It's our metaphor that makes it something bad. So it's restructuring our metaphor—taking something that we regard as bad and reframe it into "heroic exploration", "scientific curiosity," "marvelous

"Turning the Metaphor into something good."

skill'' or something like that. We reframe it and give the child the gift of being competent and successful and creative and good. Contaminating the metaphor is the opposite of that.

Implication
(Just Toss Her The Towel)

So nonevents are very useful. If a kid does something and you really wouldn't like them repeating it a lot—if it's manageable, you can give it the cold shoulder.

> *Woman: With my daughter, instead of making a big deal over spilling something, I say, "Well, people make mistakes. What's important is that we clean it up and go on."*

JG: There you go.

> *Woman: I teach her how to clean it up. I think my earlier response would have been, "Oh My God, I told you not to do that, you spilled it." Now I can say, "It's all right. What's important is that we clean it up." So it's not that big a deal.*

JG: Now you can even use Implication in a situation like that. You could say nothing about it, just toss the towel to her, while you're continuing the conversation. You imply, by your behavior, that a certain behavior is going to take place,[4] and nine times out of ten it will. You haven't even asked them. They just do it—and they don't feel coerced.

When You Get To Grad School,
We'll Deal With That

JG: You can do it verbally as well as nonverbally. "When you get to grad school, we'll deal with that." You say that when they're in the seventh grade. You don't say another word, and it will sink down into their unconscious. They're going to be the person to go to grad school. How can they argue against it? How can they build any defenses against it? You've just taken it for granted. And you get that long-term effect.

> *Woman: They'd never fall for that one!*

JG: Well, if you've got smart kids!

> *Woman: You don't know how I've been plotting and planning my kid's school career—!*

JG: Actually, the way we did it was like this: We had started Duane off in kindergarten a year early for various reasons. Then when he was around ten or twelve we told him: "You are a year ahead of yourself in school, so when you graduate from high school, you can take a year off and do anything you please."

"Anything you please!" And you can imagine how he planned and fantasized and savored in imagination the delight of spending a whole year doing anything he pleased! There never was any question about finishing high school, that was taken for granted. It was a foregone conclusion.

So Duane got to go to Europe on his own with Youth for Understanding in the band. He took a whole year off! Wow!

He went alone, that is to say, with the band. It was in the sixties. It was the height of the Cold War—late sixties. All kinds of terrible things were happening in Europe. He was in Yugoslavia, and we got this telegram, this terrible telegram, that said, "Passport and all my money stolen." We were utterly incapable of helping him. There was nothing we could do. When he got home, he told us the whole story. He said that he had left his jacket with the passport and the American Express Checks on his seat while he went out of his seat. I don't know whether he went to the bathroom or what, on the train. When he came back, it was gone. He had thought it was perfectly safe. It was a car full of band people. They took him—the secret police picked him up and he flew alone sitting beside a secret police agent, all the way back to the capital, Belgrade, where he was interrogated and then got his passport back and rejoined his group.

Sabrina: Somebody had found it and turned it in?

JG: No. In fact I don't know whether they gave it back to him or created a new one or what they did, but they allowed him to continue on his tour. He was sixteen or seventeen years old. When he came back, he was a man!

Donald: When you said a free year off I was just going to comment about a year in Europe. Probably more educational than five years in most high schools in the United States.

JG: He was a man! But that particular intervention, the groundwork for that sequence of events was laid twelve years earlier. The nice thing about interventions like that is that nobody knows you've done it. I don't know whether you would call it a verbal intervention or a combined verbal and nonverbal intervention, but certainly to the kids it was just "a free year." To us, it was a guarantee that they were going to graduate from high school.

This art of communication ranges from the very brief, second-by-second interactions all the way up to an entire lifetime. Eventually, as your kids get older, they begin to catch on. As they get into their thirties, they begin to realize, ''Oh!! You did that on purpose!'' Then you begin to recover some of the status and prestige that you deliberately lost earlier playing Flaky Parent and doing some of these other strategies.

What Is An Event?

Sabrina: Dirk took Timmy to the botanical garden on Monday. The best thing he liked about it was the peanut butter and jelly sandwiches in the car!

JG: That's what the Botanical Garden was to him! Not plants. Forget the plants. He may have vaguely noticed that there were some plants there.

C: He did like the berries. He took the berries out—till we got yelled at. He picked them and smashed them like that.

JG: It really gets to very fundamental stuff, like, ''What is an experience? What is an event?''

Getting Into The Child's World

The crux of the whole problem is getting into the child's world. The secret is the ability to switch your monitoring from monitoring yourself to monitoring the other person. Where when you look at the child, you are deliberately doing something to get into their world rather than viewing his experiences from your own perspective or your own agenda.

Learn To Use Your Own Kid Part

BG: If you find that it's hard for you to be playful with your kids—for example, as you're trying to help them learn things—it may mean that you need to encourage the playful part of your own personality in order to get into that with them. Often you can get kids to do things that they need to do and you can help them keep the flow of positive feelings by playing along with them.

Are There Some Flowers On The Bottom Of Your Soup Dish?

JG: Remember last week we were talking about little Sarah and the soup?

"The crux of the whole problem is getting into the child's world."

She was saying, "I want thome thoup!" and her Mom told us, "Oh, I get so tired of telling her to eat her soup that by the end of the day I'm lithping too!" —which I thought was kind of a negative approach to this charming child. Mom was forever saying, "Eat your soup! Eat your soup!" John said, "Are there some flowers on the bottom of your bowl? Can you find the letters in your alphabet soup?" Playing with the kid around the thing that you want them to do. If you're being playful yourself, it doesn't seem like a chore or a task. It's really fun for you, too.

What's He Going To Be Like When He's Older?

BG: And there aren't any great implications about the future. When they're twenty-one they will not slurp their soup, because there are other factors—for example, girl friends and boy friends have tremendous influence on kids. They clean themselves up. They cut their hair. They really do take care of themselves when they start getting peer pressure. Just because you let a four-year-old slurp his soup doesn't mean he's gonna do it when he's twenty-one. A lot of parents feel like, "Oh, if I don't teach him now, what's he gonna be like when he's older?" By then he will have forgotten it and will be observing other things. You don't have to worry about the future now, just get through the present as best you can! There aren't necessarily any long-range problems down the road if you're keeping up with the daily flow and acknowledging the person as you go along.

When Is A Cookie?

Sabrina: It's so hard though to sit there—I put a whole plate of food in front of him. He doesn't want his squash. He doesn't want any of it, and then he says—"I'm done," pushes away his plate and then he wants a cookie. I think, "Oh, I can't do this."

Donald: Yes. "He's gonna starve."

Sabrina: He'll starve before he gets that cookie!

JG: You can try some interesting variations. You can bake the squash in the cookies. Just because it's shaped like a cookie, it doesn't have to be totally devoid of what you want him to eat.

BG: You can make a one-pound cookie and have squash and carrots and all kinds of interesting things in the cookies.

Donald: If you don't have time to bake, there's a bakery here in town that has marvellous cookies made out of whole wheat, hand-baked. So even if you don't have time to cook, you can go there and get some good-tasting, good-for-you type of pastries.

JG: What we're talking about here is a very subtle thing but it's a really important thing to grasp if you want to do good communication. That is that when a kiddie eats a cookie, they're not eating a cookie, they're eating the mental model of a cookie that they have in their head. If it has squash in it, they still see a cookie. As long as there isn't too much squash in it, it's gonna taste like a cookie, look like a cookie—it is a cookie for them. They demanded a cookie, and they got it. They are successful.

You want their experience to be the experience of success, not failure. You want them to have that solid satisfaction that comes from knowing that they can ask for a cookie because they feel like eating a cookie and they can get a cookie and eat it and be successful. And you put a little squash in it and you're successful, too.

Is It Omelette Or Broccoli?

Donald: Our son Juan went through a stage where if you mentioned the word, ''Broccoli'', he'd say, ''No broccoli! No broccoli!'' But he loves omelettes and we put tons of broccoli in our omelettes and he loves it. He thinks it's great.

JG: It's not broccoli. It's an omelette!

You've Got To Really Be On Their Side

JG: Just remember, if you're doing it for yourself, you run the risk that they will psych out your motives. If you're doing it for them, they will know that it's for them. These methods do not work at all well if they are an attempt to impose your own personal motive structure on somebody else. In fact if you continue with them, you'll reach the point where they will kick back and sometimes they kick back really hard. So it must be in their best interests—and that has to be a definition that is fairly free of your own personal biases about what their best interest is. This is not a way of creating robots.

You're Really Not Quite Old Enough For That

JG: Here's one I like a lot. It's called Restraining a Change, or Building

Anticipation. When you really want them to do something, you use expressions like, ''Well, you're really not quite old enough for that.''

Arthur: My wife Sally runs around the house all day long doing that to Brett.

JG: You mean you deliberately do this in order to get him to do things?

Arthur: Um-hmm.

Sally: ''Oh, you're not big enough to take a bath and wash yourself all by yourself.'' He hops in the tub, starts scrubbing himself up.

JG: Boy, when he catches on to you!

Sally: I don't use it for a lot of other things. I just use it when he has to take a bath, and few other things.

JG: You're absolutely right. This is the way to do it.

Sally: ''You're not big enough to buckle teddy bear up, are you?'' So he buckles himself and teddy bear up.

JG: And you can say—

Sally: ''What a big boy you are. You surprised me.''

JG: ''You surprised me,'' that's right.

Spinach Is For Grownups
(The Extended Tom Sawyer Maneuver)

JG: Now, if Dad is always going off to his room to play with his Macintosh computer—gee, that must be fun, because the adults are into it. That's the Tom Sawyer Maneuver. I don't know whether cleaning out the chicken house—you could possibly—but that's stretching it, isn't it, Beth?

Too Clean For The Chicken Coop

BG: What he means is: When I was a little kid on the farm I used to wear my Sunday dresses a lot, because I figured my parents were less likely to tell me to clean out the chicken house if I was all dressed up!

JG: That's a really ingenious strategy, but I don't know what name to call it!

Forbidden Thrills

JG: Anything that the parents are really interested in, you can bet the kid is going to watch that piece of behavior very carefully and evaluate it very seriously for its Gratification Potential. Particularly if Mom and Dad are doing it secretly. The door is locked when they do it, they don't want to talk about it.

"Now, look, Dad is gonna go upstairs and play with his computer, and we don't want any of you guys hanging around!"

Louise: Oh, yeah! We use that one!

JG: Sound familiar? You're inadvertently using it!

BG: Your kid's gonna be a really determined something or other when he gets older.

JG: The musician Handel was an example of this. His parents forbade him to play music. They put the organ in the attic. The kid would get up at night and go up and play the forbidden music. They would punish him if they caught him.

That's the Tom Sawyer Maneuver. Remember how Tom got all the kids to help him whitewash the fence, even paying him for the privilege? If you want them to be interested in it, make it a little hard to get. Make it a little bit forbidden, and give the nonverbal signals that you're interested—

"Spinach is for grownups!" But isn't the same thing true of olives and anchovies and stuff that kids usually hate? There comes a point in their life when they say—maybe they're twelve, fifteen—"There must be something to it. What kind of secret kicks are the grownups getting out of that?"

Louise: Our baby already likes black olives!

JG: There you go!

Did Mom Throw The Buttons?

Karla: I have to tell you something that happened last week. I was sewing a button on my pants and Bridget was causing a conflict. She wanted to sew too. I was in a hurry. I didn't have time for her to sew. She grabbed the buttons and she held them up in the air. She started halfway into a tantrum and the buttons flew and the sewing-case hit the floor. Her brother turned around and asked, "What happened?"

I said, "I think I knocked the buttons off the couch." Then Bridget started laughing and said, "I threw the buttons." Her brother said, "Mom, did you throw the buttons?" I said, "Well, I think they were on the couch and that I bumped them." Bridget walked away whispering, "I threw them."

Woman: *You hadn't given her credit for that big effect.*

Karla: *I didn't know why I said it, it was just that I didn't want this conflict. She thought I didn't see her hold them up in the air so she really thought that I thought I knocked them off the couch.*

JG: Tricky! You don't always have to be totally rational about these things. That's marvelous!

Karla: *She just walked away but I heard her mumbling, "I threw the buttons." That's all. She had to make sure that she knew she had thrown—*

JG: Do you know what you did? You threw into question her model of reality. She thought she did something and you read back to her an interpretation that wouldn't fit.

Karla: *Well, she told me about three times, "I threw them down there!" I said, "Well, they were sitting right here. I think I bumped it off."*

JG: You don't mind going for the big time, do you?

Karla: *Well, I—I—I didn't want a tantrum right then, I was trying to get out the door.*

JG: Yeah! You challenged her reality.

Karla: *She was smiling but she was also—I could tell she really had started to wonder if I thought she threw them or not.*

JG: What you did was raise an issue that was even deeper than the power struggle. Namely, am I seeing reality right? I like that!

BG: You're ingenious!

Karla: *She was saying, "I threw 'em." Her brother had 'em all cleaned up and put away. He says, "Well, Mom, I'll help you pick 'em up and—". He cleaned it all up because he thought I really had bumped them off the couch on to the floor. She was just standing there trying to convince me that she threw them.*

BG: —and wanting to get a rise out of you.

> *Karla: Right. To see what I was gonna do if she had convinced me that she had thrown them. She just walked away smiling about it. I don't know what she finally concluded in her own mind.*

JG: That's a very, very—

BG: Astute!

JG: —powerful intervention!

> *Karla: I just couldn't take a tantrum right then.*

BG: Right!

> *Karla: I didn't think about what I was gonna do. I knew she was edging towards what was eventually gonna happen but I wasn't sitting there thinking, "Well, what am I gonna do here?" It just kinda came out. I just kinda said that I had dropped the buttons.*

JG: You knew enough not to run straight into the trap. She was setting up a trap to have a fight with you.

> *Karla: Well, I think six months ago I would have jumped up and ripped the buttons out of her hand and said, "You're not gonna throw these on the floor!"*

JG: You knew what she was expecting—

> *Karla: "I'm gonna put them on top of the refrigerator so you can't reach 'em." Then we would really have been into it.*

BG: *Real confrontation!*

Make A U-Turn

JG: You're like the rabbit that jumps into the briar patch when he's expected to run in another direction. You suddenly just did a U-turn.

BG: Poor Brer Fox couldn't get him. Too many thorns.

JG: Now, that's being unpredictable!

> *Karla: Well, that's what I think I was trying to do, because she's so smart that she knows what I'm gonna do before I know what I'm gonna do. The tantrums are hardly ever—I mean I'm pretty good at avoiding them now. I*

can see them coming ten minutes before she's even getting to the stage where she's starting to get upset.

BG: Um-hmm. It's kind of a decision on your part that you're gonna sleuth her out without having a confrontation?

We'll Wake You When It's Time

Naomi: After the first time Jordan came into our room, we were going to say, ''OK, you can come in again. We'll wake you up when it's time.'' We had figured out what we were going to say. ''It's time to come into our room now. We know you'd like to come in. It's time now.'' I thought, ''Either he'll buy that and he'll sleep through or we'll wake him up when it's time.'' He slept through the whole night, till seven o'clock! I mean, we didn't even get to try it.

Woman: But that was just one night.

JG: Then did it start again?

Naomi: Well, last night, he woke up at 11:30 and 12:00, but then he slept until seven. I could take that.

JG: So he's back to what you'd say is a reasonable level of interruptions?

Naomi: Yes, because we were just going to sleep. But if he starts doing this at 3 or 4 in the morning again, every few minutes, I'm going to do it. The only thing we also did differently was to put him to bed about 9 o'clock. We'd had him at the table with our dinner and fed him more. So maybe he wasn't hungry.

Often It's Enough Just To Know That You've Got The Strategy

JG: You've brought up a point that is really significant. I don't know how to teach it. I really don't know how to get it across until you've actually had this experience. You won't believe me anyway. Often it's enough just to know that you've got the strategy, because kids have radar.

They will pick it up. They will detect the fact, ''Gosh, what's going on here? Mom and Dad are—somehow they are different tonight. I better not raise my head tonight. I better stay right in that bed.'' Somehow they know.

Rita: We planned it and talked about it, and when vacation came we were going to do it. Bert kept saying, ''We've got nothing to lose.''

"Often it's enough just to know you've got the strategy, because kids have radar."

JG: You can talk in eight syllable words right over their head. You'd swear they can't understand a thing you're saying.

It Works Even If You Don't Buy It

JG: It's like those electronic bedwetting alarms. I have recommended those on occasions. I have had the kid sitting there with Dad or Mom listening as I explain to Dad how the thing works, and how the kid will not have to sleep in a wet bed, because the instant there's the slightest bit of moisture, the alarm will go off.

I remember one case, I didn't see the parents again for six months or so, and I said, "Oh, by the way, how did that alarm work?" They said, "We didn't buy it." "Well, why not?" They said, "Well, it was $19.00 and we didn't want to buy it. We didn't want to pay for it. So we waited, and that night he didn't wet his bed. We waited another night, and he didn't wet his bed that night. We waited a week and he didn't wet his bed. A month later we decided we didn't need it."

It's amazing. This is a device that works even if you don't buy it.

Naomi: Well, I wanted to try that new strategy, we were all set.

JG: You were all set. He frustrated you. It's almost enough to make you wish they would do something, so you could try one of these strategies, just to see if it works.

And I heard you use the magical sentence. "I know how much you like to do 'X'." "We know you'd like to come in."

The Perils Of Dawdling

Arthur: A lot of times we tell her to go get a story, pick out a story, and it takes her 10 minutes to come back with a book.

JG: Of course. Stave off this dreadful moment.

Sally: When we're leaving the house, Brett does that now. He hurriedly does everything he needs to do. "Come on, Brett, you've got to go." "One minute while I finish this."

Hidden Symmetry

JG: Now at a certain age, you can actually reverse this pattern. That is to say, you can be the one who holds them up, without saying a word about it. You can be the one that just can't quite get everything ready. You insert a Hidden Symmetry into the situation, what Milton Erickson called the absolute peril of dawdling.[5] By this spillover effect that we were talking about, it will change the situation. You don't have to say anything. If you say something you'll spoil it, because then it becomes punishment, then it becomes a matter of honor on the child's part to resist it and fight against it. Punishment is almost always self-defeating.[6]

But if Mom and Dad have a behavior pattern that involves the kid wanting to get somewhere, or to get something done in a hurry, and Mom and Dad are struggling and hurrying and delaying, that'll be a pattern that the kid hates. They may hate it in themselves, particularly if they do it more and discover that Mom and Dad get worse. Kids try to psych out the way the universe works. They try to psych out cause and effect. At some unconscious level they may actually believe that because they're dawdling more, Mom and Dad are dawdling more.

One By One They
Fell Asleep In Their Tracks

JG: My pediatrician—that is to say my teacher when I was in training in pediatrics—had six kids. He was a very scientifically active person. He wrote a lot of scientific papers. His pattern with his kids—he and his wife agreed on this, so you understand this was by mutual agreement—they would all eat supper together. Then he would push the dishes away and bring out his scientific papers and begin to write. He would write his scientific papers from 7:30 till 8:30, till 9:30, 10:30, 11:30, 12:30, and 1:30 and 2:30 in the morning because he was a very energetic, scientifically-oriented person.

He didn't pay a bit of attention to the kids. They played all around the dining room table. They played in the living room. They made noise and it didn't bother him. The older ones did their homework on the floor in the living room. It didn't bother him. One by one they would fall asleep in their tracks, until finally at 2:30 in the morning, there were bodies scattered all over the dining room and the living room.

And that's the way those kids slept. They never had to go to bed. They decided how much sleep they needed. The older kids would wander off to their own bedroom and go to sleep when they were ready. Now granted, that's a rather drastic approach.

Woman: *But it worked!*

JG: If you have a spouse that can stand lack of sleep, this method is worth thinking about.

Finally, She Puts Me To Bed!

Sally: That's what we finally did with Brett. We got so frustrated with fighting over his going to bed, that after a while I took away his nap, because he wasn't really needing it. Then, when he would start going into his usual pattern, when he would normally take a nap, I'd just get something really exciting to do. Keep him up! By about 8:30 he'll be sitting on the couch resisting sleep, the next thing you look at him, he's snoring. We take him upstairs and put him to bed. He hasn't given us a hassle about bed time since.

JG: It's just a delight to have you folks here!

Sally: Now he almost requests going to bed—I put him to bed the other night before he fell asleep and he was like—"Ahhh! finally, she puts me to bed!"

JG: You have given him the opportunity to learn the feeling that you have when you really need to go to sleep.

Woman: Elegant!

Mimi: "Is it my bedtime yet, Mom?"

JG: "No, not yet, honey, stay up a little longer!"

Playing The Seesaw

JG: You can get on the opposite side and you can play it back and forth, if you develop the technique of using your footwork. You can be on this side and you can be on that side, and they don't know where you're gonna be from one time to the next. When they realize that they can't predict you, then they really know that you are the parents, that you really do know more than they do.

This is the best class I think we've ever had!

Arthur: Isn't that one of your techniques?

JG: You'll never know!!! And the delight of this is that you can be perfectly sincere!

Chapter 20
Why Not Learn To Fly The Real Thing

Redefining School

JG: You can redefine anything so that it will tend in a constructive direction, but you have to have some skill in redefining. You have to practice it. Most of us have never done that in a constructive way. When somebody says to you, "Your child is a predelinquent,"—or something like that—they're defining the situation. Well, why should they be the ones to define the situation? You come back with a definition of your own—a redefinition if you like—that is even stronger than theirs.

Kay: Do you have one for that?

Jamming Their Game

JG: Well, that particular statement has the quality of an accusation to it. It implies, "You should feel guilty. You should feel ashamed." And you know how hard it is to fight off an accusation. You're stuck with trying to prove a negative. You get defensive. You say, "No, he's not," and there's no way out.

For that situation you can use a special strategy that redefines the whole situation. You use the strategy called, "Jamming The Game of Accuser/Defender."[1] You say, "He's under medical care, but the doctor can't help him."

Cora: If you say things like that to people like my parents—like my mother—she'd be furious. "Oh, you're being sarcastic with me!"

JG: Isn't that just the point, though? You've been unfairly attacked. You've been put on the defensive.

287

Ralph: You can say, "Well, gosh, you should have seen what he did to his teacher last year!"

JG: You can say he's really better than he was last year! His therapist is beginning to be hopeful he can make a full recovery.

Kay: Have they taken this course before? They've got it down!

JG: You will all be consultants in another six weeks!

Ralph: Now I was just really hard on teachers when I was a kid, so I suspect that I have had more experience—

Kay: Ohhh!

Nora: The ghosts in the nursery here!

Priscilla: There can be kids like this. They get kicked out of school, and they're productive people in society today.

Kay: When we went back for Ralph's tenth class reunion—I went to the same high school, so I know a lot of these people too—he remarked that it was people who were the brightest, that had the most promise, were the ones that were having the most problems at the moment. While the ones you didn't think were gonna make very much of themselves were doing the best.

School As Gulag

JG: You can even redefine schooling. School is an arrangement whereby society sits you in a seat and expects you to sit there without talking, for sixteen years. Well, that's a prison.

Ralph: School buildings are designed for effects—

JG: They look like prisons, don't they?

Kay: —no windows!

Cora: Assault proof!

Kay: Mine was granite, all the way through high school.

Ralph: Mine had this sickly green paint on the walls. This real light green for the institutional—

Kay: Right, 'cause green was—

JG: The color.

BG: Called bilious green.

JG: Call it a Cruikshank method, paint the world gray so that kids won't be tempted to go hyperactive.

> *Ralph: Yeah. Well, that was explicitly what it was at our high school. They had—it was green up to, like, here, and then beige up above—and it was supposed to make the kids be calm.*
>
> *Bobbi: You mean there was psychology behind those colors?*
>
> *Ralph: Yes!*

JG: How can you make a nation of individuals if you force them from infancy to be conformists? It's very easy to redefine the school system and make it into a Gulag, a prison. I personally felt that way about it. I dropped out twice—or was it three times? Once in third grade, once in high school, and once in college. In those days you could get back in by taking college entrance exams. Then they didn't know where to put me!

> *Kay: They didn't know where to put Ralph, even in high school, even though he went every day.*
>
> *Ralph: Yeah, eventually we settled on the arrangement whereby I could, like, leave whenever I felt like it (laughs)—*

JG: Yes! Right! That's not—that's the first little crack in the system, when they agree that there may be some people that don't profit by it.

> *Ralph: Well, actually, that wasn't it so much—*
>
> *Kay: How nice that they made an exception.*
>
> *Ralph: —as they just couldn't stand the trouble—it was more trouble than it was worth having a certain group of us in the school—*

Acknowledging The Problem

> *Bobbi: Yeah! So what did your Mom and Dad do when you decided to drop out of the third grade?*
>
> *Kay: Oh, that must have driven them crazy!*

JG: I had a tantrum! My Dad moved a lot, because he was moving up in the world. Every time he improved in position, he moved. They took me out of second grade and moved me to a new school and put me in third grade.

I just had a tantrum. I said, ''Look! They use check marks where the other teacher used X's. I'm getting all these check marks on my paper that mean that the answers are wrong. I know they're not wrong.''

I just threw a tantrum. I actually got down on the kitchen floor and raged. Well, that one I think they won, in a way. I did go back to school and within a short time I was loving it, because I was learning stuff. That was third grade.

Kay: You both won.

JG: We both won. They listened very respectfully to what I had to say. They acknowledged that I was objecting to the school and that as an autonomous individual with my own set of values, it was OK for me to do that. I really felt that they handled that well.

> *Bobbi: So in other words by just acknowledging the problem, without really having to go out and change a system, you can say to a child—or by giving them that respect and acknowledgement—they can sit there and feel better and actually go back and say, "I think I can deal with this."*

Dropping Out Of School Successfully

JG: You can get it out. You can be heard. You can have your dignity. You can be respected. Also, you have to go back to school. That one worked out quite well. I very quickly loved the new set of teachers just as I loved the old ones.

But when it came to high school, I was seventeen and I said, "I refuse to go to a literature class where they're discussing the Saturday Evening Post. I want to learn literature—real literature. I'm not going to go to a Latin class where the teacher has been unable to get the students to stop milling around and sit down. It's been six weeks and we haven't started the book yet."

I said, "I'm not going to do this." So my parents called the principal and the dean—and I was called in to this amazing meeting—and they said, "You are seventeen, you don't have to go to school. It sounds like you have some ideas of your own, so why don't you do it yourself?" I said, "Wow!"

Ralph: What a high!

JG: "You mean I can quit school?" They said, "Yes." Basically they said, "We have a lot of confidence in you. You've got a good record, so go home, do it yourself."

So I did. Greatest thing that ever happened to me. They were validating my dignity as a separate human being. They weren't saying,

"Look, you're shaming your parents. You'll be a delinquent, you're gonna be a dropout, next thing you know—"

The "Gentleman's 'C'"

Nora: I'm just anticipating Roxanne not doing well in that, because she can hardly sit still. She's just so fidgety, I don't know what to do with her. What is she gonna do, sitting there all day?

JG: You can tell her, "You vigorous, energetic, physical people, you really don't have a very easy time of it in school." You say, "Do what you can, I'll be satisfied with a 'C'." You remember back in the old days—do they still do this?—a "gentleman's 'C'" is the correct grade for a person to get in college—

Ralph: Hah! Well, I don't know, I don't think—

Kay: No!

Ralph: I've not known very many families who adhered to that! (laughs)

Kay: Not mine!

JG: I was raised on that tradition—

Kay: "C" is OK?

JG: —and when Duane's grades began to fall, in law school—

BG: —in law school, because teaching technical English and trying to go to law school—

JG: Right. I wrote him a letter back and the letter was only one page. It said, "A gentleman's 'C' is all that can be expected of a person in graduate school. If you want to make a higher grade, you'll have to do it yourself." Basically I was telling him, "It doesn't matter to me whether you make an "A", a "B", or a "C". If you want that distinction, do it yourself. I'm just proud that you're in Law School." His grades promptly came right up and stayed up.

BG: Well, and I also had my foot in that one.

JG: Oh, you did?

Kay: Oh-oh! (Laughter)

JG: Well, what strategy did you use?

BG: He was telling me on the phone how bad he felt because he had gotten one "C", and he was afraid that his grades were gonna drop below the graduate school expectations of a "B".

I said, "But what about the evaluations that have come in from all your technical writing students? How would you rate them on a grade level?" Well, he said, "They're all 'A-plusses'." The students that he had thought he was a super teacher. They were all doing beautifully. They were all getting "A"s. He didn't even have hardly a curve in his class. I said, "That should count for something." But he says it doesn't count in law school. I said, "Well, all right. I'm sorry about that, but balance against that, the fact that you are an absolutely marvelous teacher." And I don't know if that bit of self-esteem helped—

Kay: Oh, he was working on his self-esteem—

JG: It sure did.

BG: To be able to say, "Well, I can hack this law stuff if I can be as good a teacher as that to all those students." He had a huge class. He was having to grade papers all the time. That was what was taking his time.

Single Vision

JG: We live in a civilization where linear rational thought is supreme. If a person is doing a marvelous job of being a teacher while they are simultaneously going to law school, the fact that they get a grade lower in the law school—the law school will only look at that. They have this single vision.

You can go back all the way to William Blake. He said, "From single vision and from Newton's sleep, Good Lord, deliver us." Linear, rational thinking. But a person is a real person, in multidimensions with multiple activities. You can't make 'em ride or fall, sink or swim, on the basis of one thing that they're doing. So, when it comes to parenting, you judge every facet. You take into account every facet, and you redefine these impasses in terms of that whole person. You bring in the positive qualities, and you use that when you interact.

So you don't act towards them the way the school system is acting towards them. You don't act towards them the way the neighbors are acting towards them. You take everything into account, and then you use that to provide a basis for an interaction that will maintain their dignity and their self-esteem.

She Petted A Duck

BG: Well, let me give them a break. I'll tell a story.

JG: Go ahead.

BG: We saw a child that was being aggressive, physically energetic, bopping other kids in nursery school, and kicking her mother in the shins . . . just being generally difficult to deal with. John was able to reframe this family around this child's behavior, saying that she must be extremely bright, probably very frustrated by the restrictions and inhibitions that are being imposed on her at this age—I think she was nineteen months or not quite two. She was biting the other kids and this was really difficult. They didn't know what to do.

I think John suggested that the mother might need to spend some special time with her, going outdoors and doing really vigorous physical things . . . doing different things than she was getting in the nursery school setting.

I think she was three when she went up to a wild duck out by a pond and petted this duck. It sat there and just let her pet it. It was one of these wild ducks that usually move off when someone comes close. She got real excited. She could see the sheen on the colors of the head of the duck and the duck responded. I guess it finally got up and waddled back to the water, but it was so exciting for her. She came back and said, "Mommy! Mommy! I petted a duck! I petted a duck!"

John said, "Well, encourage that! Get her a bug barn or something. Let her do the naturalist sort of thing." It just happened we had a book about the lady that did genetics. She's eighty-three years old—Barbara—

JG: —McClintock.

BG: —McClintock. Barbara McClintock. We just happened to have an extra copy of this book around. I gave it to them to read. The parents got very excited, because that was what that lady's parents had done—

JG: That's exactly her life story.

BG: Back in the early 1900's her mother had taken her up north in the lakes region and let the kid just roam. She kept an eye on her, but she just let her explore and do things with the creatures that were in the environment. So they did this with this little girl, got a bunch of guinea pigs, and did just all kinds of naturalist type things. This just took off. She didn't have any more trouble in nursery school because she was so busy thinking about what else she was going do later and the next day that she could put up with a couple of hours of nursery school, conforming to their system.

JG: How old was she when you saw her last . . . when we went over there?

BG: That was this last summer, she must have been—seven now.

JG: The first thing she said when we walked in the door, she said, ''Let me show you my Cecropia moth!''

Kay: Wow!

BG: She had one that had laid eggs, and she was waiting for them to hatch. Seven years old. She could turn out to be a real naturalist.

JG: That's a lovely story. What I said at nineteen months was something to the effect of, ''She doesn't like people all that much. Maybe she's a scientist.''

Kay: Well, that's the way Barbara McClintock is. She just keeps going. She lives all by herself. She shoos people away. She won't have anything to do with other people. I imagine she's pretty hard to get along with, but she's a brilliant scientist.

JG: Actually, I think the word I used was, ''inner-directed.'' I said, ''She doesn't want to mess with these pre-schoolers—''

Cora: —and rules.

JG: ''She's inner-directed. She's probably a scientist.'' That's reframing. ''Unsociable behavior'' (which is the frame her preschool teachers were starting to use) is being reframed as a positive attribute. If you pick the right reframe, you've got the person in a frame that they like—that's mutually comfortable. The parents can be proud of it and the child can feel comfortable with it.

BG: There are many directions. For example, an active child could be a gymnast. It doesn't have to be any one special thing.

JG: Right. You may find that you have made the wrong choice—that that frame isn't really the one that is most comfortable—

BG: —it doesn't fit her, so you try something else.

JG: The way this little girl ended up, her backyard was a fairly junglelike arrangement over here on the west side. They had guinea pigs outdoors—being raised outdoors—and the whole place was just turning into kind of a terrarium I guess you might say.

BG: They had the wild rabbits that were feeding. The neighbors of course didn't like that because—

    Cora: *Rabbits in the garden!*

JG: The thing was, she would spontaneously take over this stuff because she was really interested.

Don't Stand In Front Of The Locomotive

The parents had found which way this little plant was going to grow. They had found the area in which this little person could blossom and develop to the fullest, and so they just had to sit back. There was nothing more they needed to do because they had tapped into the energy of this growing child. That energy was going in this direction—why stand in front of it and try to stop it? Stand aside—find where it can go. Create the conditions and then step aside. That's all you need to do. Mother Nature will do the rest.

BG: It isn't any harder doing it right. I mean, figuring it out and going with the flow is probably less energy-consuming than to be fighting it all the time.

JG: That's the purpose of knowledge and thinking—to avoid having to do things the hard way. You figure it out. You find out where it's going. It's like Bucky Fuller says, ''Don't oppose forces. Go with them. Use them.''

But there are times when you have to make an intervention, or at least you think you have to make an intervention, for safety or for some other purpose. Being able to do that—to deliberately move in and alter the direction that a child is going without setting up an adversary relationship, without getting into the position of being the bad guy who's stopping them from having their fun—there you have to have specific strategies. You have to know how to do these things. I think I've told some of you about the hang-glider, haven't I?

K: No. I haven't heard about that.

JG: We regarded that as a very serious development. Our kids were growing up. They'd been avid model airplane enthusiasts ever since they were seven years old—which is another story by the way—how we kept them from becoming—

BG: —motorcycle fiends.

Why Not Learn To Fly The Real Thing?

JG: —motorcycle fiends. You can tell 'em about that. Dave at the age of fourteen, said, "I want a motorcycle." He'd already taken a used car apart and left it in the back yard. We were thinking, "Oh, my God. Another motorcycle fiend."

Then Beth did this amazing thing, just on the spur of the moment. She said, "What do you want to mess around with motorcycles for? You've been a model airplane builder all your life. Why don't you learn to fly the real thing?"

God, this fourteen year old, he just practically—"My Mom is gonna let me fly airplanes!!! Not motorcycles—airplanes!!!" She said, "I'll take you down to Willow Run, and we'll do a trial flight today, right now."

BG: They had those five-dollar, come-on things—

JG: She drove this fourteen year old out to Willow Run—

Kay: On the spur!

JG: On the spur of the moment, located the pilot and said, "My son wants to fly!"

BG: Plunked down five dollars and said, "We want your demonstration ride."

JG: She sat out on the tarmac and watched. We already knew something about this boy. I'll tell you later.

Cora: But it's the pilot who flies the plane?

JG: No!!

Ralph: No?

JG: No. The pilot takes off,—

BG: The pilot takes it off—

JG: —and with an adult trainee, of course, there comes a point where the pilot says, "Would you like to try the stick?"

BG: It's dual control.

JG: But a fourteen year old—never in a thousand years. Anyway the plane went off, up—flew off into the distance. Beth waited—

BG: Half an hour—

JG: Half an hour went by. The time was up for the five dollars. Forty-five minutes, fifty minutes, an hour—

Ralph: You sure got your five dollars worth, didn't you?

BG: Yes!

JG: —and she began to wonder, where did they go?

BG: I was really getting worried.

Kay: He was having a ball with it.

JG: —worried, did they crash? Then the plane appeared and began to wobble back towards the airport and wobblingly circled the airport and wobbingly came down and bounced a little bit and came to a stop and—out jumped Dave! He ran across—"Mom, I flew it! I flew it!"

BG: —and he landed it! I couldn't believe—

JG: Yes! He landed the airplane. Without a single lesson!

BG: The pilot gave him the stick.

JG: But he'd been building airplanes all his life. He knew what they were all about.

BG: On the radio-controlled model airplanes, the controls are exactly like a real airplane.

Cora: Oh, so it's all familiar—

BG: —and this guy had the feel for the real thing. He has the kinesthetics—

Cora: Unh-hunh. The aerodynamics, the—

JG: —but we knew that before.

BG: —Like me! He's kinesthetic, like me.

Kay: —like you!

I Don't Think So

JG: —because I had tried to get him interested in golf, which is my game. I took him out when he was six? Seven?—

BG: Eight.

JG: —years old. He was a gangly kid at that age. I explained to him, "Now, this is the club. You hit the ball with this. This is the ball—" and I threw it down on the ground. I said, "The object is to knock it closer to the hole." So he picks up the club and he says, "Is this the right end?"

BG: Which hand do you put on top?

JG: I said, "Now, just let it swing gently and hit that ball." He hit the ball, and it went up in a perfect parabola, curved up in the air, went a hundred and fifty yards, landed on the green and bounced towards the cup. I said, "Wow! You're gonna play golf with me for the rest of my life!"
But he said, "I don't think so." "I don't think so."

Their Thing, Not Your Thing

JG: So we knew he had the reflexes. He never played golf. He wasn't interested. He would have been a marvelous golfer. But it had to be his thing—not my thing—his thing. So Beth knew he would be all right when he got up in that airplane.

BG: We went at it seriously. We put up the money and we said, "You can have flying lessons."

JG: When he went to Florida, he took a job on the flight line as a mechanic and used that money to pay for flying lessons. He now has five tickets including the—

BG: —commercial—

JG: —instrument rules, the commercial, the multi-engine, and so on. He's done it all himself, and there never was a word about getting a motorcycle. There never ever was another discussion because that was just—a pilot associates with trained, disciplined mature people—

BG: Well, there was one interlude down in Florida. He bought himself a motorcycle—

JG: Oh sure! But by then he was twenty-seven.

> ***Bobbi:*** *By then it's their own problem!*

JG: Yeah!

BG: He told me afterwards—he was a little sheepish about it. He said, "You know, you can't take a girl on a date on a motorcycle, especially when it rains."

JG: Right!

BG: I think it had happened to him—

JG: —and the reason why preteeners and early teeners like motorcycles is because it keeps them distant from girls. When they get past that stage, then they realize that the thing is an impediment rather than a help—

BG: —It's not any fun, really.

JG: Do you recognize the strategy involved? That's the point.

That's My Hang-glider!

JG: Let me tell you the story about the hang-glider because I think it's pertinent.

Duane also had been in the basement for twelve years learning how to make model airplanes. He didn't want to imitate his younger brother and fly airplanes. He wanted to be a hang-glider person! One day he came home with this mass of bolts and screws and rods and Nylon—

BG: It looked like the sail for a big huge sailboat draped over this little Saab.

JG: At first we thought he had brought home a piece of a sailboat. I said, "What on earth is that?" He said, "Dad, that's my hang-glider. I'm gonna be a hang-glider person!" I don't know if you've ever experienced that sinking feeling, but it's an awful feeling—Oh, my God!

Ralph: Like—*"We're gonna move to Kansas!"*

BG: Where there aren't any hills.

JG: He said, "I've saved my money. I've saved twenty five hundred dollars."

Kay: God!

JG: He really put out the effort for this. "—and I bought this and it's mine, and I want you to see how beautiful it is. So will you come out in the back yard with me and let me show you as I assemble it."

At that point—not knowing of any strategy—I used diplomacy, pacing, and positive connotation. I said, "Well, sure." I didn't let him see how pale my face was. We went out into the back yard. He proceeded to put this thing together from three o'clock to four o'clock and from four o'clock to five o'clock and from five o'clock to six o'clock. We sat there and the sun went over the sky and set. We turned on the backyard lights and here is this gigantic bat-like creature growing in the twilight till finally it's looming up there like some kind of a—

BG: Rainbow colors—

JG: To me it looked like a giant bat. When he got it all put together he said, "Here's what you do. You lie right here"—with that leather strap— "and then you can fly!" I said, "Wow!" It was too dark that night, so he dismantled it—

BG: Ummh-hmm.

JG: —took him till midnight. He dismantled it, and put it away. Then a few days later the opportunity came and he said, ''Take me down to the golf course, because I want to show you how this thing flies, it's really neat.''

BG: If any of you know the golf course over there.

Cora: Yeah. I figured it had to be on a golf course.

BG: ''Suicide Hill''—there's one—

JG: Number Seventeen or thereabouts, where you tee off and there's a cliff—

I went out there with my heart sinking, smiling and—Duane had his own car at that time, didn't he?

BG: Well, I let him use the Saab most of the time—little thing. It looked so funny.

JG: It looked like a car with wings, with this thing sticking on the Saab. He put it together right there on the tee-off, got into it, strapped himself in, backed up all the way back so as to get a good running start, and he ran—again it was about twilight—he ran and leaped off the cliff.

And the thing flew! And I could just see what an experience this was for him. It was only about a half inch off the ground, but it was flying. Maybe he got up to a foot or two. Then it ran out of wind and it came to the ground. It hit really hard and bent the struts. Duane was thrown forward onto the ground. He didn't break anything, but he was out of breath. He stood up and he said, ''See! It flies!''

I said, ''That's great!'' It was too dark to try again, so we went home. A couple of days later he announced he was going to take it up to Sleeping Bear Dunes.

Ralph: It's actually probably about the best place you could go to—

Cora: They have big competitions up there.

JG: Yes. There was a cold snap that Fall, and he didn't actually get to take it up there. He went up there once and watched the others hang glide but—it wasn't—

Kay: Land in the water?

Ralph: You wouldn't want to land in the water!

Cora: Some little beach?

BG: You run off the dunes and fly around and hopefully land on the beach. There's a wind off Lake Michigan that—

Cora: Yeah. Yeah.

JG: He didn't actually do it, and God! did we feel relieved. Anyway, Winter set in, and he rolled up the hang glider and put it in the garage—

BG: —diagonally. It was twenty-four feet long.

JG: We're talking about the early days of hang gliding. It didn't have anti-stall on it. It would stall and fall straight down—

BG: —one of the earliest models. It was a terrible thing.

JG: We didn't know what to do. We just looked at each other. But that Winter . . . he fell in love. He met the girl that he later married. And the courtship proceeded very quickly. It was only a few weeks until he had reached the stage of bringing her home to introduce her to the family and show her around the family estate—all quarter acre of it. He was proudly doing this with Barbara and they came to the garage. She looked up and saw this thing and she said, "What's that?"

JG: We were listening behind the door!

BG: We were in the kitchen.

JG: I will admit it. Because they were engaged. There was this long silence from the garage, and then we heard the fatal words. She said, "Death-toy! Either it goes or I go!"

Bobbi: —You said—

Cora (shouting): "You love this girl!! Marry her!!"

JG: You should have seen us! We didn't dare to say anything. That was the end of that. He never touched it again. It rotted in place. Beth got rid of it last year. That was the end of hang-gliding.

Duane went on to become a champion model airplane racer, a designer of racing model airplanes, an editor of the model racers' magazine, and an organizer of model racing societies.

A Stronger Voice

JG: What is the strategy represented here? It's very simple. If you don't have the power to tell them something, find somebody whose voice is stronger.[2]

> *Kay: The girlfriend!*

BG: Yep!

JG: That's right. She was in a position where she could carry it out. She had leverage. We didn't. You tell a young adult that something is too risky for them, what are they going to say?

> *Kay: "You don't know anything."*

JG: "You don't know anything. I'm competent. I'll show you."

> *Ralph: Do you think it helped that you didn't say, "No"?*

That Ancient Pattern

JG: Absolutely. That's the thing that would have killed it, because then we would have fallen into that ancient pattern of the wise old parent who's dull and boring telling the young hero that they can't do their heroic deeds. You can't get anywhere that way. If they listen to you, they have betrayed their own self-confidence. You're asking them to give up something that's very precious. So you don't ask them to obey you when they are young adults. What you do is let them show you what they can do. But you can let somebody else come in and tell them a thing or two.

". . . then we would have fallen into that ancient pattern of the wise old parent who's dull and boring telling the young hero that they can't do heroic deeds."

Chapter 21
The Miracle That Your Child Is

Make A Little Change
(Penny On The Rails)

JG: I think that kids often recognize that their parents are not pleased by some aspect of their behavior, but the conditioning—whatever it is, that the parents themselves may not know about—that conditioning is continuing. It continues to trigger the undesired behavior. They find themselves willy-nilly doing what offends their parents. They can't stop because they're not aware that the triggers are still being fired because they're behaving in the same way. Then something comes along and changes the situation in a very small way, and all of a sudden the whole thing has changed. The corresponding strategy is called, "Make A Little Change." Instead of trying to get the whole thing to change, change some little tiny insignificant part of it. This is that snowball effect again.[1] You may discover that what you have done is kind of like putting a penny on the rails of the locomotive. It's a small change, but it can produce a big effect. You know, if you're starting to ski down a hill, you can make a small change this way or that way and you may find yourself on the other side of the mountain by the time you get to the bottom of the hill.

Chaos

JG: How many of you have seen the TV program Nova? Do you ever watch Nova? Have you seen the episode called "Chaos"? It's one of the newest ones.

Back in the 50's one of the great prophecies that was made about the brave new world was that we'd be able to predict the weather two weeks in advance. You'll notice that it hasn't happened yet. Right?

Man: They can't predict it for 24 hours!

305

JG: Right! This was thought to be due to the fact that there wasn't enough information. So, as the computer age came along; and as there began to be thousands of weather stations around the world with instantaneous feed-in into a central gigantic computer, they figured, "OK, with enough information, we'll be able to predict the weather two weeks in advance." But what actually happened was, the prediction quality didn't improve. They still could predict three days, but they could not predict two weeks.

Finally it dawned on a weather person, a meteorologist, to check this out from a mathematical standpoint. He was able to show that it is in principle unpredictable. It's not a matter of having detailed information. You can't do it, no matter how much information you have.

This is what is called Chaos. We start with our deterministic world model in which you have all the data, and unexpected events will still happen. I'm not going to try to go through the intricacies of that because it involves some sophisticated math that I didn't understand, but it explains why the weather man comes on the day after predicting a big snowstorm and says, "Gee, that's funny. We got a big rainstorm way over here instead of a snowstorm over there, and it took place twelve hours earlier than we predicted."

It's because you make a little change, so small that it's in the 12th decimal place. Somewhere way out there. It's at the limits of the instruments. That little change, by the process of consecutive re-iteration of differential equations, will generate a gigantic difference in the outcome.[2]

So, you go down the slope and you turn your skis a little bit this way or a little bit this way, and you end up in a far different place. OK, human behavior is like that. If you understand that, and accept it, then you can realize that you can make enormous changes if you can just get a person to make a little change.

So don't go for the end result all at once. Don't tell your kid when he's seven, "I demand that you commit yourself to Harvard graduate school." Just be happy with one little change. Maybe ten minutes more study—or ten minutes less study, because you don't know which way they are going to go. Just practice making a little change.

Lifting The Spell

BG: That should release some of us who have the idea that parenting is such a heavy responsibility—that if you don't do X when the kid is a toddler, he's going to turn out to be a juvenile delinquent down the road. And blah, blah, blah!

Arthur: That's what my mom thought.

BG: Yes!

JG: That's that deterministic model. Where if you start out on a certain path, it's like iron rails.

Sally: "Don't pick that baby up, he'll get spoiled and will just have control of you for the rest of your lives!"

JG: Right.

BG: There's the track lying right up there.

JG: Now if you believe that, then your own mother has induced a small change in you, which can actually make that come true by a process of self-fulfilling prophecy.

Sally: Well, actually it worked out real well for us. My father was there and he said, "No, No, No, they've changed child-rearing since we did it!"

BG: That's kind of like breaking the spell. The kiss of the prince.

Breaking The Chain

Arthur: I find myself still trying to break out of the trend I've always been in up till now—you know, the way my Mom thought it ought to be—especially since I've been taking this class.

BG: Yes. You seem to—

JG: How did you notice it? How did you become aware of it?

Arthur: Probably after about three classes. I found that I was still on the same wave length.

Sally: On the same track.

Arthur: Same track—same mode, I guess.

Sally: Using the same repertoire. "Here we go again."

Arthur: I came to this class, and we were talking about all these different ways to diagnose ego states, and the fact that I could change back and forth from one ego state to another. It just seems like my mother is constantly in a criticizing mode, a critical ego state, all the time. Always critical, straight across the board. That was it, and I found myself, even still today, trying to get out of cringing and rebelling. Still!

Sally: So do I. But it's funny, when Arthur deals with the kids, he will have a tendency a lot of the time to be critical himself. And his own mother, when she's with her mother, she's always cringing and rebelling. With everybody else, in every other situation, she'd always be the one to do the criticizing.

Arthur: This has gone right down through the generations.

JG: It's kind of spooky, isn't it? Generation to generation.

Arthur: I'm gonna break it.

JG: How's that?

Arthur: I'm here to say I'm going to break the chain.

JG: To break the chain! I bet you there's a half a dozen people in this room who respond to that. How many saw Roseanne the other night? Do you ever watch that program?

Sally: I watched that once.

Arthur: It's a great show.

JG: Remember Roseanne's husband is a contractor, and his dad is a salesman.

Woman: I saw that one.

JG: You saw that one? Dad began to harp on the old sore point. It didn't take five minutes before they were really upset. Roseanne's husband had to leave the dinner table, go out to the garage and recover himself.

BG: Even when the dad tried to change, he still was in this same mode. It was tragic to see this reaction where they were right into it again. You know he was trying to quit.

Samantha: The son didn't get suckered into it the second time, though. He picked up the dish of carrots and said, "Here, try the carrots."

JG: Do a little different thing. Even so small a thing as that. Just do something a little different.

We're Going To Figure Out Something Else

Morilla: Now when you were raising your children, were you attuned to this, or—

JG: We were raw beginners!

BG: We made a whole bunch of mistakes! And we've asked our kids to forgive us and they have!

JG: That's a useful thing to do when they get up to be around twenty-eight. We told them, ''We realize we did primitive things. We weren't really tuned in, we didn't understand what we were doing.''

BG: We did stop spanking them, with a conscious decision. They were about four and two, and the older one was beating on the little one. Then I would spank the older one because he was beating on the little one. John came home one night and I said, ''This doesn't make any sense at all!'' I said, ''Here I am, beating on him for beating on his little brother, and it just doesn't make any sense at all! Period!! What are we going to do?''

JG: So we decided—

BG: We said, ''Well, we're going to quit spanking, period! We're going to figure out something else!''

JG: Obviously we're touching on something here that's a very live issue that we all need to develop skills with.

> *Louise: Yes. I see it more as my problem, rather than my son's. I have to learn to live with him, rather than the other way around.*

JG: A good way to think of it. Well, it's mutual. It goes both ways. The child has to do some learning. The parents can do some too.

That's Just The Way Things Are

> *Priscilla: My husband and I took this class a couple of months ago together. We were leaving the class one Sunday and we decided—it was really weird, we both were raised by the rule that you eat what's put on the table in front of you. Eat it, it doesn't matter if you like it or not!*

> *Louise: You eat all of it!*

> *Priscilla: My father—I don't like tomatoes, and if there was a salad and it was lettuce and tomatoes, if I didn't take at least one piece of tomato, he would put five in my bowl and I'd have to eat 'em.*

> *Louise: Oh, God!*

Priscilla: That's the way he was. My husband and I discussed it. We were planning on having a spinach quiche for supper that night and we got to thinking. It didn't seem right, all of a sudden, that we would make the kids eat that. We knew they didn't like it, and yet that was what we were having. So we decided that if they didn't like that, they could have something else. They're certainly big enough to make their own peanut butter sandwiches. They'll eat peanut butter three times a day, but we started giving them the option of, "Well, we're having this. Do you want this or would you rather have a hot dog or a sandwich or something like that?" Now we don't have to fight with them at all about eating any more. They'll eat. They tell us what they want, and they'll go ahead and eat.

Theodore: It's amazing how this continues generation after generation.

Morilla: I know, it's amazing.

Theodore: —and you don't realize until you find yourself doing exactly what your parents did.

BG: The tapes are playing.

Theodore: The tapes are playing, but there's a point at which all of a sudden, you think, "What am I doing? I'm an adult!"

Ralph: My parents started that same way. But an incident with me dissuaded them, because at one point they gave me rhubarb, which I just had never had before. I tasted a little bit of it and had a real serious reaction to it. They said, "You have to eat your rhubarb." I said, "If I eat the rest of this, I'm going to throw up!" My mother, who was a little more on the ball about this than my father, said, "I think he might be serious about this!" But father said, "No, he's got to eat it!" So I did, and I threw up. After that they were a little less rigid.

Morilla: Backed off a little bit?

Theodore: Did you throw up in their shoes?

Ralph: I don't remember about that, but I never had rhubarb again.

Priscilla: My husband's aunt went so far as to—they were having vegetable soup for supper one night and my husband—he was just a child—said he didn't want it, he wasn't going to eat it. And she said, "Well, you either eat that tonight or you will get it for breakfast tomorrow morning." He was about thirteen, I guess, so he decided to call her bluff. The next morning he woke up and smelled bacon and pancakes and everything cooking. He got up and there was his bowl of vegetable soup, waiting for him to eat it, and she made him eat it. To this day he will not touch vegetable soup.

Stomachaches Every Day

BG: Some families are so removed from their feelings and their own desires. We had a girl whose mother called in and wanted a medical appointment for the daughter who was having stomachaches. The girl was thirteen at the time. She was having stomachaches every day.

John started to question what the circumstances were. "Well, I have a stomachache every day as soon as I get up in the morning, and then just before lunch and just before supper I get this terrible stomachache." There was another sister, and the father was in the hospital at the time. He had had a cardiac arrest and subsequently died, so we thought that maybe there was something in connection with the emotional upset and fear in the family. But when we finally got down to it, it turned out that this was just plain hunger. In this family that had never been either discussed, recognized or acknowledged in a way where a person would know that when they felt hungry it was OK to eat.

JG: They didn't recognize the bodily sensations that were hunger. They did not recognize hunger, they ate when the clock said it was time.

BG: This was a very rigidly scheduled family. This girl was getting hungry, and the pain in her stomach was hunger. We talked about it afterwards. It seems hard to believe, but that was the case.

JG: That process of dissociation is one of the ways in which we bring it about that in rearing our own children, we carry out exactly what was done to us.

She Never Told Us That
She Loved Us

Kay: My Mom and I have always had—have always been—we get along, but we don't get along. I never really understood why she did some of the things she did until my grandfather—her father—came to live with us after my grandmother died. It was so clear then that this was something that was just passed down. She was not a hugging person. She never told us, either me or my sister, that she loved us, or anything—but she did in other ways. She just never said it. That was just the same relationship that she had with her own father. That really was an eye-opener. Luckily I was old enough—I was in college at the time—to understand what was going on at that point. That really helped.

I just wish I had learned earlier than that.

JG: If you're really stumped about a piece of behavior, call in the nearest relatives and check them out. You may learn something totally unexpected.

Little Pieces, Little Changes, Little Victories

Mimi: Going along with this "make a little change," and back to the problem, I can throw all these problems together and now I've got this one big one—and—and—

JG: You like big cheese balls!

Mimi: I find that what helps is if I start breaking it apart, taking pieces of it, just making the problem smaller, and just working with a solvable portion of it.

JG: Very good.

Mark: You want to treat the world in terms of little victories.

JG: You've got it.

BG: That's beautiful.

Sally: I can eat chocolate tomorrow! I can diet one day at a time.

Mark: Large chunks—two, three year time frames. You try and encompass it all at one shot. You're overwhelmed. So you break the task up into manageable chunks, and you don't sweat what comes afterwards.

JG: That's the way it is with childrearing too. What you want to do is, no matter what your child does, you redefine it as a little victory so that you stay away from all this heavy stuff, this disaster stuff.

What A Good Burp!

Linda: It's hard to do that though, like with Kevin being real cranky. It's real hard to see any victories, it's all—it's all just—

Mark: So you sat up the other night—

Linda: I went shewwww—

JG: "Gee, you managed to pass that gas real well!"

Mimi: "What a good burp!"

You Validate Their Essential Goodness

JG: "That was a really good burp. You're a good kid." You validate their essential goodness, their essential worthwhileness, no matter what it is.

Wendy: Can you do it with something negative, like, "That was the best whining you've done all week?"

"Whine Along With Me!"

JG: "You're really getting good at whining, aren't you?" You Praise the Achievement, and then go into the "practice it" routine.

Sally: What is that, to have them whine more?

JG: Sure, and the child comes home—

Arthur: Whine along with them.

JG: "Whine along with me!"

Mimi: Actually I did that. Lydia would go, "Unnnhn, uhnnnhn!" and I would just go, "Uhnnhn! Uhnnnhn!" It was really funny, how it gets higher and higher and all of a sudden we were singing.

JG: This corresponds to that Japanese martial art. Which one is it?

Beth: Aikido?

JG: Where you let their own momentum carry them—

Woman: Aikido.

JG: —farther than they expected. Yeah, that's what this is. Everything is a little victory.

Arthur: Brett started hitting me this morning and I started crying. All of a sudden I got him to cry.

JG: You plopped down on his perch.

Sally: I've learned to say, "Oh, you're hurting me. Now you've got to give me a hug." So now it's almost like what you said about the kid who would hit his mom to get sent up to his room. He'll hit me lightly once on the arm and then give me a hug (laughs).

JG: You can see the incredible power of these techniques. You can produce almost any behavior that you want.

The Learning Tantrum

BG: There's something else, too, that kids get into when they're either growing fast or going into a new stage. It may be Kevin's got some of this going right now. He's really trying hard to creep, and he's getting sick and tired of lying around like a little baby.

Mark: Yeah. He hates that.

BG: —and that may be a lot of his frustration. When they're going into a new developmental stage, they feel overwhelmed—like you say, you get a three-year assignment and you're thinking about it and it's all coming down on your head. A baby who's into a new stage of development will do this. It happens several times at different stages. When he gets to trying to walk, he may go through another real cranky stage.

Kim: Margaret did that. When she tried to crawl she got really really frustrated. She'd just yell and get angry. She'd turn red and then when she started walking the same thing would happen. Every time she'd fall down she'd sit there, she'd cry and she'd look at me like, "How could you let that happen to me! How dare you make me fall—it's all your fault!"

Linda: It's hard to get out of the mind-set, though. You think, "He's such a cranky kid I can't stand him!" It's hard to see a lot of the positive—

Mimi: I do the same thing with Heidi, she's so shy.

Linda: I'm getting to where I expect it every day. Every day . . . I'm dreading every day . . . so it's like, "Oh God, he's going to be cranky again today. I can't stand one more day of this."

Mimi: Yeah.

Linda: He was well—after he went through the screaming for the first hour.

Small Fish

JG: Did any of you read about the revolt of the dolphins? I think there's a good lesson there. You know how the Sea World stuff was done. Karen Pryor's ideas made it possible to do these incredible shows of the killer whale leaping nineteen feet into the air to grab a fish. Maybe you remember in the book that they tried a—what was it?—a small fish, and the killer whales went on strike.

They refused to do it. It had to be a large mackerel, because it was a big trick and they had to have a big reward.[3]

The Revolt Of The Dolphins

Then at least one of these shows was taken over by a giant international conglomerate, so that this was just a subsidiary unit, run by an executive vice president who really didn't know anything about Sea World. They were upping the schedule and running it more and more relentlessly in order to maximize profits. The dolphins and the whales were working more and life was turning into a endless round of performances. And they literally rebelled. They went out of control and seriously injured one of the trainers. Something that had never ever happened before. What the managers had been doing was to push too hard on the system. They'd been trying to get a product out of it for themselves, without paying attention to the legitimate needs of the dolphins.

Mimi: I'll have to tell that to my boss!

Mark: He'll just say, "I can always get more dolphins!"

JG: If you use these techniques as a cold blooded manipulation to benefit yourself, they will backfire on you. You can get hurt. So you've got to be real sure that you're doing it for the other person as well as for yourself.

Three Cranky Nights And He Jumps Ahead

Sally: I was just thinking a kid can put too much pressure on themselves, too. Maybe that's part of the reason why the crankiness comes out. Fred started getting into a sleepless cycle where for three nights in a row I'm up every hour with him. On the third night he'll have a little jump in his development. Just recently he started picking up things with a pincer grasp. He can do it with one hand or the other. For a while I didn't know what was going on. Last week we had three nights where I literally did not get any sleep. Then I noticed he had been doing it sort of with one hand and then I noticed, "Hey wait a second, now he's doing it with both hands and he's doing it well!"

JG: And he's practicing.

Sally: It never connected with me until I saw him doing that. I hate the nights without the sleep, but—!"

JG: When you realize what it means . . . when you understand that this is actually what you might call the shadow side of the advance. This is the regression that goes with the advance.

> *Sally: I hadn't been pressuring him or even trying to get him to do that though.*

Give Them A Free Regression

JG: He was doing it himself. He felt that motivation to move forward. A kid will move forward real fast. They will scare themselves, and they will need to have a regression. That's where the real savvy parent will encourage them to regress.[4] No matter what it is, bed wetting or anything at all. You will encourage them to regress because that leaves the door open. They're moving forward so fast they scare themselves. They're moving away from babyhood at rocket speed. They look back and they say, "My God, I'll never be able to be a baby again. I need to be a baby for a while." You let them regress. It's the yin and yang. It's the oscillations of the machine. You have the advance. You have the fallback and then the advance again. It's a very wise parent who will allow that and even encourage it.

So you Encourage a Regression. "Of course you want to be a baby! Here, let's get out your old blanket."

> *Louise: Should you just put the diapers on him, or say, "Would you like to try that?" He started doing it and he's having all kinds of accidents all the time.*

JG: Ask him if he wants his diapers on.

> *Louise: He doesn't. I ask him and he cries, "No, No, No! I don't want them!"*

JG: There you are. He doesn't want them.

> *Louise: So I shouldn't?*

JG: Right. "You want to be a baby but you don't want to have diapers on. We'll just put 'em in the bureau here by your bed." He can say, "No, No, No! I don't want 'em in my room!" "Oh, you don't want them in your room. Where would you like them to be?" No matter what he does, he's stuck with the darn diapers, because he's regressing and you are helping him.

"They're moving away from babyhood at rocket speed . . ."

Cora: You could just say, ''Well, why don't we just keep them nearby just in case you change your mind. It would be a good thing to have them around.''

JG: You could ask him if he would like that. Then he could say yes or he could say no. You keep the options open. You keep your own options open, and you keep his options open, until finally he works himself into a situation that is satisfactory to you both.

That's what has been wrong with the text books on child rearing from the 19th century on. They label an isolated piece of behavior. They call it lying, stealing, viciousness, rebelliousness, refusal to sleep—whatever. Then they treat it as if it was some kind of a thing, instead of seeing it as part of the whole process of growing up. It's as much a part of that process of moving ahead as the concavity of the wave is, that makes the next wave. You have to have it. If you know that, you can encourage it. Then the kid says, ''Ahhh! I can still be a baby! But wait a minute, I'd rather be grown up.'' So he moves ahead again. You let him move back and move forward again. He's happy. He feels comfortable. And you feel comfortable—except for those three nights in a row!

Cherished Ideals

JG: Now one thing most parents have is cherished ideals for what the child is going to be like . . . what the child is going to do. ''They're going to make me feel really proud, because they are going to grow up and go to Harvard Business School.''

''Let Me Be How I Grow''

There's a great trap there—because the essence of every human being is to be an individual, and to not be the embodiment of someone else's dreams.[5] The child's life position is, ''Let me be how I grow.''[6]

BG: Or disappointments. I mean if the parents didn't make it somewhere, they push the kid real hard.

JG: The child will try. They will consciously try, if you convey to them by overt and covert messages that you expect them to be such and such. The more they love you, the harder they will try to do this. It is possible to induce a child to give up being who they were spontaneously destined to be. I don't know what the word is, but they'll give up their own true nature—in order to try to be the person that you expect them to be—or the opposite. If you really come on strong about that, they will try real hard to do that. They may never discover until their 50's or 60's or later, that they have thrown away the potential of a real human being, in order to become the imitation of something that you wanted.

Sally: Or they'll do it to their kids.

JG: Or they will do it to their kids.

Sally: "I could have been this if I had been allowed to. Now I'm going to make you do it."

JG: You expect it. The child picks up that expectation. They'll either rebel against it or they will try to conform. Then that becomes one of the big things that is filling up their life. Rebelling against an expectation or trying to fulfill the expectation. But the third thing, the thing that is not mentioned, is their own spontaneous self-expression. What they might have done if they didn't have that issue.

How do you foster a child to be who they're destined to be rather than to be who you want them to be? That takes a subtle touch. As Joseph Campbell says, "You help the child to follow his bliss." When Bill Moyers asked Campbell, "How can those of us who are parents help our children recognize their bliss?" Campbell replied, "You have to know your child and be attentive to the child . . . you can see the eyes open and the complexion change."[7]

Learning To Be Stochastic

JG: So, in regard to your expectations for your child, let your expectations be guided by them, not by you; by what you see, by what your child spontaneously does. Let your ambitions and hopes change from year to year and even from day to day, depending on what you see the child doing. Then eventually, as time goes on, your hopes and expectations will turn out to be exactly what the child is becoming. You'll be satisfied and the child will be satisfied.

BG: That's keeping alive your own sense of wonder, the child part of you that says, "Oh wheee!" watching the miracle that your child is.

"Whee! The miracle that your child is!"

Notes and References

Page (in italics) indicates the text page on which the work is cited.

Foreword

1. Satir, Virginia. In: Goulding, Mary McClure and Robert L. Goulding (1979) *Changing Lives Through Redecision Therapy.* New York. Brunner/Mazel. *Page ix*
2. White, E. B. (1989). *The Second Tree From The Corner.* New York. Harper, p. 195. *Page xi*

Preface

1. Mead, Margaret (1928). *Coming of Age in Samoa.* New York. New American Library edition 1949, pp. 24–26. *Page xxiii*
2. Faber, Adele and Elaine Mazlish (1980). *How to Talk So Kids Will Listen and Listen So Kids Will Talk.* New York. Avon *Page xxiii*
3. Crary, Elizabeth (1979). *Without Spanking or Spoiling. A Practical Approach to Toddler and Preschool Guidance.* Seattle. Parenting Press *Page xxiii*
4. Clarke, Jean Illsley (1978). *Self-Esteem. A Family Affair.* Minneapolis. Winston Press *Page xxiii*
5. Gordon, Thomas (1970). *P.E.T. Parent Effectiveness Training. The Tested New Way To Raise Responsible Children.* New York. New American Library (1975) *Page xxiii*
6. While scholarly documentation may seem out of place in a book intended for general readership, we believe it is too important to omit. Both of us believe strongly in the continuity of culture—in the importance of crediting those who preceded our generation and upon whose labors the progress of our own generation is based. However, finding the earliest printed references to these strategies would involve a

massive bibliographic search beyond our present resources to carry out. And so far as we know, no one has attempted a systematic documentation of the origins of these strategies. That deficiency itself is a telling commentary on the general unawareness of their importance or even of their existence. *Page xxiv*

7. Watzlawick, Paul, John Weakland, & Richard Fisch (1974). Change. Principles of Problem Formation and Problem Resolution. New York. Norton, p. 160 *Page xxv*

Chapter 1
In Real life It's The Fox

1. (Only One Strategy). Satir, Virginia & Michele Baldwin (1983). *Satir Step by Step. A Guide to Creating Change in Families.* Palo Alto, California. Science and Behavior Books, pp. 160–169. *Page 3*

Chapter 2
He Just Gave A Little Chirp

1. (You Can't Not Communicate). Watzlawick, Paul, Janet Helmick Beavin, and Don D. Jackson (1967). *Pragmatics of Human Communication. A Study of Interactional Patterns, Pathologies, and Paradoxes.* New York. Norton, pp. 48–50. *Page 11*
2. ("Humans cannot not metacommunicate.") Satir, Virginia (1964. Revised, 1967). *Conjoint Family Therapy.* Third Edition 1983. Palo Alto, California. Science and Behavior Books, Inc., p. 97. *Page 11*
3. (Infant Signals). Givens, D. (1978). "Social Expressivity During the First Year of Life." *Sign Language Studies* 20, 251–274. *Page 11*

See also: Sanger, S., and John Kelly (1985). *You And Your Baby's First Year.* New York. Bantam. (Contains a good bibliography of original articles relating to infant communication).

4. (Signal that a baby gives before they start rooting). Givens, D. (1978). "Social Expressivity During the First Year of Life." *Sign Language Studies* 20, 251–274. *Page 15*
5. (Indirectly Directing Attention). Erickson, Milton H. and Ernest Rossi. "The Indirect forms of Suggestion." In. Rossi, Ernest L. (Ed.) (1980). *The Collected Papers of Milton H. Erickson on Hypnosis.* Volume I. *The Nature of Hypnosis and Suggestion,* pp. 456–7. *Page 19*

6. (Graded Series of Negative Responses). Givens, D. (1978). ''Social Expressivity During the First Year of Life.'' *Sign Language Studies* 20, 251–274. *Page 20*

7. (Parent tapes). Woollams, S. and Michael Brown (1978). *Transactional Analysis.* Dexter, Michigan. Huron Valley Institute Press, pp. 15–18. *Page 21*

8. (Infant Scientists). Bower, T. G. R. (1977). *A Primer of Infant Development.* San Francisco. Freeman. p. 42. Bower refers to earlier work by Watson, J. S. (1973). ''Smiling, Cooing, and 'the Game.''' Merrill-Palmer *Quarterly of Behavior and Development* 18, 323–339. Also Papousek, H. (1969). ''Individual Variability in Learned Responses in Human Infants. In R. J. Robinson (Ed.), *Brain and Early Behavior.* London. Academic Press. *Page 22*

9. (Infant Reaching). Bower, T. G. R. (1977). *A Primer of Infant Development.* San Francisco. Freeman. p. 27. *Page 22*

10. (Baby Sonar). Bower, T. G. R. (1977). *A Primer of Infant Development.* San Francisco. Freeman. pp. 104–105. *Page 24*

11. (How The Professor Does It) Gall, John C. (1986) ''Infant Mental Health As A Performing Art. I. The Effective Use Of The Prenatal Interview.'' Presented before the Washtenaw Chapter of the Michigan Association Of Infant Mental Health, January 17, 1986. *Page 25*

12. (Stonewalling the baby). Brazelton, T. Berry and Bertrand G. Cramer (1990). *The Earliest Relationship. Parents, Infants, and the Drama of Early Attachment.* Reading, Massachusetts. Addison-Wesley. See especially Chapter 12. Still-Face Studies. *Page 26*

13. (Inborn temperament). Thomas, Alexander, and Stella Chess (1977). *Temperament and Development.* New York. Brunner/Mazel. *Page 31*

14. (Pacing). Laurens Van der Post reports that C. G. Jung was deliberately using Pacing as a technique while still at the Burghoelzli mental hospital, ca. 1900–1910. Van der Post, Laurens (1975). ''Jung and the story of our time.'' New York. Pantheon, p. 114. *Page 32*

Chapter 3
A Sore Spot From Your Past

1. Caffey, John (1946). ''Multiple Fractures in the Long Bones of Infants Suffering from Chronic Subdural Hematoma.'' *Am. J. Roentgenology* 56 (2): 163–173. *Page 38*

2. (Reality Of Child Abuse). Masson, Jeffrey M. (1984) *The Assault on Truth. Freud's Suppression of the Seduction Theory.* New York. Penguin, pp. 51–54. *Page 38*

3. ''To abuse is to treat in a harmful, injurious, or offensive way; to attack in words; to speak insultingly, harshly, and unjustly to or about a person; to revile. Abuse was further defined to refer particularly to unnecessary or avoidable acts or words of a negative nature inflicted by one person on another person or persons.'' From: Silver Henry K., and Anita Duhl Glicken. *Medical Student Abuse. Incidence, Severity, and Significance.* Washtenaw County Medical Society Bulletin, Vol. 41, No. 8 (April) 1990, pp. 3–12. *Page 41*

Chapter 4
How Do You Get Into Another Person's World?

1. (Sensory Channels). Grinder, John, Judith Delozier, and Richard Bandler (1977). *Patterns of the Hypnotic Techniques of Milton H. Erickson, M.D.* Vol. II. Cupertino, California. Meta Publications. p. 11. *Page 43*
2. (Parent Tapes). Woollams, S. and Michael Brown (1978). *Transactional Analysis.* Dexter, Michigan. Huron Valley Institute Press, pp. 15–18. *Page 48*
3. (Incongruity). Satir, Virginia (1967). *Conjoint Family Therapy.* Third edition, 1983. Palo Alto, California. Science and Behavior Books. p. 45. *Page 51*
4. (Best Channels). Gordon, David, and Maribeth Meyers-Anderson (1981). Phoenix. *Therapeutic Patterns of Milton H. Erickson.* Cupertino, California. Meta Publications, pp. 34–38. *Page 52*
5. (Telephone ear). Grinder, J., and Richard Bandler (ca. 1977). (Reference lost.) *Page 52*
6. (Face approach). Givens, D. (1978). ''Social expressivity during the first year of life.'' *Sign Language Studies*, 20, 251–274. *Page 57*
7. (Representational Systems). Grinder, John, and Richard Bandler (1976). *The Structure of Magic. II.* Palo Alto, California. Science and Behavior Books. p 6ff. *Page 59*
8. (Visual accessing cues). Bandler, Richard, and John Grinder (1979). *Frogs into Princes. Neuro Linguistic Programming.* Moab, Utah. Real People Press. p. 25. *Page 59*

Chapter 5
That Lovely Feeling Of Being Understood

1. Miller, G. A. (1956). ''The magical number seven, plus or minus two: some limits on our capacity for processing information.'' *Psychological Review*, 63, 81–97. *Page 69*

2. (Parallel Accessing). Zeig, J. (Ed.) (1980). A Teaching Serminar With Milton H. Erickson. New York. Brunner/Mazel, p. 64. *Page 76*

See also: Erickson, Milton H. "The 'Surprise' and 'My-Friend-John' Techniques of Hypnosis: Minimal Cues and Natural Field Experimentation." *Amer. J. Clin. Hypn.* 6, 1964, 293–307.

Chapter 6
Where Have I Seen This Before?

1. (Mental Model). Bandler, Richard, and John Grinder (1975). *The Structure of Magic. I. A Book about Language and Therapy.* Palo Alto, California. Science and Behavior Books. p. 7. *Page 80*
2. (Punctuation). Bateson, Gregory (1942). "Social Planning and the Concept of Deutero-Learning." In Bateson, Gregory (1972). *Steps to an Ecology of Mind.* New York. Ballantine, p. 163ff. *Page 87*
3. (Tracking The Sequence). Crary, Elizabeth (1979). *Without Spanking or Spoiling. A Practical Approach to Toddler and Preschool Guidance.* Seattle, Washington. Parenting Press. *Page 87*
4. (Calibrated Communication). Bandler, Richard, John Grinder, and Virginia Satir (1976). *Changing With Families. A Book About Further Education for Being Human.* Palo Alto, California. Science and Behavior Books, p.108. *Page 88*
5. (Calibration). Bateson, Gregory (1979). *Mind and Nature. A Necessary Unity.* New York. Dutton. pp. 195–202. *Page 88*
6. (Executive Control over Ego States). Woollams, Stan and Michael Brown (1978). *Transactional Analysis.* Dexter, Michigan. Huron Valley Institute Press. pp. 32–36. *Page 89*
7. (The Message Sent Is Not Necessarily the Message Received). Satir, Virginia (1964). *Conjoint Family Therapy.* Palo Alto, California. Science and Behavior Books. p. 129. *Page 90*
8. ("Hyperactivity"). Bandler, R., & John Grinder (1979). *Frogs Into Princes.* Moab, Utah. Real People Press, p. 92. *Page 97*

Chapter 7
A Twenty-First Century Way

1. Ashby, W. Ross (1961). *An Introduction to Cybernetics.* London. Chapman and Hall. *Page 99*
2. Keeney, Bradford P. (1983). *Esthetics of Change.* New York. Guilford. *Page 99*

3. (Seed Model versus Threat and Reward Model). Satir, Virginia, and Michele Baldwin (1983). *Satir Step by Step. A Guide to Creating Change in Families.* Palo Alto California. Science and Behavior Books, pp. 160–169. *Page 102*

4. ("Augment the Pathology"). Whitaker, Carl (1973). "My Philosophy of Psychotherapy." *Journal of Contemporary Psychotherapy* 6(1), 49–52. Reprinted by permission in Neill, John R. and David Kniskern (Eds.) (1982). *From Psyche to System. The Evolving Therapy of Carl Whitaker.* New York. Guilford, p. 33. *Page 102*

5. (Positive Connotation). Palazzoli, Mara Selvini, L. Boscolo, G. Cecchin, and G. Prata (1978). *Paradox and Counterparadox. A New Model in the Therapy of the Family in Schizophrenic Transaction,* p. 55ff. *Page 102*

6. (Making it a Chore). Mehrabian, A. (1970). *Tactics of Social Influence.* Englewood Cliffs, New Jersey. Prentice-Hall, pp. 59–60. *Page 104*

7. (Punishment leads to the desire to get back, to get even). Bettelheim, Bruno (1987). *A Good Enough Parent. A Book on Child-Rearing.* New York. Random House, p. 125. *Page 105*

8. (Cigarettes in the Attic). Zeig, J. (Ed.) (1980). *A Teaching Serminar With Milton H. Erickson.* New York. Brunner/Mazel, p. 195. *Page 112*

See also: Gordon, David and Maribeth Meyers-Anderson (1981). *Phoenix. Therapeutic Patterns of Milton H. Erickson.* Cupertino, California. Meta Publications, pp. 21–22.

Chapter 8
Polar Opposites—And The Space Between

1. (Taking Possesion of the Symptom) Hoffman, Lynn (1981). *Foundations of Family Therapy. A Conceptual Framework for Systems Change.* New York. Basic Books, p. 236. *Page 120*

2. Madanes, C. (1985). *Finding a Humorous Alternative.* In J. K. Zeig (Ed.), *Ericksonian Psychotherapy, Volume II: Clinical Applications,* pp. 24–43. New York. Brunner/Mazel. *Page 125*

3. (Distraction). Erickson, Milton H., and Ernest Rossi. "Two-Level Communication and the Microdynamics of Trance and Suggestion." In. Rossi, E. (Ed.) (1980). *The Collected Papers of Milton H. Erickson on Hypnosis. Volume I. The Nature of Hypnosis and Suggestion,* pp. 430–451. See especially "Distraction in the Dynamics of Two-Level Communication," pp. 432–433. *Page 127*

4. (Use Everything). Erickson, Milton H. (1959). "Further Clinical Tech-

niques of Hypnosis. Utilization Techniques.'' *American Journal of Clinical Hypnosis* 2, 3–21. *Page 128*

Chapter 9
How To Tie Them Up In Nots

1. (No analogue or iconic signal for ''not''). Bateson, Gregory (1964). ''The Logical Categories of Learning and Communication.'' In Bateson, Gregory (1972). *Steps to an Ecology of Mind.* New York. Ballantine, p. 291

   See also: Laing, R. D. (1969). ''Rules and Metarules.'' In Laing, R. D. (1972). *The Politics of the Family and Other Essays.* New York. Vintage, pp. 103–116. *Page 129*
2. (''With the word, 'But', you can kill anything.''). Perls, Fritz (1975). *Legacy From Fritz.* Palo Alto, California. Science and Behavior Books, p. 126. *Page 136*
3. (Fright Face). Svejda, M. J.(November,1981). ''The Development of Infant Sensitivity to Affective Messages in the Mother's Voice.'' Unpublished doctoral dissertation, University of Denver, Colorado. *Page 138*
4. (Yes Set). Erickson, Milton H. (1964). Quoted without further reference in Erickson, Milton H., E, L. Rossi, and S. I. Rossi (1976). *Hypnotic Realities. The Induction of Clinical Hypnosis and Forms of Indirect Suggestion.* New York. Irvington, pp. 58–59. *Page 139*
5. (The Best Interests of the Child). Erickson, M. H. (1958). ''Pediatric Hypnotherapy.'' *The American Journal of Clinical Hypnosis* 1, pp. 25–29. *Page 142*

Chapter 11
The Flaky Moms' And Dads' Club

1. (Specialty Slots). Satir, V. (1964. Revised, 1967). *Conjoint Family Therapy.* Third Edition 1983. Palo Alto, California. Science and Behavior Books, Inc., p. 71. *Page 157*
2. (Benevolent Sabotage). Watzlawick, Paul, John Weakland, and Richard Fisch (1974). *Change. Principles of Problem Formation and Problem Resolution.* New York. Norton, pp. 142–146. *Page 157*
3. (Humility). Satir, Virginia, and Michele Baldwin (1983). *Satir Step By Step. A Guide To Creating Change in Families.* Palo Alto, California. Science and Behavior Books, Inc., p. 229. *Page 162*

4. ("Guard your impotence as one of your most valuable weapons.")
   Whitaker, Carl (1976). "The Hindrance of Theory in Clinical Work."
   In P. J. Guerin (Ed.), *Family Therapy: Theory and Practice*. New York.
   Gardner Press. Reprinted by permission in Neill, John R. and David
   P. Kniskern (Eds.) (1982). *From Psyche to System. The Evolving Therapy
   of Carl Whitaker*. New York. Guilford, p. 329. *Page 162*

Chapter 12
Who Has The Problem?

1. (Drivers). Kahler, Taibi. The Miniscript. In Graham Barnes (Ed.) (1977).
   *Transactional Analysis after Eric Berne. Teachings and Practices of Three
   Schools*. New York. Harper, pp. 223–256. *Page 171*
2. ("If it gets under your skin . . ."). Whitmont, Edward C. (1969). *The
   Symbolic Quest. Basic Principles of Analytical Psychology*. Princeton, NJ.
   Princeton University Press, p. 60. *Page 179*

Chapter 13
The Magic Door

1. Margaret Mead. "Cybernetics of Cybernetics." In *Esthetics of Change*.
   Bradford P. Keeney. New York. Guilford Press, 1983, p. 76. Original
   ref. is in *Purposive Systems*. H. von Foerster, H. Peterson, J. White and
   J. Russell (Eds). New York. Spartan Books, 1968. *Page 185*
2. Pryor, Karen (1984). *Don't Shoot the Dog! The New Art of Teaching and
   Training*. New York. Bantam. *Page 186*
3. (The Miscommunication Principle). Watzlawick, Paul, Janet Helmick
   Beavin, and Don D. Jackson (1967). *Pragmatics of Human Communica-
   tion: A Study of Interactional Patterns, Pathologies, and Paradoxes*. New
   York. Norton, pp. 94–95. *Page 188*

Chapter 14
Some Babies Are Like That

1. (Basic temperament). Thomas, Alexander, and Stella Chess (1977).
   Temperament and Development. New York. Brunner/Mazel. *Page 195*
2. (Difficult children). Thomas, Alexander, Stella Chess, and Herbert G.
   Birch (1968). *Temperament and Behavior Disorders in Children*. New York.
   New York University Press, pp. 75–84. *Page 199*

3. (Avoiding Power Struggles). Erickson, L., Elliott, B., Erickson, A., Erickson, R., Klein, R., & Erickson, K. (Panelists) (1985). "Erickson family panel: the child-rearing techniques of Milton H. Erickson." In J. K. Zeig (Ed.), *Ericksonian Psychotherapy I: Structures*, pp. 619–637. New York. Brunner/Mazel. *Page 205*

Chapter 15
The Bear In The Bathroom

1. (Discipline and Double Binds). Sluzki, C., and Veron, E. (1971). "The Double Bind as a Universal Pathogenic Situation." *Family Process* 10: 397–417. *Page 207*
2. (Requisite Variability). Ashby, W. Ross (1961). *An Introduction to Cybernetics*. London. Chapman and Hall, p. 206. *Page 208*
3. (Maximizing Options). von Foerster, Heinz, in Paul Watzlawick (1984). *The Invented Reality*. New York. Norton, p. 60. *Page 208*
4. (To Change Others, Change Yourself). Keeney, Bradford P. (1983). *Aesthetics of Change*. New York. Guilford, p. 133. *Page 208*
5. (Joining Children's Fantasy). *See also:* Lustig, Herbert S. "The Enigma of Erickson's Therapeutic Paradoxes." In Jeffrey K. Zeig (Ed.) (1985), *Ericksonian Psychotherapy. Volume II. Clinical Applications*. New York. Brunner/Mazel, pp. 249–250. Cf: "Erickson Family Panel: The Child-Rearing Techniques of Milton Erickson." In Jeffrey K. Zeig (Ed.) (1985). *Ericksonian Psychotherapy. Volume I. Structures*. New York. Brunner/Mazel, p. 626. *Page 213*
6. (What The Monster Is). Fraiberg, Selma H. (1959). *The Magic Years. Understanding and Handling the Problems of Early Childhood*. New York. Scribner's, pp. 16–23. *Page 214*
7. (Stretching The Umbilical Cord). Gall, John C. (1990). "The Art of Examining a Child. Use of Naturalistic Methods in the Pediatric Physical Examination." In Stephen R. Lankton (Ed.) *Ericksonian Monographs. Number 7. The Broader Implications of Ericksonian Therapy*. New York. Brunner/Mazel, p. 83. *Page 215*

Chapter 16
The Meaning Of A Tantrum

1. (A More Horrible Example). Compare the story entitled "Ruth", in Rosen, Sidney (Ed.). (1982). *My Voice Will Go With You. The Teaching Tales of Milton H. Erickson*. New York. Norton, pp. 229–231. *Page 220*

2. (Dolphin Tantrums). Pryor, Karen (1984). *Don't Shoot the Dog! The New Art of Teaching and Training.* New York. Bantam, pp. 100–103. *Page 223*

3. (Reverse Set Double Bind). Erickson, Milton H., Ernest L. Rossi, and S. I. Rossi (1976). *Hypnotic Realities. The Induction of Clinical Hypnosis and Forms of Indirect Suggestion.* New York. Irvington. *The Reverse Set Double Bind,* pp. 72–73. Contains an anecdote about Erickson's "first well-remembered intentional use of the double bind" in his early boyhood. The anecdote was published in Erickson, M. and Rossi, E. (1975). "Varieties of Double Bind." *American Journal of Clinical Hypnosis* 17, pp. 143–157. *Page 224*

Chapter 17
Sigmund Freud's Little Brother

1. (Sigmund Freud's Little Brother). Jones, Ernest (1953). *The Life and Work of Sigmund Freud.* Volume I. New York. Basic Books, pp. 7–8. *Page 236*

2. (The Fantasies They Don't Like To Talk About). Whitaker, Carl R. and William M. Bumberry (1988). *Dancing With The Family. A Symbolic-Experiential Approach.* New York. Brunner/Mazel, pp. 22, 121, 182. *Page 239*

3. Faber, Adele, and Elaine Mazlish (1987). *Siblings Without Rivalry.* New York. Norton. *Page 243*

Chapter 18
Lemmings Are Consistent

1. (Making A U-Turn). Fisch, Richard, John H. Weakland, and Lynn Segal (1982). *The Tactics Of Change. Doing Therapy Briefly.* San Francisco. Jossey-Bass, pp. 166–167. *Page 247*

2. (Providing A Secure Reality). Haley, Jay (1973). *Uncommon Therapy. The Psychiatric Techniques of Milton H. Erickson, M.D.* New York. Norton, pp. 213–221. *Page 256*

Chapter 19
Toying With The Reality

1. (Redefining Gravity). Wilk, James (1985). "Ericksonian Therapeutic Patterns: A Pattern Which Connects." In Zeig, Jeffrey K. (Ed.). *Ericksonian Psychotherapy. Volume II: Clinical Applications.* New York. Brunner/Mazel, p. 214. *Page 261*

2. (Bellac Ploy). Watzlawick, Paul , John Weakland, and Richard Fisch (1974). *Change. Principles of Problem Formation and Problem Resolution.* New York. Norton, pp. 130–133. *Page 267*

3. (Contaminating The Metaphor). Palazzoli, M. Selvini, L. Boscolo, G. Cecchin, and G. Prata (1978). *Paradox and Counterparadox. A New Model in the Therapy of the Family in Schizophrenic Transaction.* New York and London. Jason Aronson, Inc. (Originally published in Italy by Feltrinelli Editore, Milan, 1975), pp. 150–152. *Page 268*

4. (Psychological Implication). Erickson, Milton H., Ernest L. Rossi, and S. I. Rossi (1976). *Hypnotic Realities. The Induction of Clinical Hypnosis and Forms of Indirect Suggestion.* New York. Irvington, pp. 59–62. *Page 271*

5. (Hidden Symmetry). Haley, Jay (Ed.) (1985) *Conversations with Milton H. Erickson, M.D. Volume III. Changing Children and Families.* Triangle Press, pp. 90–92. *Page 284*

6. Satir, Virginia (1972). *Peoplemaking.* Palo Alto, California. Science and Behavior Books, Inc., pp. 209–210. *Page 284*

Chapter 20
Why Not Learn To Fly The Real Thing?

1. (Jamming Their Game). Fisch, Richard, John Weakland, and Lynn Segal (1982). *Tactics of Change. Doing Therapy Briefly.* San Francisco. Jossey-Bass, pp. 156–158. *Page 287*

2. (A Stronger Voice). Cooper, Duff (1932). *Talleyrand.* Republished in 1986 by Fromm International Publishing Corporation, New York, pp. 263–265. *Page 303*

Chapter 21
The Miracle That Your Child Is

1. (Snowball Effect). Gordon, David and Maribeth Meyers-Anderson (1981). Phoenix. *Therapeutic Patterns of Milton H. Erickson.* Cupertino, California. Meta Publications, pp. 122–123. *Page 305*

2. Ian Stewart. *Does God Play Dice? The Mathematics of Chaos.* Cambridge, Mass: Basil Blackwell, 1989 *Page 306*

3. (A Big Enough Incentive). Pryor, Karen (1984). *Don't Shoot the Dog! The New Art of Teaching and Training.* New York. Bantam, p. 31. *Page 315*

4. (Encouraging a Relapse). Haley, Jay (1973). *Uncommon Therapy. The Psychiatric Techniques of Milton H. Erickson, M.D.* New York. Norton, pp. 30–31. *Page 316*

5. Satir, Virginia (1972). *Peoplemaking.* Palo Alto, California. Science and Behavior Books, Inc., pp. 205–207. *Page 318*
6. Grossman, Jean Schick (1948). *Life With Family. A Perspective on Parenthood.* New York. Appleton-Century-Crofts, Inc., p. 41. *Page 318*
7. Campbell, Joseph (1988). *The Power Of Myth.* New York. Doubleday, p. 118. *Page 319*

Appendix A:
Strategies List

Items are listed in approximately the sequence in which they happened to be mentioned in this seminar. There is no deep significance to their sequence.

Notice how these strategies overlap. One implies others. They blend into each other. Basically, it's all one thing!

There is no one-to-one correspondence between a strategy and an actual intervention. Many interventions are a blend of several strategies. For example, the intervention in the story entitled, "The Worst Tantrum in the World," embodies elements of more than twenty of the strategies listed below. See if you can verify that for yourself!

. . . and you can have the delightful anticipation of wondering which of these strategies will work best for you!

1. Matching Channels (Pacing)

Includes Verbal Pacing.

Gordon, David, and Maribeth Meyers-Anderson (1981). Phoenix. *Therapeutic Patterns of Milton H. Erickson.* Cupertino, California. Meta Publications. pp. 34–38.

2. Indirectly Directing Another Person's Attention (Indirect Associative Focussing)

Closely related to Distraction.

Erickson, Milton H. and Ernest Rossi. "The Indirect forms of Suggestion." In. Rossi, Ernest L. (Ed.) (1980). *The Collected Papers of Milton H. Erickson on Hypnosis. Volume I. The Nature of Hypnosis and Suggestion,* pp. 456-7.

3. Face Approach (For Babies)

Givens, David (1978). "Social expressivity during the first year of life." *Sign Language Studies* 20, 251–274. See especially pp. 260–261, "Eye Contact (*en face* position).

4. Parallel Accessing

(Talking about your own experiences to cause others to access their own similar experiences).

Zeig, Jeffrey K. (Ed.) (1980). *A Teaching Seminar With Milton H. Erickson.* New York. Brunner/Mazel, p. 64.

5. Playing The Resistance (Elegant Reversals)

Erickson, Milton H., Ernest L. Rossi, and S. I. Rossi (1976). *Hypnotic Realities. The Induction of Clinical Hypnosis and Forms of Indirect Suggestion.* New York. Irvington. *The Reverse Set Double Bind,* pp. 72–73. Contains an anecdote about Erickson's "first well-remembered intentional use of the double bind" in his early boyhood. The anecdote was published in Erickson, M. and Rossi, E. (1975). "Varieties of Double Bind." *American Journal of Clinical Hypnosis* 17, 143–157.

6. Restraining A Change (Building Anticipation)

Used when you want them to do it. "You're really not quite old enough for that!"

"Encouraging a Response by Frustrating It." Haley, Jay (1973). *Uncommon Therapy. The Psychiatric Techniques of Milton H. Erickson, M. D.* New York. Norton. p. 31.

7. Being Mysterious And Unpredictable

See also:

Whitaker, Carl (1976). "The hindrance of theory in clinical work." In P. J. Guerin (Ed.), *Family Therapy: Theory and Practice.* New York: Gardner Press.

See also:
". . . the importance of being inconsistent." Whitaker, Carl and David V. Keith. "Symbolic-Experiential Family Therapy." From Gurman, A., and D. Kniskern (Eds.) (1981). *The Handbook of Family Therapy.* New York. Brunner/Mazel. Reprinted by permission in Neill, John R., and David P. Kniskern (1982). *From Psyche to System. The Evolving Therapy of Carl Whitaker.* New York. Guilford, p. 358.

8. Distraction

(It's half of a strategy)

Erickson, Milton H., and Ernest Rossi. ''Two-Level Communication and the Microdynamics of Trance and Suggestion.'' In. Rossi, E. (Ed.) (1980). *The Collected Papers of Milton H. Erickson on Hypnosis. Volume I. The Nature of Hypnosis and Suggestion,* pp. 430–451. See especially ''Distraction in the Dynamics of Two-Level Communication,'' pp. 432–433.

9. Yin And Yang (They Need Both Sides Of Every Equation)

Erickson, Milton H. (1959). ''Further clinical techniques of hypnosis. Utilization techniques.'' *American Journal of Clinical Hypnosis* 2, 3–21.

10. Selective Blindness (Nonevents)

If Mom and Dad don't notice that anything has happened, there's no payoff.

''The Benefits of Inattention.'' Watzlawick, Paul, John Weakland, and Richard Fisch (1974). *Change. Principles of Problem Formation and Problem Resolution.* New York. Norton. pp 146–149.

11. Higher And Higher (Pace Them Right Into It)

You just join them until they decide this is going too far.

Whitaker, Carl (1973). "My Philosophy of Psychotherapy." *Journal of Contemporary Psychotherapy* 6 (1), 49–52. Reprinted by permission in Neill, John R. and David Kniskern (Eds.) (1982). *From Psyche to System. The Evolving Therapy of Carl Whitaker.* New York. Guilford, p. 33.

12. Plopping On Their Perch.

Move in and take over the child's Family Career Slot. Be a bigger scaredy-cat or whatever.

See also:
Role-function discrepancy, in: Satir, V. (1972). *Peoplemaking.* Palo Alto, California. Science & Behavior Books, p. 167.

13. Taking Possession Of The Symptom (Making It Mom's Thing Or Dad's Thing)

Any behavior can become a chore if required on schedule.

See also:

Bateson, G., D. D. Jackson, J. Haley, and J. Weakland, "Toward a Theory of Schizophrenia," *Behavioral Science* 1 (1956), 251–264. Reference in: Hoffman, Lynn (1981). *Foundations of Family Therapy. A Conceptual Framework for Systems Change.* New York. Basic Books, p. 236.

14. Putting The Kids In Control

(Use this one carefully. Follow the General Principle of allowing kids to have as much control as they can handle.)

15. Natural Consequences
(Consequences, Not Punishment)

(Letting the child's behavior result in inconvenience to the child, not to the parent.)

See also:
Milton Erickson's famous "bad boy" intervention in: Haley, Jay (Ed.). *Conversations with Milton H. Erickson, M. D.* Volume III. *Changing Children and Families.* Triangle Press. 1985, pp. 107–109.

16. Offering A Less And Less
Desirable Alternative.

See also:

"Providing a Worse Alternative." Haley, Jay (1973). "Uncommon therapy." *The Psychiatric Techniques of Milton H. Erickson, M. D.* New York. Norton, p. 25.

17. Speaking To Two Parts At Once

''Humans cannot not metacommunicate.''

Satir, Virginia (1964. Revised, 1967). *Conjoint Family Therapy.* Third Edition 1983. Palo Alto, California. Science and Behavior Books, Inc., p. 97.

18. Eliciting The ''Yes'' Set

Erickson, Milton H. (1964). Quoted without further reference in Erickson, Milton H., E, L. Rossi, and S. I. Rossi (1976). *Hypnotic Realities. The Induction of Clinical Hypnosis and Forms of Indirect Suggestion.* New York. Irvington, pp. 58–59.

See also:
Erickson, Milton H., and Ernest L. Rossi (1979). *Hypnotherapy. An Exploratory Casebook.* New York: Irvington. p. 2, p. 32.

And also:
Erickson, Milton H., and Ernest L. Rossi (1981). *Experiencing Hypnosis: Therapeutic Approaches to Altered States.* New York: Irvington, p. 8, p. 165.

19. Environmental Control
(The Architect Did It)

A very elegant and vastly underused method of preventing problems from arising.

20. Using Children's Games To Play With Them

21. The Flaky Moms' And Dads' Club

(The old folks try so hard to be helpful but they just can't get it right. It's easier to do it ourselves.)

See also:

''Benevolent Sabotage'' Watzlawick, Paul, John Weakland, and Richard Fisch (1974). *Change. Principles of Problem Formation and Problem Resolution.* New York. Norton, pp 142–146.

See also:
''Mommy will protect me''. Fisch, Richard, John Weakland, and Lynn Segal (1982). *The Tactics of Change. Doing Therapy Briefly.* San Francisco. Jossey-Bass, p. 143.

22. Using Your Weakness

''Guard your impotence as one of your most valuable weapons.'' Whitaker, Carl (1976). ''The hindrance of theory in clinical work.'' In P.J. Guerin (Ed.), *Family Therapy: Theory and Practice.* New York: Gardner Press. Reprinted by permission in Neill, John R. and David P. Kniskern (Eds.) (1982). *From Psyche to System. The Evolving Therapy of Carl Whitaker.* New York. Guilford, p. 329.

Satir, Virginia, and Michele Baldwin (1983). *Satir Step By Step. A Guide To Creating Change in Families.* Palo Alto, California. Science and Behavior Books, Inc. pp.226–231.

23. Letting Them Win Once In A While

Whitmont, Edward C. (1969). *The Symbolic Quest. Basic Principles of Analytical Psychology.* Princeton, NJ. Princeton University Press, p. 248: ". . . growth therefore depends upon at least a minimal disobedience of and revolt against parental values."

24. Learning To Say, "I Wonder If—?" (Going One-down To Get One-up)

25. Putting The Critic In Charge

26. Letting Them Make Some Mistakes

See also:

27. "Let Me Be How I Grow"

"Let me be how I grow". Grossman, Jean Schick (1948). *Life With Family. A Perspective on Parenthood.* New York. Appleton-Century-Crofts, Inc., p. 41.

28. The Magic Door (Location Change, Or Picnic In The Bedroom)

Sometimes just shifting the scene of the action from one room to another is enough. Also known as "Get Out of My Kitchen." A way to produce a shift of ego state.

Related to:

"The Use of Space and Position." Haley, Jay (1973). *Uncommon Therapy. The Psychiatric Techniques of Milton H. Erickson, M. D.* New York. Norton. pp.32–33.

29. Linkage

Binding the desired behavior to a pleasurable activity. The bedtime story starts in the bathroom as the children begin brushing their teeth.

See also:

Pryor, Karen (1985). *Don't Shoot The Dog! The New Art of Teaching and Training.* New York. Simon and Schuster.

30. Keep Your Body Between Them

You just keep them physically separated.

31. Providing A Secure Reality

The parent gently but firmly enfolds the child and won't let go.

''Providing a Secure Reality.'' Haley, Jay (1973). *Uncommon Therapy. The Psychiatric Techniques of Milton H. Erickson, M. D.* New York. Norton, pp. 213–221. (The story of Joe.)

32. Stretching The Little Old Umbilical Cord

(Using Distance)

Gall, John C. (1990). ''The Art of Examining a Child. Use of Naturalistic Methods in the Pediatric Physical Examination.'' In Stephen R. Lankton (Ed.) *Ericksonian Monographs. Number 7. The Broader Implications of Ericksonian Therapy.* New York. Brunner/Mazel, p. 83. The expression, ''Stretching the Little Old Umbilical Cord,'' was used in a cartoon sequence by Mell Lazarus in his cartoon strip entitled, ''Momma.'' (date lost).

33. Leaving The Scene

34. Providing A More Horrible Example (''Mother, Don't Do that!'')

''Providing a Worse Alternative.'' Haley, Jay (1973). *Uncommon Therapy. The Psychiatric Techniques of Milton H. Erickson, M. D.* New York. Norton. p. 25.

35. Knock 'Em Out With Novelty

36. It's Time For Your Tantrum
(Anticipation, Or Messing Up The Sequence)

Offer it before they're ready for it. There's nothing worse than a good meal when you're not hungry. You're giving them what they want, but somehow it's just not as satisfying as it was before.

Erickson, Milton H. In S. Rosen. (Ed.) (1982). *My Voice Will Go With You. The Teaching Tales of Milton H. Erickson.* New York. Norton, pp. 252–253.

37. Detoxifying Fantasies

Whitaker, Carl R. and William M. Bumberry (1988). *Dancing With The Family. A Symbolic-Experiential Approach.* New York. Brunner/Mazel, pp. 22, 121, 182.

38. Shaking The Foundations (A)

(Are Mom and Dad about to crack up? Are they gonna split?)

Madanes, Cloe (1981). *Strategic Family therapy.* San Francisco. Jossey-Bass, pp. 136–137.

39. Shaking The Foundations (B)

Can I trust my own perceptions?

40. Encouraging A Regression
(The Good Old Ways)

''Of course you want to be a baby and pee your pants. Here, let's get out your old diapers again.'' There's always a part that's conservative and wants to go back to the good old ways. Talk to that part, validate it!

''Encouraging a Relapse.'' Haley, Jay (1973). *Uncommon Therapy. The Psychiatric Techniques of Milton H. Erickson, M. D.* New York. Norton. pp. 30–31.

41. Changing The Metaphor

(Studying gravity again, eh?)

Watzlawick, Paul, John Weakland, and Richard Fisch (1974). *Change. Principles of Problem Formation and Problem Resolution.* New York: Norton. Chapter Eight: ''The Gentle Art of Reframing,'' pp. 92–109.

42. Learning To Make A U-Turn, Fast Or Slow, As the Occasion Requires, But Gracefully

''Making a 'U-Turn'.'' Fisch, Richard, John H. Weakland & Lynn Segal (1982). *The Tactics of Change. Doing Therapy Briefly.* San Francisco: Jossey-Bass, p. 166.

43. Future Pacing

A form of Implication relating to future events.

Satir, Virginia. ''A Family of Angels.'' An Interview with Virginia Satir. In Haley, Jay and Lynn Hoffman (Eds.) (1967). *Techniques of Family Therapy.*

Five Leading Therapists Reveal Their Working Styles, Strategies and Approaches. New York. Basic Books, p. 98.

Grinder, John and Richard Bandler (1981). *Trance-formations. Neuro-Linguistic Programming and the Structure of Hypnosis*. Moab, Utah. Real People Press, p. 159.

Bandler, Richard and John Grinder (1982). *Reframing. Neuro-Linguistic Programming and the Transformation of Meaning*. Moab, Utah. Real People Press, p. 115.

Erickson, Milton H., and Elizabeth M. Erickson (1941). ''Concerning the Nature and Character of Posthypnotic Behavior.'' *Journal of Genetic Psychology* 24, 95–133. Reprinted with permission in Ernest L. Rossi (Ed.) (1980). *The Collected Papers of Milton H. Erickson on Hypnosis. Volume I. The Nature of Hypnosis and Suggestion*, by Milton H. Erickson. New York. Irvington, pp. 381–412.

44. Nonverbal Pacing

45. ''Gee, You're Wonderful'' (The Bellac Ploy)

Watzlawick, Paul, John Weakland, and Richard Fisch (1974). *Change. Principles of Problem Formation and Problem Resolution*. New York: Norton. pp. 130–133.

46. The Dark Side Of Reframing (Contaminating The Metaphor)

''Anorexia is a female disease.''

Palazzoli, M. Selvini, L. Boscolo, G. Cecchin, and G. Prata (1978). *Paradox and Counterparadox. A New Model in the Therapy of the Family in Schizophrenic Transaction.* New York and London. Jason Aronson, Inc. (Originally published in Italy by Feltrinelli Editore, Milan, 1975), pp. 150–152.

47. Implication

"Psychological Implication." Erickson, Milton H., Ernest L. Rossi, and S. I. Rossi (1976). *Hypnotic Realities. The Induction of Clinical Hypnosis and Forms of Indirect Suggestion.* New York. Irvington, 59–62.

48. The Extended Tom Sawyer Maneuver

(The grownups are having so much fun doing that, it must be fun. Let me try that!)

Watzlawick, Weakland, and Fisch (1974). *Change,* pp 92–93.

49. Hidden Symmetry

"I Don't Has To." and "Garbage." Rosen, Sidney (1982). *My Voice Will Go With You. The Teaching Tales of Milton H. Erickson.* New York. Norton, pp. 238–241.

"The Perils of Dawdling." Haley, Jay (Ed.) (1985) *Conversations with Milton H. Erickson, M. D.* Volume III. *Changing Children and Families.* Triangle Press, pp. 90–92.

50. Letting Them Hear It From Someone Whose Voice Carries More Weight

Cooper, Duff (1932). *Talleyrand.* Republished in 1986 by Fromm International Publishing Corporation, New York, pp. 263–265.

51. Making A Little Change

"The Great Effects of Small Causes." Watzlawick, Paul, John Weakland, and Richard Fisch (1974). *Change. Principles of Problem Formation and Problem Resolution.* New York. Norton. pp. 127–130.

Haley, Jay (1973). *Uncommon Therapy. The Psychiatric Techniques of Milton H. Erickson, M. D.* New York. Norton. p. 35.

52. Intermittent Reinforcement

You reward only the most outstanding examples of the behavior you want.

Pryor, Karen. (1985) *Don't Shoot the Dog! The New Art of Teaching and Training.* New York. Simon and Schuster.

53. Switching Sensory Channels

"We wrote notes and posted them on his bedroom door."

54. Pre-emptive Frame-Setting

Forestalling problems by setting the right tone at the beginning.

55. Whipsaw Technique

If Mom and Dad are at opposite ends of the see-saw, which one shall I resist?

56. Too Clean For The Chicken Coop

How NOT to get picked for the job.

57. "Jamming" The Game Of Accuser/Defender

Challenge them to guess when you're really guilty and when you're just pretending.

Richard Fisch, John Weakland, and Lynn Segal (1982). *Tactics of Change. Doing Therapy Briefly.* San Francisco. Jossey-Bass, pp. 156–158.

58. Just Wait For The Next Level Of Development

(Dr. Ken Owings calls this the Charley Brown approach to problem-solving.)

59. Confusion Technique

Related to:
Shaking The Foundations, Humor, Mistaken Identity, Quick Switches, Making A U-Turn, Speaking To Two Parts At Once. Probably present to some degree in every effective strategy.

60. Beyond Strategies

"The only completely successful strategy to use with another person is to get to the place where neither of you is concerned with strategy at all."

Carl Whitaker in: "The Growing Edge. An Interview with Carl A. Whitaker, M. D." Chapter 4 of Haley, Jay, and Lynn Hoffman (1967). *Techniques of Family Therapy. Five Leading Therapists Reveal Their Working Styles, Strategies, and Approaches.* New York. Basic Books. p. 321.

FOR EXPERTS ONLY

Things not to do unless you really know how to use them constructively:

61. Nagging
(The Repetition Of Unsuccessful Requests)

Nag them to do what you want them to stop doing!

62. Bribery

(The price keeps going up, and anyway, it's an attempt to reward behavior that hasn't happened yet.)

63. Accusations

Don't do this to a child—it's dirty fighting. The more they deny your accusations, the less convincing they are. The child will end up believing there must be a grain of truth in the accusations and he just can't see it— thereby destroying his trust in his own perceptions.

Constructive use of Accusation usually involves the element of humor or irony.

"Sneaking off to do your homework again, eh? How many times have I told you to go outside and play and leave your homework to the last minute like any normal kid?"

(See Erickson's famous case called "Cinnamon Face" in Gordon, David and Maribeth Meyers-Anderson (1981). Phoenix. *Therapeutic Patterns of Milton H. Erickson.* Cupertino, California. Meta Publications, pp. 79–80.)

64. Attributions
(You're the one who . . .)

These are accusations at an even higher level of sneakiness—taken for granted as just a fact of life. The worst attributions are so-called "medical" diagnoses—hyperactivity, learning disorder, schizophrenia. Who can defend themselves against that? But that doesn't mean they can't respond. Typical responses:

a. *Apathy.* Hopeless about the possibility of change.
b. *Low self-esteem.* Accepting self as a flawed inferior being.
c. Embracing with exasperated enthusiasm a negative career as a handicapped person, criminal, schizophrenic, etc.

Constructive application: "You always have such good ideas."

65. Explanations

Any explanation more than five words long is too long. Children don't have that much Verbal Model to work with. However, a long-winded explanation can sometimes be used to achieve a constructive goal. (Use with caution.)

66. Ex Cathedra Demands

"Do it because I said so." Want your child to give up thinking? This will do it. "Give up your will. Submit to mine—because I'm bigger." But again, constructive use of this strategy is possible: "Open your mouth and close your eyes, and I'll give you a nice surprise." (Be sure it really is a nice surprise.)

67. "Not-Doing" Something

In general, this is impossible. Provide an acceptable alternate pathway. But you can say, "You don't need to bother doing your homework tonight."

68. Indirect Verbal Attacks

Certain specific phrases should immediately raise a red flag of warning in your mind. Examples: "If you really . . ."; "Don't you even care . . ."; "Even you should . . ." It's probably wise never to use such language with your child.

For the complete list, see:

Elgin, Suzette Haden (1980). *The Gentle Art of Verbal Self-Defense.* New York. Prentice-Hall.

Appendix B: Principles List

1. Learn To Pay Attention To Feedback

2. Learn Problem Location

It's not cricket to ask the child to change if the problem is basically your own.

3. Switch Strategies Freely

If at first you don't succeed, give up. Do something else. Switch to a different strategy. Don't waste energy pushing interventions that aren't working.

Mead, Margaret. Cybernetics of Cybernetics. In H. von Foerster, H. Peterson, J. White, and J. Russell (Eds.). *Purposive Systems.* New York. Spartan Books 1968. (Reference in Keeney, op. cit., p. 76.)

Ashby, W. Ross (1952). *Design for a Brain.* New York. Wiley. p. 108.

4. Nonverbal Modelling Is Usually Better Than Verbal

Never do explicitly what you can do implicitly. The child's verbal model of the universe is extremely crude. (So is ours—just a little less so!) Use behavior—or as Beth Gall says, "Behavior Behavior".

5. Don't Explain Everything

It's easy to give away your power by talking. There are times when it's better not to explain. Your interventions are much more powerful if they don't know what's going to happen. Build anticipation. That way, you will know you have their full attention.

6. Learn To Speak To Two Parts At Once

7. Learn Multilevel Communication

8. Learn To Be Actors And Actresses

After you have learned your lines and used them successfully three times, you won't be "acting" any more.

9. Learn More Lines! (Requisite Variety)

Increase Your Repertoire. The more strategies you have at your fingertips the better equipped you will be to meet any situation. The Principle Of Requisite Variety states that in any System, control is exercised by the element with the greatest variety of behavioral responses.

W. Ross Ashby (1961). *An Introduction to Cybernetics*. London. Chapman and Hall, p. 206.

10. Learn Verbal Pacing

"You don't want to clean up your room. You want to go out and play." Validate their position. That way, they will know that you really understand the situation.

11. If You Don't Want It To Be In Their Repertoire, Don't Talk About It

Why give them an explicit verbal model of things you don't want them to do? Don't talk about "avoiding juvenile delinquency," "staying out of trouble", etc. They know how you feel about such things.

12. Minimize Constraints

A rigid insistence that the problem must be solved within a specific set of parameters may merely indicate that you as a parent have a problem with rigidity. Take a good look at what you're asking, and why. The child may be merely trying to stay out of your overly rigid system. He may even be trying to help you overcome your rigidity by showing you a wider range of behavior than you had thought possible. Is the problem really due to the healthy refusal of the child to internalize and thus take upon himself what is properly a social problem or even a parental problem? Examples: "Achievement", "Doing Well" in school, etc. In raising a child, an ounce of spontaneity is worth a pound of obedience.

13. Don't Get Polarized. Stay Flexible

Ruthless application of permissiveness is still ruthlessness. Extremism in the defense of liberty is still extremism.

14. Stay Out Of The Fairness Trap

As a parent, you are obligated to provide to each child what that child needs. A new baby needs more attention than an older sibling. As a parent, you decide who needs what and how much, and you cannot be blackmailed by complaints of unfairness. Of course it's unfair!

15. Be Selective.
Ignore Unimportant Stuff

A parent who treats everything as equally important (equally ominous) conveys Catastrophic Expectations. (See Avoiding Rigidity, above.)

16. Parents Should Take Care Of
Their Own "Child" Needs First

These are parental needs for security, comfort, validation, rest, recreation, etc. Don't try to get these from the child. That turns the world upside down and stands things on their head. (Comment of a 17-year-old unwed mother on the first day of her baby's life: "He's already being good to me.")

Cf. The Needy Parent Syndrome: often seen just after the birth of the first, second, third, fourth, or fifth child: no resources, no help, no one to take shifts with, on call all the time and burned out. Also known as Cabin Fever or Stir Crazy. In such a setting, problems have even tighter constraints than usual: the child's not sleeping is really a problem of the parents being too exhausted. If you as the parent feel put upon, you may be suffering from this syndrome.

17. Learn To Get In Touch With The Kid
Part Of Yourself And Use That Part
In Communicating With Your Children

18. Use Consequences, Not Punishment. (Natural Consequences)

Don't be a victim. Let the child's failure to learn the desired responses get in his way, not yours.

See also:
Milton Erickson's famous "bad boy" intervention in: Haley, Jay (Ed.). *Conversations with Milton H. Erickson, M. D. Volume III. Changing Children and Families.* Triangle Press. 1985, pp. 107–109.

19. Praise The Achievement, Don't Criticize The Shortcoming

Children always do poorly at first what they later will do well. If you criticize the shortcoming, you merely diminish motivation and fixate the child's behavior pattern at the level of poor performance.

20. Let The Child Have As Much Control As She Or He Can Handle Without Feeling Overwhelmed

Remember, the reason you are doing all these things is so you can have a feeling of being in control. Why not let him enjoy that, too, in his way and at his level?

21. Don't Ask For Performances

Some kids are little hams and will repeat their latest achievements on request. Most kids don't like this and won't do it. You'll save yourself a lot of grief if you just don't ask them to perform.

22. Utilize The Spontaneous Offerings Of The Child

That's the behavior they already know how to do. The behavior they are already exhibiting. Find a way to put it to good use. If the child exhibits skill and satisfaction in resisting you, let him resist you. But set things up so that in resisting you, he is accomplishing something you want accomplished.

23. If Your Child's Behavior Seems Malicious Or Crazy, Remember That This Means A Basic Miscommunication Has Occurred Somewhere

Or else there is actually craziness somewhere, either in the family or the school, or somewhere. Make it your assignment to find out where the miscommunication has taken place. Don't ask, find out for yourself.

"The Miscommunication Principle." Satir, Virginia (1964). *Conjoint Family Therapy.* Third edition. Palo Alto, California. Science and Behavior Books. p. 125.

Satir, Virginia, Watzlawick, Paul, Janet Helmick Beavin, and Don D. Jackson (1967). *Pragmatics of Human Communication. A Study of Interactional Patterns, Pathologies, and Paradoxes.* New York. Norton. pp. 94–95.

24. Respect Inborn Temperament

Let them be how they grow, even if it's a little strange.

25. Respect Infant Preferences

26. Respect The Developmental Level Of The Child

a. "Lying" versus reality testing. If there's a bear in the bathroom, deal with the bear, don't give a sermon on lying.
b. Impulse control. When it's developmentally not there, don't try to elicit it. Keep sibs physically apart.
c. Autonomic control (sphincters, etc.) Same idea. When it's developmentally not there, don't try to elicit it.
d. Sharing. First comes possession, then comes sharing! Give them time— lots of time! Like eight or ten years! Would you be willing to share your new sports car?

Fraiberg, Selma H. (1959). *The Magic Years. Understanding and Handling the Problems of Early Childhood*. New York. Scribner's.

27. Anticipate And Encourage A Relapse

Understand that a relapse may be a signal that you have made a successful intervention. They are escalating their old responses to find out what went wrong, why the old methods aren't working. . . . Then they can frustrate you by not having one.

Haley, Jay (1973). *Uncommon Therapy. The Psychiatric Techniques of Milton H. Erickson, M. D.* New York. Norton. pp. 30–31.

28. Understand That Learning Proceeds By Fits And Starts

Sudden advances are followed by long periods of little change. And often the first indication that a major advance is about to take place is the occurrence of restless, irritable behavior—the Learning Tantrum.

Pryor, Karen (1984). *Don't Shoot the Dog! The New Art of Teaching and Training.* New York. Bantam, pp. 100–103.

29. You Are Always Fundamentally On Their Side

Your task as a parent is to help them get past the sticky points, to facilitate their own mastery of their current developmental tasks and so to move on to the next developmental level.

Erickson, Milton H. (1958). "Pediatric Hypnotherapy." *The American Journal of Clinical Hypnosis* 1, 25–29.

Haley, Jay (1973). *Uncommon Therapy. The Psychiatric Techniques of Milton H. Erickson, M. D.* New York. Norton. p. 42.

30. Help Them To Move To The Next Higher Level of Development

31. Set Them Up To Succeed Whenever Possible

32. Don't Give Away Your Power Unless That's Part Of Your Strategy

Don't negotiate with a child who is too young to negotiate. A two-year-old has a very rudimentary idea of the meaning of compromise, much less of promise, contract, obligation. Forget it! On the other hand, they often do understand barter (exchange).

33. Learn To Deliberately Use Your Own Failure And Powerlessness

(Allow children to succeed in getting the better of you and doing what you really wanted them to do all along.)

34. Learn to Make A *Little* Change

It will snowball.

Appendix C:
Case Histories List

Chapter 2

Chapter 3

Chapter 4

Chapter 5

Chapter 10

Chapter 11

Chapter 12

Chapter 13

Chapter 14

Chapter 15

Chapter 16

Chapter 17

Chapter 18

Chapter 19

Chapter 20

Chapter 21

Bibliography

Ashby, W. Ross (1961). *An Introduction to Cybernetics*. London. Chapman and Hall.

Bandler, Richard, and John Grinder (1975). *The Structure of Magic. I. A Book about Language and Therapy*. Palo Alto, California. Science and Behavior Books.

——, John Grinder, and Virginia Satir (1976). *Changing With Families. A Book About Further Education for Being Human*. Palo Alto, California. Science and Behavior Books.

—— and John Grinder (1979). *Frogs into Princes. Neuro Linguistic Programming*. Moab, Utah. Real People Press.

—— and John Grinder (1982). *Reframing. Neuro-Linguistic Programming and the Transformation of Meaning*. Moab, Utah. Real People Press.

Bateson, Gregory (1979). *Mind and Nature. A Necessary Unity*. New York. Dutton.

—— (1942). "Social Planning and the Concept of Deutero-Learning." In: Bateson, Gregory (1972). *Steps to an Ecology of Mind*. New York. Ballantine, p. 163ff.

—— (1964). "The Logical Categories of Learning and Communication." In: Bateson, Gregory (1972). *Steps to an Ecology of Mind*. New York. Ballantine.

Bergman, Joel S. (1985). *Fishing For Barracuda. Pragmatics of Brief Systemic Therapy*. New York. Norton.

Bower, T. G. R. (1977). *A Primer of Infant Development*. San Francisco. Freeman.

Brazelton, T. Berry and Bertrand G. Cramer (1990). *The Earliest Relationship. Parents, Infants, and the Drama of Early Attachment*. Reading, Massachusetts. Addison-Wesley.

Caffey, John (1946). "Multiple Fractures in the Long Bones of Infants Suffering from Chronic Subdural Hematoma." *Am. J. Roentgenology* 56(2): 163–173.

Campbell, Joseph (1988). *The Power Of Myth*. New York. Doubleday.

Clarke, Jean Illsley (1978). *Self-Esteem. A Family Affair*. Minneapolis. Winston Press.

Cooper, Duff (1932). *Talleyrand*. Republished in 1986 by Fromm International Publishing Corporation, New York

Crary, Elizabeth (1979). *Without Spanking or Spoiling. A Practical Approach to Toddler and Preschool Guidance*. Seattle, Washington. Parenting Press.

Elgin, Suzette Haden (1980). *The Gentle Art of Verbal Self-Defense*. New York. Prentice-Hall.

Erickson, L., Elliott, B., Erickson, A., Erickson, R., Klein, R., & Erickson, K. (Panelists) (1985). "Erickson family panel: the child-rearing techniques of Milton H. Erickson." In J. K. Zeig (Ed.), *Ericksonian Psychotherapy I: Structures*, pp. 619–637. New York. Brunner/Mazel.

Erickson, M. and Rossi, E. (1975). "Varieties of Double Bind." *American Journal of Clinical Hypnosis* 17, 143–157.

——— (1958). "Pediatric hypnotherapy." *The American Journal of Clinical Hypnosis* 1, 25–29.

——— (1959). "Further clinical techniques of hypnosis. Utilization techniques." *American Journal of Clinical Hypnosis* 2, 3–21.

——— (1964). "The 'Surprise' and 'My-Friend-John' Techniques of Hypnosis: Minimal Cues and Natural Field Experimentation." *Amer. J. Clin. Hypn.* 6, 293–307.

—— and Ernest Rossi. "The Indirect Forms of Suggestion." In: Rossi, Ernest L. (Ed.) (1980). *The Collected Papers of Milton H. Erickson on Hypnosis. Volume I. The Nature of Hypnosis and Suggestion,* pp. 456–7.

—— and Ernest Rossi. "Two-Level Communication and the Microdynamics of Trance and Suggestion." In: Rossi, E. (Ed.) (1980). *The Collected Papers of Milton H. Erickson on Hypnosis. Volume I. The Nature of Hypnosis and Suggestion,* pp. 430–451.

——, E. L. Rossi, and S. I. Rossi (1976). *Hypnotic Realities. The Induction of Clinical Hypnosis and Forms of Indirect Suggestion.* New York. Irvington.

Faber, Adele and Elaine Mazlish (1980). *How to Talk So Kids Will Listen and Listen So Kids Will Talk.* New York. Avon.

Faber, Adele and Elaine Mazlish (1987). *Siblings Without Rivalry.* New York. Norton.

Ferber, Richard (1985). *Solve Your Child's Sleep Problems.* New York. Simon and Schuster.

Fisch, Richard, John Weakland, and Lynn Segal (1982). *Tactics of Change. Doing Therapy Briefly.* San Francisco. Jossey-Bass

Fraiberg, Selma H. (1959). *The Magic Years. Understanding and Handling the Problems of Early Childhood.* New York. Scribner's.

Gall, John C. (1990). "The Art of Examining a Child. Use of Naturalistic Methods in the Pediatric Physical Examination." In: Stephen R. Lankton (Ed.) *Ericksonian Monographs. Number 7. The Broader Implications of Ericksonian Therapy.* New York. Brunner/Mazel.

Givens, D. (1978). "Social expressivity during the first year of life." *Sign Language Studies* 20, 251–274.

Gordon, David and Maribeth Meyers-Anderson (1981). Phoenix. *Therapeutic Patterns of Milton H. Erickson.* Cupertino, California. Meta Publications.

Gordon, Thomas (1970). *P.E.T. Parent Effectiveness Training. The Tested New Way To Raise Responsible Children.* New York. New American Library (1975).

Goulding, Mary McClure and Robert L. Goulding (1979) *Changing Lives Through Redecision Therapy.* New York. Brunner/Mazel.

Grinder, John, and Richard Bandler (1976). *The Structure of Magic. II.* Palo Alto, California. Science and Behavior Books.

————, Judith Delozier, and Richard Bandler (1977). *Patterns of the Hypnotic Techniques of Milton H. Erickson, M. D.* Vol. II. Cupertino, California. Meta Publications.

Grossman, Jean Schick (1948). *Life With Family. A Perspective on Parenthood.* New York. Appleton-Century-Crofts, Inc.

Haley, Jay (1973). *Uncommon Therapy. The Psychiatric Techniques of Milton H. Erickson, M. D.* New York. Norton.

———— (Ed.) (1985). *Conversations with Milton H. Erickson, M. D. Volume III. Changing children and Families.* Triangle Press. Distributed by W. W. Norton. New York.

Hilgard, Ernest R. (1977, 1986). *Divided Consciousness. Multiple Controls in Human Thought and Action.* Expanded Edition. New York. Wiley.

Hoffman, Lynn (1981). *Foundations of Family Therapy. A Conceptual Framework for Systems Change.* New York. Basic Books.

Jones, Ernest (1953). *The Life and Work of Sigmund Freud.* Volume I. New York. Basic Books.

Jung, C. G. (1921). "Psychological Types." In: *The Basic Writings of C. G. Jung* (1959). Edited and with an Introduction by V. S. de Laszlo. New York. Modern Library.

Kahler, Taibi. "The Miniscript." In: Graham Barnes (Ed.) (1977). *Transactional Analysis after Eric Berne. Teachings and Practices of Three Schools.* New York. Harper.

Keeney, Bradford P. (1983). *Aesthetics of Change.* New York. Guilford.

Laing, R. D. (1969). *The Politics of the Family and Other Essays.* New York. Random House.

Madanes, Cloe (1981). *Strategic Family Therapy.* San Francisco. Jossey-Bass.

Masson, Jeffrey M. (1984) *The Assault on Truth. Freud's Suppression of the Seduction Theory.* New York. Penguin.

Mead, Margaret (1928). *Coming of Age in Samoa.* New York. New American Library edition 1949.

Mehrabian, A. (1970). *Tactics of Social Influence.* Englewood Cliffs, New Jersey. Prentice-Hall.

Miller, A. (1983). *For Your Own Good. Hidden Cruelty in Child-rearing and the Roots of Violence* (H. Hannum & H. Hannum, Trans.). New York. Farrar Strauss Giroux. (Originally published in German under the title: *Am Anfang war Erziehung. Frankfurt am Main. Suhrkamp Verlag* (1980)).

——— (1986). *Thou Shalt Not Be Aware. Society's Betrayal of the Child.* New York and Scarborough, Ontario. New American Library. (Originally published in German under the title *Du sollst nicht merken. Frankfurt am Main. Suhrkamp Verlag* (1981)).

Palazzoli, M. Selvini, L. Boscolo, G. Cecchin, and G. Prata (1978). *Paradox and Counterparadox. A New Model in the Therapy of the Family in Schizophrenic Transaction.* New York and London. Jason Aronson, Inc. (Originally published in Italy by Feltrinelli Editore, Milan, 1975).

Papousek, H. (1969). "Individual variability in learned responses in human infants." In: R. J. Robinson (Ed.), *Brain and Early Behavior.* London. Academic Press.

Parkinson, C. N. (1957). *Parkinson's Law and Other Studies in Administration.* Boston. Houghton Mifflin.

Pryor, Karen (1984). *Don't Shoot the Dog! The New Art of Teaching and Training.* New York. Bantam.

Rosen, Sidney (Ed.) (1982). *My Voice Will Go With You. The Teaching Tales of Milton H. Erickson.* New York. Norton.

Sanger, S., and John Kelly (1985). *You And Your Baby's First Year.* New York. William Morrow.

Satir, Virginia (1964. Revised, 1967). *Conjoint Family Therapy.* Third Edition 1983. Palo Alto, California. Science and Behavior Books, Inc.

―――― (1972). *Peoplemaking*. Palo Alto, California, pp. 205–207.

―――― and Michele Baldwin (1983). *Satir Step By Step. A Guide To Creating Change in Families*. Palo Alto, California. Science and Behavior Books, Inc.

Silver, Henry K., and Anita Duhl Glicken. "Medical Student Abuse. Incidence, Severity, and Significance." Washtenaw County Medical Society Bulletin, Vol 41, No. 8 (April) 1990, pp. 3–12.

Stewart, Ian. *Does God Play Dice? The Mathematics of Chaos*. Cambridge, Mass. Basil Blackwell. 1989.

Svejda, M. J. (November,1981). "The development of infant sensitivity to affective messages in the mother's voice." Unpublished doctoral dissertation, University of Denver, Colorado.

Thomas, Alexander, and Stella Chess (1977). *Temperament and Development*. New York. Brunner/Mazel.

――――, Stella Chess, and Herbert G. Birch (1968). *Temperament and Behavior Disorders in Children*. New York. New York University Press.

von Foerster, H., H. Peterson, J. White and J. Russell (Eds) (1968). *Purposive Systems*. New York. Spartan Books. 1968.

Watson, J. S. (1973). "Smiling, Cooing, and 'the game'." *Merrill-Palmer Quarterly of Behavior and Development* 18, 323–339.

Watzlawick, Paul, Janet Helmick Beavin, and Don D. Jackson (1967). *Pragmatics of Human Communication. A Study of Interactional Patterns, Pathologies, and Paradoxes*. New York. Norton.

――――, John Weakland, and Richard Fisch (1974). *Change. Principles of Problem Formation and Problem Resolution*. New York.

――――, (1984). *The Invented Reality*. New York. Norton.

Whitaker, Carl (1973). "My Philosophy of Psychotherapy." *Journal of Contemporary Psychotherapy* 6 (1), 49–52. Reprinted by permission in Neill, John R. and David Kniskern (Eds.) (1982). *From Psyche to System. The Evolving Therapy of Carl Whitaker*. New York. Guilford.

————, (1976). "The hindrance of theory in clinical work." In: P. J. Guerin (Ed.) (1976). *Family Therapy: Theory and Practice.* New York. Gardner Press.

———— and William Bumberry (1988). *Dancing With The Family. A Symbolic-Experiential Approach.* New York. Brunner/Mazel.

Whitmont, Edward C. (1969). *The Symbolic Quest. Basic Principles of Analytical Psychology.* Princeton, NJ. Princeton University Press.

Wilk, James (1985). "Ericksonian Therapeutic Patterns: A Pattern Which Connects." In: Zeig, Jeffrey K. (Ed.). *Ericksonian Psychotherapy. Volume II: Clinical Applications.* New York. Brunner/Mazel, p. 210–233.

Woollams, Stan and Michael Brown (1978). *Transactional Analysis.* Dexter, Michigan. Huron Valley Institute Press.

Zeig, J. (Ed.) (1980). *A Teaching Seminar With Milton H. Erickson.* New York. Brunner/Mazel.

Index